On The Edge
Literature And Imagination

☆

Edited by

Arthur Haberman

and Fran Cohen

Toronto
OXFORD UNIVERSITY PRESS
1993

Oxford University Press, 70 Wynford Drive
Don Mills, Ontario, M3C 1J9

Toronto   Oxford   New York   Delhi   Bombay   Calcutta   Madras   Karachi
Kuala Lumpur   Singapore   Hong Kong   Tokyo   Nairobi   Dar es Salaam
Cape Town   Melbourne   Auckland   Madrid

and associated companies in
Berlin Ibadan

This book is printed on permanent (acid-free) paper. ∞

Canadian Cataloguing in Publication Data

Main entry under title:

On the edge: literature and imagination

ISBN 0-19-540890-X

1. Readers (Secondary). I. Haberman, Arthur, 1938-
II. Cohen, Fran.

PE1121.06 1993   808.8   C92-095412-X

OXFORD is a trademark of Oxford University Press.

Cover: The woodcut on which this cover is based is commonly attributed to an
anonymous German artist of the 16th century. Some sources believe it to be a
19th-century interpretation of the cosmology of the 16th century.

Editor: Loralee Case
Designer: Marie Bartholomew
Typesetter: Trigraph
Printed in Canada by The Bryant Press

1   2   3   4   5   97   96   95   94   93

Contents

✿

Heritage: Turn and Face the Stranger 93

Self—and Other 119

Language and Power 163

Risk 193

Contents

Selections by Other Themes

✡

History, Society, and Culture

Media

The Nature of Art

Quests

Values

Change

Arthur Haberman is Associate Professor of History and Humanities at York University. He has been a consultant to the Ontario and British Columbia Ministries of Education and the National Faculty of Humanities, Arts, and Sciences. He has extensive experience working with teachers and students and is the author of several works used in secondary schools.

Fran Cohen has taught at the elementary, secondary, and university levels. She is currently an instructor in Humanities at York University and a writing consultant and editor in educational publishing.

The authors would like to thank the following people for reviewing the manuscript and offering their insights: Judith Barker-Sandbrook, Sir Oliver Mowat Collegiate, Scarborough; John Lord, Stephen Leacock Collegiate, Scarborough; and Stephen Goss, Cartier McGee–Louis St. Laurent Classic School, Edmonton. Special thanks to Neil Anderson of West Hill Collegiate, Scarborough, for providing his media expertise.

To Jan and Alan

Preface

✩

Imagination holds a place in our lives that is of abiding interest to most individuals, and indeed, to all cultures. Dreams, symbols, myths, stories, and even scientific speculations about the nature of our universe all arise from the imagination. Each of these, in its own way, tells us something about who we are, where we come from, and what we ought to be and do.

Through art and literature, this book explores the power of the imagination and its relationship to issues of human nature and social values. By reflecting on such issues as the meaning of madness, language and power, dreams and their role in our understanding, heritage and its ambiguities, or other worlds and the problem of order and chaos, we can learn much about ourselves and the way we construct reality and shape our lives.

On the Edge is organized around a number of themes. Each theme begins simply enough, reflecting commonly held concepts or views. However, as the theme progresses, it raises new questions and provokes alternate perspectives and approaches. Ideas begin to "bend" so that they can be considered afresh. The questions raised in this manner have no simple answers, of course, but each lends itself to examination from many points of view and disciplines. To the search for understanding of some of these ideas central to our lives, readers bring their own knowledge of story and non-fiction, of art, of history, of science, and of media.

Imagination has many uses, among them to provide us with new ways of understanding. The materials in this book are intended to open old questions, to renew how we think about our past, our ethics, our relationships, and ourselves.

We appreciate the insights and suggestions of a number of individuals who contributed to the development of this book: Alan Davies, Jan Rehner, Diana Cooper-Clark, and Richard Teleky; and Anthony Luengo and Loralee Case of Oxford University Press.

Madness

Madness. To be mad; bizarre; crazy; strange; dangerous; unconventional. There is a fascination with the idea of madness that has made it an important theme in art and literature, and a magnet for viewers and readers. Perhaps this fascination stems from questions and doubts about our sanity. Most of us have thought ourselves mad at one time or another, perhaps because we believe we are relating to the world differently than others, or perhaps because we feel that madness is an escape from an ordinary and increasingly banal world.

In fact, the borderline between sanity and insanity may be quite obscure. Many heroes have been thought to be "mad"—religious leaders, creative thinkers, revolutionaries, dissenters—people who seem to be marching to their own drummer. Sometimes, the mad person is seen to have special wisdom or insight, only articulated in an unusual way. If, like Emily Dickinson, we come to see that "much madness is divinest sense," we may perceive our world differently and with greater understanding.

The Cry

✡

Edvard Munch

The Starry Night

(1889)

☆

Vincent van Gogh

The Granger Collection, New York

Selected Letters

✡

Vincent van Gogh

St. Rémy

My dear Theo,   [*28 January 1889*]
Only a few words to tell you that my health and my work are not progressing so badly.

It astonishes me already when I compare my condition today with what it was a month ago. Before that I knew well enough that one could fracture one's legs and arms and recover afterward, but I did not know that you could fracture the brain in your head and recover from that too.

I still have a sort of "what is the good of getting better?" feeling about me, even in the astonishment aroused in me by my getting well, which I hadn't dared hope for. . . .

Since it is still winter, look here, let me go quietly on with my work; if it is that of a madman, well, so much the worse. I can't help it.

However, the unbearable hallucinations have ceased, and are now getting reduced to a simple nightmare,. . .

[*3 February 1889*]

. . .I have no illusions about myself any more. I am feeling very well, and I shall do everything the doctor says, but. . .

When I came out of the hospital. . .I thought that there had been nothing wrong with me, but *afterward* I felt that I had been ill. Well, well, there are moments when I am twisted by enthusiasm or madness or prophecy, like a Greek oracle on the tripod. . . .

I must tell you this, that the neighbors, etc., are particularly kind to me, as everyone here is suffering either from fever, or hallucinations, or madness, we understand each other like members of the same family. Yesterday I went to see the girl I had gone to when I was out of my wits. They told me there that in this country things like that are not out of the ordinary. She had been upset by it and had fainted but had recovered her calm. And they spoke well of her, too.

But as for considering myself as completely sane, we must not do it. People here who have been ill like me have told me the truth. You may be old or young, but there will always be moments when you lose your head.

So I do not ask you to say of me that there is nothing wrong with me, or that there never will be. . . .

[*May 1889*]

I wanted to tell you that I think I have done well to come here; first of all, by seeing the *reality* of the life of the various madmen and lunatics in this menagerie, I am losing the vague dread, the fear of the thing. And little by little I can come to look upon madness as a disease like any other. Then the change of surroundings does me good, I think. . . .

The idea of work as a duty is coming back to me very strongly, and I think that all my faculties for work will come back to me fairly quickly. Only work often absorbs me so much that I think I shall always remain absent-minded and awkward in shifting for myself for the rest of my life too.

[*10 September 1889*]

My work is going very well, I am finding things that I have sought in vain for years, and feeling this, I am always thinking of that saying of Delacroix's that you know, namely that he discovered painting when he no longer had any breath or teeth left.

Well, I with my mental disease, I keep thinking of so many other artists suffering mentally, and I tell myself that this does not prevent one from exercising the painter's profession as if nothing were amiss.

Vincent

☆

Don McLean

Starry starry night
Paint your palette blue and grey
Look out on a summer's day
With eyes that know the darkness in my soul
Shadows on the hills
Sketch the trees and the daffodils
Catch the breeze and the winter chills
In colours on the snowy linen land

Now I understand
What you tried to say to me
How you suffered for your sanity
And how you tried to set them free
They would not listen
They did not know how
Perhaps they'll listen now

Starry starry night
Flaming flowers that brightly blaze
Swirling clouds in violet haze
Reflect in Vincent's eyes of china blue
Colours changing hue
Morning fields of amber grain
Weathered faces lined in pain
Are smoothed beneath the artist's loving hand

Now I understand
What you tried to say to me
And how you suffered for your sanity
And how you tried to set them free
They would not listen
They did not know how
Perhaps they'll listen now

For they could not love you
But still your love was true
And when no hope was left inside
On that starry starry night
You took your life as lovers often do
But I could have told you Vincent
This world was never meant
For one as beautiful as you

Starry starry night
Portraits hung in empty halls
Frameless heads on nameless walls
With eyes that watch the world and can't forget
Like the strangers that you've met
The ragged men in ragged clothes
The silver thorn, the bloody rose
Lie crushed and broken on the virgin snow.

Now I think I know
What you tried to say to me
And how you suffered for your sanity
And how you tried to set them free
They would not listen
They're not listening still
Perhaps they never will.

Much Madness is divinest Sense

✡

Emily Dickinson

Much Madness is divinest Sense—
To a discerning Eye—
Much sense—the Starkest Madness—
'Tis the Majority
In this, as All, prevail—
Assent—and you are sane—
Demur—you're straightway dangerous—
And handled with a Chain—

The Yellow Wallpaper

☆

Charlotte Perkins Gilman

It is very seldom that mere ordinary people like John and myself secure ancestral halls for the summer.

A colonial mansion, a hereditary estate, I would say a haunted house, and reach the height of romantic felicity—but that would be asking too much of fate!

Still I will proudly declare that there is something queer about it.

Else, why should it be let so cheaply? And why have stood so long untenanted?

John laughs at me, of course, but one expects that in marriage.

John is practical in the extreme. He has no patience with faith, an intense horror of superstition, and he scoffs openly at any talk of things not to be felt and seen and put down in figures.

John is a physician, and *perhaps*—(I would not say it to a living soul, of course, but this is dead paper and a great relief to my mind)—*perhaps* that is one reason I do not get well faster.

You see he does not believe I am sick!

And what can one do?

If a physician of high standing, and one's own husband, assures friends and relatives that there is really nothing the matter with one but temporary nervous depression—a slight hysterical tendency—what is one to do?

My brother is also a physician, and also of high standing, and he says the same thing.

So I take phosphates or phospites—whichever it is, and tonics, and journeys, and air, and exercise, and am absolutely forbidden to "work" until I am well again.

Personally, I disagree with their ideas.

Personally, I believe that congenial work, with excitement and change, would do me good.

But what is one to do?

I did write for a while in spite of them; but it *does* exhaust me a good deal—having to be so sly about it, or else meet with heavy opposition.

I sometimes fancy that in my condition if I had less opposition and more society and stimulus—but John says the very worst thing I can do is to think about my condition, and I confess it always makes me feel bad.

So I will let it alone and talk about the house.

The most beautiful place! It is quite alone, standing well back from the road, quite three miles from the village. It makes me think of English places that you read about, for there are hedges and walls and gates that lock, and lots of separate little houses for the gardeners and people.

There is a *delicious* garden! I never saw such a garden—large and shady, full of box-bordered paths, and lined with long grape-covered arbors with seats under them.

There were greenhouses, too, but they are all broken now.

There was some legal trouble, I believe, something about the heirs and coheirs; anyhow, the place has been empty for years.

The spoils of my ghostliness, I am afraid, but I don't care— there is something strange about the house—I can feel it.

I even said so to John one moonlight evening, but he said what I felt was a *draught*, and shut the window.

I get unreasonably angry with John sometimes. I'm sure I never used to be so sensitive. I think it is due to this nervous condition.

But John says if I feel so, I shall neglect proper self-control; so I take pains to control myself—before him, at least, and that makes me very tired.

I don't like our room a bit. I wanted one downstairs that opened on the piazza and had roses all over the window, and such pretty old-fashioned chintz hangings! but John would not hear of it.

He said there was only one window and not room for two beds, and no near room for him if he took another.

He is very careful and loving, and hardly lets me stir without special direction.

I have a schedule prescription for each hour in the day; he takes all care from me, and so I feel basely ungrateful not to value it more.

He said we came here solely on my account, that I was to have perfect rest and all the air I could get. "Your exercise depends on your strength, my dear," said he, "and your food somewhat on your appetite; but air you can absorb all the time." So we took the nursery at the top of the house.

It is a big, airy room, the whole floor nearly, with windows that look all ways, and air and sunshine galore. It was nursery first and then playroom and gymnasium, I should judge; for the windows are barred for little children, and there are rings and things in the walls.

The paint and paper look as if a boys' school had used it. It is stripped off—the paper—in great patches all around the head of my bed, about as far as I can reach, and in a great place on the other side of the room low down. I never saw a worse paper in my life.

One of those sprawling flamboyant patterns committing every artistic sin.

It is dull enough to confuse the eye in following, pronounced enough to constantly irritate and provoke study, and when you follow the lame uncertain curves for a little distance they suddenly commit suicide—plunge off at outrageous angles, destroy themselves in unheard of contradictions.

The color is repellent, almost revolting; a smouldering unclean yellow, strangely faded by the slow-turning sunlight.

It is a dull yet lurid orange in some places, a sickly sulphur tint in others.

No wonder the children hated it! I should hate it myself if I had to live in this room long.

There comes John, and I must put this away,—he hates to have me write a word.

We have been here two weeks, and I haven't felt like writing before, since that first day.

I am sitting by the window now, up in this atrocious nursery, and there is nothing to hinder my writing as much as I please, save lack of strength.

John is away all day, and even some nights when his cases are serious.

I am glad my case is not serious!

But these nervous troubles are dreadfully depressing.

John does not know how much I really suffer. He knows there is no *reason* to suffer, and that satisfies him.

Of course it is only nervousness. It does weigh on me so not to do my duty in any way!

I meant to be such a help to John, such a real rest and comfort, and here I am a comparative burden already!

Nobody would believe what an effort it is to do what little I am able,—to dress and entertain, and order things.

It is fortunate Mary is so good with the baby. Such a dear baby!

And yet I *cannot* be with him, it makes me so nervous.

I suppose John never was nervous in his life. He laughs at me so about this wall-paper!

At first he meant to repaper the room, but afterwards he said that I was letting it get the better of me, and that nothing was worse for a nervous patient than to give way to such fancies.

He said that after the wall-paper was changed it would be the heavy bedstead, and then the barred windows, and then that gate at the head of the stairs, and so on.

"You know the place is doing you good," he said, "and really, dear, I don't care to renovate the house just for a three months' rental."

"Then do let us go downstairs," I said, "there are such pretty rooms there."

Then he took me in his arms and called me a blessed little goose, and said he would go down to the cellar, if I wished, and have it whitewashed into the bargain.

But he is right enough about the beds and windows and things.

It is an airy and comfortable room as any one need wish, and, of course, I would not be so silly as to make him uncomfortable just for a whim.

I'm really getting quite fond of the big room, all but that horrid paper.

Out of one window I can see the garden, those mysterious deepshaded arbors, the riotous old-fashioned flowers, and bushes and gnarly trees.

Out of another I get a lovely view of the bay and a little private wharf belonging to the estate. There is a beautiful shaded lane that runs down there from the house. I always fancy I see people walking in these numerous paths and arbors, but John has cautioned me not to give way to fancy in the least. He says that with my imaginative power and habit of story-making, a nervous weakness like mine is sure to lead to all manner of excited fancies, and that I ought to use my will and good sense to check the tendency. So I try.

I think sometimes that if I were only well enough to write a little it would relieve the press of ideas and rest me.

But I find I get pretty tired when I try.

It is so discouraging not to have any advice and companionship about my work. When I get really well, John says we will ask Cousin Henry and Julia down for a long visit; but he says he would as soon put fireworks in my pillow-case as to let me have those stimulating people about now.

I wish I could get well faster.

But I must not think about that. This paper looks to me as if it *knew* what a vicious influence it had!

There is a recurrent spot where the pattern lolls like a broken neck and two bulbous eyes stare at you upside down.

I get positively angry with the impertinence of it and the everlastingness. Up and down and sideways they crawl, and those absurd, unblinking eyes are everywhere. There is one place where two breaths didn't match, and the eyes go all up and down the line, one a little higher than the other.

I never saw so much expression in an inanimate thing before, and we all know how much expression they have! I used to lie awake as a child and get more entertainment and terror out of blank walls and plain furniture than most children could find in a toy-store.

I remember what a kindly wink the knobs of our big, old bureau used to have, and there was one chair that always seemed like a strong friend.

I used to feel that if any of the other things looked too fierce I could always hop into that chair and be safe.

The furniture in this room is no worse than inharmonious, however, for we had to bring it all from downstairs. I suppose when this was used as a playroom they had to take the nursery things out, and no wonder! I never saw such ravages as the children have made here.

The wall-paper, as I said before, is torn off in spots, and it sticketh closer than a brother—they must have had perseverance as well as hatred.

Then the floor is scratched and gouged and splintered, the plaster itself is dug out here and there, and this great heavy bed which is all we found in the room, looks as if it had been through the wars.

But I don't mind it a bit—only the paper.

There comes John's sister. Such a dear girl as she is, and so careful of me! I must not let her find me writing.

She is a perfect and enthusiastic housekeeper, and hopes for no better profession. I verily believe she thinks it is the writing which made me sick!

But I can write when she is out, and see her a long way off from these windows.

There is one that commands the road, a lovely shaded winding road, and one that just looks off over the country. A lovely country, too, full of great elms and velvet meadows.

This wall-paper has a kind of sub-pattern in a different shade, a particularly irritating one, for you can only see it in certain lights, and not clearly then.

But in the places where it isn't faded and where the sun is just so—I can see a strange, provoking, formless sort of figure, that seems to skulk about behind that silly and conspicuous front design.

There's sister on the stairs!

Well, the Fourth of July is over! The people are all gone and I am tired out. John thought it might do me good to see a little company, so we just had mother and Nellie and the children down for a week.

Of course I didn't do a thing. Jennie sees to everything now.

But it tired me all the same.

John says if I don't pick up faster he shall send me to Weir Mitchell in the fall.

But I don't want to go there at all. I had a friend who was in his hands once, and she says he is just like John and my brother, only more so!

Besides, it is such an undertaking to go so far.

I don't feel as if it was worth while to turn my hand over for anything, and I'm getting dreadfully fretful and querulous.

I cry at nothing, and cry most of the time.

Of course I don't when John is here, or anybody else, but when I am alone.

And I am alone a good deal just now. John is kept in town very often by serious cases, and Jennie is good and lets me alone when I want her to.

So I walk a little in the garden or down that lovely lane, sit on the porch under the roses, and lie down up here a good deal.

I'm getting really fond of the room in spite of the wall-paper. Perhaps *because* of the wall-paper.

It dwells in my mind so!

I lie here on this great immovable bed—it is nailed down, I believe—and follow that pattern about by the hour. It is as good as gymnastics, I assure you. I start, we'll say, at the bottom, down in the corner over there where it has not been touched, and I determine for the thousandth time that I *will* follow the pointless pattern to some sort of a conclusion.

I know a little of the principle of design, and I know this thing was not arranged on any laws of radiation, or alternation, or repetition, or symmetry, or anything else that I ever heard of.

It is repeated, of course, by the breadths, but not otherwise.

Looked at in one way each breadth stands alone, the bloated curves and flourishes—a kind of "debased Romanesque" with *delirium tremens*—go waddling up and down in isolated columns of fatuity.

But, on the other hand, they connect diagonally, and the sprawling outlines run off in great slanting waves of optic horror, like a lot of wallowing seaweeds in full chase.

The whole thing goes horizontally, too, at least it seems so, and I exhaust myself in trying to distinguish the order of its going in that direction.

They have used a horizontal breadth for a frieze, and that adds wonderfully to the confusion.

There is one end of the room where it is almost intact, and there, when the crosslights fade and the low sun shines directly upon it, I can almost fancy radiation after all,—the interminable grotesques seem to form around a common centre and rush off in headlong plunges of equal distraction.

It makes me tired to follow it. I will take a nap I guess.

I don't know why I should write this.

I don't want to.

I don't feel able.

And I know John would think it absurd. But I *must* say what I feel and think in some way—it is such a relief!

But the effort is getting to be greater than the relief.

Half the time now I am awfully lazy, and lie down ever so much.

John says I mustn't lose my strength, and has me take cod liver oil and lots of tonics and things, to say nothing of ale and wine and rare meat.

Dear John! He loves me very dearly, and hates to have me sick. I tried to have a real earnest reasonable talk with him the other day, and tell him how I wish he would let me go and make a visit to Cousin Henry and Julia.

But he said I wasn't able to go, nor able to stand it after I got there; and I did not make out a very good case for myself, for I was crying before I had finished.

It is getting to be a great effort for me to think straight. Just this nervous weakness I suppose.

And dear John gathered me up in his arms, and just carried me upstairs and laid me on the bed, and sat by me and read to me till it tired my head.

He said I was his darling and his comfort and all he had, and that I must take care of myself for his sake, and keep well.

He says no one but myself can help me out of it, that I must use my will and self-control and not let any silly fancies run away with me.

There's one comfort, the baby is well and happy, and does not have to occupy this nursery with the horrid wall-paper.

If we had not used it, that blessed child would have! What a fortunate escape! Why, I wouldn't have a child of mine, an impressionable little thing, live in such a room for worlds.

I never thought of it before, but it is lucky that John kept me here after all, I can stand it so much easier than a baby, you see.

Of course I never mention it to them any more—I am too wise,— but I keep watch of it all the same.

There are things in that paper that nobody knows but me, or ever will.

Behind that outside pattern the dim shapes get clearer every day.

It is always the same shape, only very numerous.

And it is like a woman stooping down and creeping about behind that pattern. I don't like it a bit. I wonder—I begin to think—I wish John would take me away from here!

It is so hard to talk with John about my case, because he is so wise, and because he loves me so.

But I tried it last night.

It was moonlight. The moon shines in all around just as the sun does.

I hate to see it sometimes, it creeps so slowly, and always comes in by one window or another.

John was asleep and I hated to waken him, so I kept still and watched the moonlight on that undulating wall-paper till I felt creepy.

The faint figure behind seemed to shake the pattern, just as if she wanted to get out.

I got up softly and went to feel and see if the paper *did* move, and when I came back John was awake.

"What is it, little girl?" he said. "Don't go walking about like that—you'll get cold."

I thought it was a good time to talk, so I told him that I really was not gaining here, and that I wished he would take me away.

"Why darling!" said he, "our lease will be up in three weeks, and I can't see how to leave before.

"The repairs are not done at home, and I cannot possibly leave town just now. Of course if you were in any danger, I could and would, but you really are better, dear, whether you can see it or not. I am a doctor, dear, and I know. You are gaining flesh and color, your appetite is better, I feel really much easier about you."

"I don't weigh a bit more," said I, "nor as much; and my appetite may be better in the evening when you are here, but it is worse in the morning when you are away!"

"Bless her little heart!" said he with a big hug, "she shall be as sick as she pleases! But now let's improve the shining hours by going to sleep, and talk about it in the morning!"

"And you won't go away?" I asked gloomily.

"Why, how can I, dear?" It is only three weeks more and then we will take a nice little trip of a few days while Jennie is getting the house ready. Really dear you are better!"

"Better in body perhaps—" I began, and stopped short, for he sat up straight and looked at me with such a stern, reproachful look that I could not say another word.

"My darling," said he, "I beg of you, for my sake and for our child's sake, as well as for your own, that you will never for one instant let that idea enter your mind! There is nothing so dangerous, so fascinating, to a temperament like yours. It is a false and foolish fancy. Can you not trust me as a physician when I tell you so?"

So of course I said no more on that score, and we went to sleep before long. He thought I was asleep first, but I wasn't, and lay there for hours trying to decide whether that front pattern and the back pattern really did move together or separately.

On a pattern like this, by daylight, there is a lack of sequence, a defiance of law, that is a constant irritant to a normal mind.

The color is hideous enough, and unreliable enough, and infuriating enough, but the pattern is torturing.

You think you have mastered it, but just as you get well underway in following, it turns a back-somersault and there you are. It slaps you in the face, knocks you down, and tramples upon you. It is like a bad dream.

The outside pattern is a florid arabesque, reminding one of a fungus. If you can imagine a toadstool in joints, an interminable string of toad-stools, budding and sprouting in endless convolutions—why, that is something like it.

That is, sometimes!

There is one marked peculiarity about this paper, a thing nobody seems to notice but myself, and that is that it changes as the light changes.

When the sun shoots in through the east window—I always watch for that first long, straight ray—it changes so quickly that I never can quite believe it.

That is why I watch it always.

By moonlight—the moon shines in all night when there is a moon—I wouldn't know it was the same paper.

At night in any kind of light, in twilight, candle light, lamplight, and worst of all by moonlight, it becomes bars! The outside pattern I mean, and the woman behind it is as plain as can be.

I didn't realize for a long time what the thing was that showed behind, that dim sub-pattern, but now I am quite sure it is a woman.

By daylight she is subdued, quiet. I fancy it is the pattern that keeps her so still. It is so puzzling. It keeps me quiet by the hour.

I lie down ever so much now. John says it is good for me, and to sleep all I can.

Indeed he started the habit by making me lie down for an hour after each meal.

It is a very bad habit I am convinced, for you see I don't sleep.

And that cultivates deceit, for I don't tell them I'm awake—O no!

The fact is I am getting a little afraid of John.

He seems very queer sometimes, and even Jennie has an inexplicable look.

It strikes me occasionally, just as a scientific hypothesis,—that perhaps it is the paper!

I have watched John when he did not know I was looking, and come into the room suddenly on the most innocent excuses, and I've caught him several times *looking at the paper!* And Jennie too. I caught Jennie with her hand on it once.

She didn't know I was in the room, and when I asked her in a quiet, a very quiet voice, with the most restrained manner possible, what she was doing with the paper—she turned around as if she had been caught stealing, and looked quite angry—asked me why I should frighten her so!

Then she said that the paper stained everything it touched, that she had found yellow smooches on all my clothes and John's, and she wished we would be more careful!

Did not that sound innocent? But I know she was studying that pattern, and I am determined that nobody shall find it out but myself!

Life is very much more exciting now than it used to be. You see I have something more to expect, to look forward to, to watch. I really do eat better, and am more quiet than I was.

John is so pleased to see me improve! He laughed a little the other day, and said I seemed to be flourishing in spite of my wall-paper.

I turned it off with a laugh. I had no intention of telling him it was *because* of the wall-paper—he would make fun of me. He might even want to take me away.

I don't want to leave now until I have found it out. There is a week more, and I think that will be enough.

I'm feeling ever so much better! I don't sleep much at night, for it is so interesting to watch developments; but I sleep a good deal in the daytime.

In the daytime it is tiresome and perplexing.

There are always new shoots on the fungus, and new shades of yellow all over it. I cannot keep count of them, though I have tried conscientiously.

It is the strangest yellow, that wall-paper! It makes me think of all the yellow things I ever saw—not beautiful ones like buttercups, but old foul, bad yellow things.

But there is something else about that paper—the smell! I noticed it the moment we came into the room, but with so much air and sun it was not bad. Now we have had a week of fog and rain, and whether the windows are open or not, the smell is here.

It creeps all over the house.

I find it hovering in the dining-room, skulking in the parlor, hiding in the hall, lying in wait for me on the stairs.

It gets into my hair.

Even when I go to ride, if I turn my head suddenly and surprise it—there is that smell!

Such a peculiar odor, too! I have spent hours in trying to analyze it, to find what it smelled like.

It is not bad—at first, and very gentle, but quite the subtlest, most enduring odor I ever met.

In this damp weather it is awful, I wake up in the night and find it hanging over me.

It used to disturb me at first. I thought seriously of burning the house—to reach the smell.

But now I am used to it. The only thing I can think of that it is like is the *color* of the paper! A yellow smell.

There is a very funny mark on this wall, low down, near the mopboard. A streak that runs round the room. It goes behind every piece of furniture, except the bed, a long, straight, even *smooch*, as if it had been rubbed over and over.

I wonder how it was done and who did it, and what they did it for. Round and round and round—round and round and round—it makes me dizzy!

I really have discovered something at last.

Through watching so much at night, when it changes so, I have finally found out.

The front pattern *does* move—and no wonder! The woman behind shakes it!

Sometimes I think there are a great many women behind, and sometimes only one, and she crawls around fast, and her crawling shakes it all over.

Then in the very bright spots she keeps still, and in the very shady spots she just takes hold of the bars and shakes them hard.

And she is all the time trying to climb through. But nobody could climb through that pattern—it strangles so; I think that is why it has so many heads.

They get through, and then the pattern strangles them off and turns them upside down, and makes their eyes white!

If those heads were covered or taken off it would not be half so bad.

I think that woman gets out in the daytime!

And I'll tell you why—privately—I've seen her!

I can see her out of every one of my windows!

It is the same woman, I know, for she is always creeping, and most women do not creep by daylight.

I see her on that long road under the trees, creeping along, and when a carriage comes she hides under the blackberry vines.

I don't blame her a bit. It must be very humiliating to be caught creeping by daylight!

I always lock the door when I creep by daylight. I can't do it at night, for I know John would suspect something at once.

And John is so queer now, that I don't want to irritate him. I wish he would take another room! Besides, I don't want anybody to get that woman out at night but myself.

I often wonder if I could see her out of all the windows at once.

But, turn as fast as I can, I can only see out of one at one time.

And though I always see her, she *may* be able to creep faster than I can turn!

I have watched her sometimes away off in the open country, creeping as fast as a cloud shadow in a high wind.

If only that top pattern could be gotten off from the under one! I mean to try it, little by little.

I have found out another funny thing, but I shan't tell it this time! It does not do to trust people too much.

There are only two more days to get this paper off, and I believe John is beginning to notice. I don't like the look in his eyes.

And I heard him ask Jennie a lot of professional questions about me. She had a very good report to give.

She said I slept a good deal in the daytime.

John knows I don't sleep very well at night, for all I'm so quiet!

He asked me all sorts of questions, too, and pretended to be very loving and kind.

As if I couldn't see through him!

Still, I don't wonder he acts so, sleeping under this paper for three months.

It only interests me, but I feel sure John and Jennie are secretly affected by it.

Hurrah! This is the last day, but it is enough. John to stay in town over night, and won't be out until this evening.

Jennie wanted to sleep with me—the sly thing! but I told her I should undoubtedly rest better for a night all alone.

That was clever, for really I wasn't alone a bit! As soon as it was moonlight and that poor thing began to crawl and shake the pattern, I got up and ran to help her.

I pulled and she shook, I shook and she pulled, and before morning we had peeled off yards of that paper.

A strip about as high as my head and half around the room.

And then when the sun came and that awful pattern began to laugh at me, I declared I would finish it to-day!

We go away to-morrow, and they are moving all my furniture down again to leave things as they were before.

Jennie looked at the wall in amazement, but I told her merrily that I did it out of pure spite at the vicious thing.

She laughed and said she wouldn't mind doing it herself, but I must not get tired.

How she betrayed herself that time!

But I am here, and no person touches this paper but me,—not *alive!*

She tried to get me out of the room—it was too patent! But I said it was so quiet and empty and clean now that I believed I would lie down again and sleep all I could; and not to wake me for dinner—I would call when I woke.

So now she is gone, and the servants are gone, and the things are gone, and there is nothing left but that great bedstead nailed down, with the canvas mattress we found on it.

We shall sleep downstairs to-night, and take the boat home to-morrow.

I quite enjoy the room, now it is bare again.

How those children did tear about here!

This bedstead is fairly gnawed!

But I must get to work.

I have locked the door and thrown the key down into the front path.

I don't want to go out, and I don't want to have anybody come in, till John comes.

I want to astonish him.

I've got a rope up here that even Jennie did not find. If that woman does get out, and tries to get away, I can tie her!

But I forgot I could not reach far without anything to stand on!

This bed will *not* move!

I tried to lift and push it until I was lame, and then I got so angry I bit off a little piece at one corner—but it hurt my teeth.

Then I peeled off all the paper I could reach standing on the floor.

It sticks horribly and the pattern just enjoys it! All those strangled heads and bulbous eyes and waddling fungus growths just shriek with derision!

I am getting angry enough to do something desperate. To jump out of the window would be admirable exercise, but the bars are too strong even to try.

Besides I wouldn't do it. Of course not. I know well enough that a step like that is improper and might be misconstrued.

I don't like to *look* out the windows even—there are so many of those creeping women, and they creep so fast.

I wonder if they all come out of that wall-paper as I did?

But I am securely fastened now by my well-hidden rope—you don't get *me* out in the road there!

I suppose I shall have to get back behind the pattern when it comes night, and that is hard!

It is so pleasant to be out in this great room and creep around as I please!

I don't want to go outside. I won't, even if Jennie asks me to.

For outside you have to creep on the ground, and everything is green instead of yellow.

But here I can creep smoothly on the floor, and my shoulder just fits in that long smooch around the wall, so I cannot lose my way.

Why there's John at the door!

It is no use, young man, you can't open it!

How he does call and pound!

Now he's crying for an axe.

It would be a shame to break down that beautiful door!

"John dear!" said I in the gentlest voice, "the key is down by the front steps, under a plantain leaf!"

That silenced him for a few moments.

Then he said—very quietly indeed, "Open the door, my darling!"

"I can't," said I. "The key is down by the front door under a plantain leaf!"

And then I said it again, several times, very gently and slowly, and said it so often that he had to go and see, and he got it of course, and came in. He stopped short by the door.

"What is the matter?" he cried. "For God's sake, what are you doing!"

I kept on creeping just the same, but I looked at him over my shoulder.

"I've got out at last," said I, "in spite of you and Jane. And I've pulled off most of the paper, so you can't put me back!"

Now why should that man have fainted? But he did, and right across my path by the wall, so that I had to creep over him every time!

Theme Questions

✿

✿ What techniques do artists use to convey the inner world of the mind?

✿ Do you agree with Emily Dickinson that "much madness is divinest sense"? Explain.

✿ What special wisdom is associated with madness in each of the selections in this section?

✿ Is it possible for madness to be different in different cultures or at different times in history? Do our perceptions of what is madness change? Explain.

Dreams: Maps of the
Inner World

Dreams lie at the edge of our consciousness. They are mysteries; they are facts. Dreaming is a part of the experience of every human being, as natural and ordinary as blinking. Our dreams express our desires, our fears, and our hopes, although we may not recognize them. The language of dreams speaks to us in symbols—a code that art and literature can help us to decipher. Through dreams we can discover essential aspects of our nature and our world, on a level far different from that of our conscious lives.

Dreams are part of the experiences of cultures as well as of individuals. When we share stories about our history as a country or a people, when we talk about what is important to us now or in the future, we are helping to pass on our dreams to others. Through these dreams, we identify more clearly who we are and what our place is within a larger community.

Whether the dream is an individual one or shared by many, it can sometimes provide a goal, even a victory over social forces outside of our control. Or it can produce such a longing that we ache for the rest of our lives.

The Dream

✩

Henri Rousseau

The Door in the Wall

☆

H.G. Wells

I

One confidential evening, not three months ago, Lionel Wallace told me this story of the Door in the Wall. And at the time I thought that so far as he was concerned it was a true story.

He told it me with such a direct simplicity of conviction that I could not do otherwise than believe in him. But in the morning in my own flat, I woke to a different atmosphere, and as I lay in bed and recalled the things he had told me, stripped of the glamour of his earnest slow voice, denuded of the focussed shaded table light, the shadowy atmosphere that wrapped about him and the pleasant bright things, the dessert and glasses and napery of the dinner we had shared, making them for the time a bright little world quite cut off from every-day realities, I saw it all as frankly incredible. "He was mystifying!" I said, and then: "How well he did it!....It isn't quite the thing I should have expected him, of all people, to do well."

Afterwards, as I sat up in bed and sipped my morning tea, I found myself trying to account for the flavour of reality that perplexed me in his impossible reminiscences, by supposing they did in some way suggest, present, convey—I hardly know which word to use—experiences it was otherwise impossible to tell.

Well, I don't resort to that explanation now. I have got over my intervening doubts. I believe now, as I believed at the moment of telling, that Wallace did to the very best of his ability strip the truth of his secret for me. But whether he himself saw, or only thought he saw, whether he himself was the possessor of an inestimable privilege, or the victim of a fantastic dream, I cannot pretend to guess. Even the facts of his death, which ended my doubts forever, throw no light on that. That much the reader must judge for himself.

I forget now what chance comment or criticism of mine moved so reticent a man to confide in me. He was, I think, defending himself against an imputation of slackness and unreliability I had made in relation to a great public movement in which he had disappointed me. But he plunged suddenly. "I have," he said, "a preoccupation—"

"I know," he went on, after a pause that he devoted to the study of his cigar ash, "I have been negligent. The fact is—it isn't a case of ghosts or apparitions—but—it's an odd thing to tell of, Redmond—I am haunted. I am haunted by something—that rather takes the light out of things, that fills me with longings. . . ."

He paused, checked by that English shyness that so often overcomes us when we would speak of moving or grave or beautiful things. "You were at Saint Athelstan's all through," he said, and for a moment that seemed to me quite irrelevant. "Well"—and he paused. Then very haltingly at first, but afterwards more easily, he began to tell of the thing that was hidden in his life, the haunting memory of a beauty and a happiness that filled his heart with insatiable longings that made all the interests and spectacle of worldly life seem dull and tedious and vain to him.

Now that I have the clue to it, the thing seems written visibly in his face. I have a photograph in which that look of detachment has been caught and intensified. It reminds me of what a woman once said of him—a woman who had loved him greatly. "Suddenly," she said, "the interest goes out of him. He forgets you. He doesn't care a rap for you— under his very nose. . . ."

Yet the interest was not always out of him, and when he was holding his attention to a thing Wallace could contrive to be an extremely successful man. His career, indeed, is set with successes. He left me behind him long ago; he soared up over my head, and cut a figure in the world that I couldn't cut—anyhow. He was still a year short of forty, and they say now that he would have been in office and very probably in the new Cabinet if he had lived. At school he always beat me without effort— as it were by nature. We were at school together at Saint Athelstan's College in West Kensington for almost all our school time. He came into the school as my co-equal, but he left far above me, in a blaze of scholarships and brilliant performance. Yet I think I made a fair average running. And it was at school I heard first of the Door in the Wall—that I was to hear of a second time only a month before his death.

To him at least the Door in the Wall was a real door leading through a real wall to immortal realities. Of that I am now quite assured.

And it came into his life early, when he was a little fellow between five and six. I remember how, as he sat making his confession to me with a slow gravity, he reasoned and reckoned the date of it. "There was," he said, "a crimson Virginia creeper in it—all one bright uniform crimson in a clear amber sunshine against a white wall. That came into the impression somehow, though I don't clearly remember how, and there were horse-chestnut leaves upon the clean pavement outside the green door. They were blotched yellow and green, you know, not brown nor dirty, so that they must have been new fallen. I take it that means October. I look out for horse-chestnut leaves every year, and I ought to know.

"If I'm right in that, I was about five years and four months old."

He was, he said, rather a precocious little boy—he learned to talk at an abnormally early age, and he was so sane and "old-fashioned," as people say, that he was permitted an amount of initiative that most children scarcely attain by seven or eight. His mother died when he was born, and he was under the less vigilant and authoritative care of a nursery governess. His father was a stern, preoccupied lawyer, who gave him little attention, and expected great things of him. For all his brightness he found life a little grey and dull, I think. And one day he wandered.

He could not recall the particular neglect that enabled him to get away, nor the course he took among the West Kensington roads. All that had faded among the incurable blurs of memory. But the white wall and the green door stood out quite distinctly.

As his memory of that remote childish experience ran, he did at the very first sight of that door experience a peculiar emotion, an attraction, a desire to get to the door and open it and walk in. And at the same time he had the clearest conviction that either it was unwise or it was wrong of him—he could not tell which—to yield to this attraction. He insisted upon it as a curious thing that he knew from the very beginning—unless memory has played him the queerest trick—that the door was unfastened, and that he could go in as he chose.

I seem to see the figure of that little boy, drawn and repelled. And it was very clear in his mind, too, though why it should be so was never explained, that his father would be very angry if he went through that door.

Wallace described all these moments of hesitation to me with the utmost particularity. He went right past the door, and then, with his hands in his pockets, and making an infantile attempt to whistle, strolled right along beyond the end of the wall. There he recalls a number of mean, dirty shops, and particularly that of a plumber and decorator, with a dusty disorder of earthenware pipes, sheet lead ball taps, pattern books of wall paper, and tins of enamel. He stood pretending to examine these things, and coveting, passionately desiring the green door.

Then, he said, he had a gust of emotion. He made a run for it, lest hesitation should grip him again, he went plump with out-stretched hand through the green door and let it slam behind him. And so, in a trice, he came into the garden that has haunted all his life.

It was very difficult for Wallace to give me his full sense of that garden into which he came.

There was something in the very air of it that exhilarated, that gave one a sense of lightness and good happening and well being; there was something in the sight of it that made all its colour clean and perfect and subtly luminous. In the instant of coming into it one was exquisitely glad—as only in rare moments and when one is young and joyful one can be glad in this world. And everything was beautiful there. . . .

Wallace mused before he went on telling me. "You see," he said, with the doubtful inflection of a man who pauses at incredible things, "there were two great panthers there. . .Yes, spotted panthers. And I was not afraid. There was a long wide path with marble-edged flower borders on either side, and these two huge velvety beasts were playing there with a ball. One looked up and came toward me, a little curious as it seemed. It came right up to me, rubbed its soft round ear very gently against the small hand I held out and purred. It was, I tell you, an enchanted garden. I know. And the size? Oh! it stretched far and wide, this way and that. I believe there were hills far away. Heaven knows where West Kensington had suddenly got to! And somehow it was just like coming home.

"You know, in the very moment the door swung to behind me, I forgot the road with its fallen chestnut leaves, its cabs and tradesmen's carts, I forgot the sort of gravitational pull back to the discipline and obedience of home, I forgot all hesitations and fear, forgot discretion, forgot all the intimate realities of this life. I became in a moment a very glad and wonder-happy little boy—in another world. It was a world with a different quality, a warmer, more penetrating and mellower light, with a faint clear gladness in its air, and wisps of sun-touched cloud in the blueness of its sky. And before me ran this long wide path, invitingly, with weedless beds on either side, rich with untended flowers, and these two great panthers. I put my little hands fearlessly on their soft fur, and caressed their round ears and the sensitive corners under their ears, and played with them, and it was as though they welcomed me home. There was a keen sense of home-coming in my mind, and when presently a tall, fair girl appeared in the pathway and came to meet me, smiling, and said 'Well?' to me, and lifted me, and kissed me, and put me down, and led me by the hand, there was no amazement, but only an impression of delightful rightness, of being reminded of happy things that had in some strange way been overlooked. There were broad steps, I remember, that came into view between spikes of delphinium, and up these we went to a great avenue between very old and shady dark trees. All down this avenue, you know, between the red chapped stems, were marble seats of honour and statuary, and very tame and friendly white doves. . . .

"And along this avenue my girl-friend led me, looking down— I recall the pleasant lines, the finely-modelled chin of her sweet kind face— asking me questions in a soft, agreeable voice, and telling me things, pleasant things I know, though what they were I was never able to recall...And presently a little Capuchin monkey, very clean, with a fur of ruddy brown and kindly hazel eyes, came down a tree to us and ran beside me, looking up at me and grinning, and presently leapt to my shoulder. So we went on our way in great happiness...."

He paused.

"Go on," I said.

"I remember little things. We passed an old man musing among laurels, I remember, and a place gay with paroquets, and came through a broad shaded colonnade to a spacious cool palace, full of pleasant fountains, full of beautiful things, full of the quality and promise of heart's desire. And there were many things and many people, some that still seem to stand out clearly and some that are a little vague, but all these people were beautiful and kind. In some way—I don't know how—it was conveyed to me that they all were kind to me, glad to have me there, and filling me with gladness by their gestures, by the touch of their hands, by the welcome and love in their eyes. Yes—"

He mused for a while. "Playmates I found there. That was very much to me, because I was a lonely little boy. They played delightful games in a grass-covered court where there was a sun-dial set about with flowers. And as one played one loved....

"But—it's odd—there's a gap in my memory. I don't remember the games we played. I never remembered. Afterwards, as a child, I spent long hours trying, even with tears, to recall the form of that happiness. I wanted to play it all over again—in my nursery—by myself. No! All I remember is the happiness and two dear playfellows who were most with me....Then presently came a sombre dark woman, with a grave, pale face and dreamy eyes, a sombre woman wearing a soft long robe of pale purple, who carried a book and beckoned and took me aside with her into a gallery above a hall—though my playmates were loth to have me go, and ceased their game and stood watching as I was carried away. 'Come back to us!' they cried. 'Come back to us soon!' I looked up at her face, but she heeded them not at all. Her face was very gentle and grave. She took me to a seat in the gallery, and I stood beside her, ready to look at her book as she opened it upon her knee. The pages fell open. She pointed, and I looked, marvelling, for in the living pages of that book I saw myself; it was a story about myself, and in it were all the things that had happened to me since ever I was born....

"It was wonderful to me, because the pages of that book were not pictures, you understand, but realities."

Wallace paused gravely—looking at me doubtfully.

"Go on," I said. "I understand."

"They were realities—yes, they must have been; people moved and things came and went in them; my dear mother, whom I had near forgotten; then my father, stern and upright, the servants, the nursery, all the familiar things of home. Then the front door and the busy streets, with traffic to and fro: I looked and marvelled, and looked half doubtfully again into the woman's face and turned the pages over, skipping this and that, to see more of this book, and more, and so at last I came to myself hovering and hesitating outside the green door in the long white wall, and felt again the conflict and the fear.

"'And next?' I cried, and would have turned on, but the cool hand of the grave woman delayed me.

"'Next?' I insisted, and struggled gently with her hand, pulling up her fingers with all my childish strength and as she yielded and the page came over she bent down upon me like a shadow and kissed my brow.

"But the page did not show the enchanted garden, nor the panthers, nor the girl who had led me by the hand, nor the playfellows who had been so loth to let me go. It showed a long grey street in West Kensington, on that chill hour of afternoon before the lamps are lit, and I was there, a wretched little figure, weeping aloud, for all that I could do to restrain myself, and I was weeping because I could not return to my dear playfellows who had called after me, 'Come back to us! Come back to us soon!' I was there. This was no page in a book, but harsh reality; that enchanted place and the restraining hand of the grave mother at whose knee I stood had gone—whither have they gone?"

He halted again, and remained for a time, staring into the fire.

"Oh! the wretchedness of that return!" he murmured.

"Well?" I said after a minute or so.

"Poor little wretch I was—brought back to this grey world again! As I realised the fulness of what had happened to me, I gave way to quite ungovernable grief. And the shame and humiliation of that public weeping and my disgraceful home-coming remain with me still. I see again the benevolent-looking old gentleman in gold spectacles who stopped and spoke to me— prodding me first with his umbrella. 'Poor little chap,' said he; 'and are you lost then?'—and me a London boy of five and more! And he must needs bring in a kindly young policeman and make a crowd of me, and so march me home. Sobbing, conspicuous and frightened, I came from the enchanted garden to the steps of my father's house.

"That is as well as I can remember my vision of that garden—the garden that haunts me still. Of course, I can convey nothing of that indescribable quality of translucent unreality, that difference from the common things of experience that hung about it all; but that—that is what happened. If it was a dream, I am sure it was a day-time and altogether extraordinary dream.... H'm!—naturally there followed a terrible questioning, by my aunt, my father, the nurse, the governess—everyone...

"I tried to tell them, and my father gave me my first thrashing for telling lies. When afterwards I tried to tell my aunt, she punished me again for my wicked persistence. Then, as I said, everyone was forbidden to listen to me, to hear a word about it. Even my fairy tale books were taken away from me for a time—because I was 'too imaginative.' Eh? Yes, they did that! My father belonged to the old school.... And my story was driven back upon myself. I whispered it to my pillow—my pillow that was often damp and salt to my whispering lips with childish tears. And I added always to my official and less fervent prayers this one heartfelt request: 'Please God I may dream of the garden. Oh! take me back to my garden! Take me back to my garden!'

"I dreamt often of the garden. I may have added to it, I may have changed it; I do not know.... All this you understand is an attempt to reconstruct from fragmentary memories a very early experience. Between that and the other consecutive memories of my boyhood there is a gulf. A time came when it seemed impossible I should ever speak of that wonder glimpse again."

I asked an obvious question.

"No," he said. "I don't remember that I ever attempted to find my way back to the garden in those early years. This seems odd to me now, but I think that very probably a closer watch was kept on my movements after this misadventure to prevent my going astray. No, it wasn't until you knew me that I tried for the garden again. And I believe there was a period—incredible as it seems now—when I forgot the garden altogether—when I was about eight or nine it may have been. Do you remember me as a kid at Saint Athelstan's?"

"Rather!"

"I didn't show any signs did I in those days of having a secret dream?"

II

He looked up with a sudden smile.

"Did you ever play North-West Passage with me?.... No, of course you didn't come my way!"

"It was the sort of game," he went on, "that every imaginative child plays all day. The idea was the discovery of a North-West Passage to school. The way to school was plain enough; the game consisted in finding some way that wasn't plain, starting off ten minutes early in some almost hopeless direction, and working one's way round through unac-

customed streets to my goal. And one day I got entangled among some
rather low-class streets on the other side of Campden Hill, and I began to
think that for once the game would be against me and that I should get to
school late. I tried rather desperately a street that seemed a *cul de sac*, and
found a passage at the end. I hurried through that with renewed hope. 'I
shall do it yet,' I said, and passed a row of frowsy little shops that were
inexplicably familiar to me, and behold! there was my long white wall
and the green door that led to the enchanted garden!

"The thing whacked upon me suddenly. Then, after all, that garden,
that wonderful garden, wasn't a dream!". . . .

He paused.

"I suppose my second experience with the green door marks the world
of difference there is between the busy life of a schoolboy and the infinite
leisure of a child. Anyhow, this second time I didn't for a moment think of
going in straight away. You see. . .For one thing my mind was full of the
idea of getting to school in time—set on not breaking my record for
punctuality. I must surely have felt *some* little desire at least to try the
door—yes, I must have felt that. . . .But I seem to remember the attraction of the door mainly as another obstacle to my overmastering determination to get to school. I was immediately interested by this discovery I
had made, of course—I went on with my mind full of it—but I went on.
It didn't check me. I ran past tugging out my watch, found I had ten
minutes still to spare, and then I was going downhill into familiar
surroundings. I got to school, breathless, it is true, and wet with
perspiration, but in time. I can remember hanging up my coat and hat. . .
Went right by it and left it behind me. Odd, eh?"

He looked at me thoughtfully. "Of course, I didn't know then that it
wouldn't always be there. School boys have limited imaginations. I
suppose I thought it was an awfully jolly thing to have it there, to know
my way back to it, but there was the school tugging at me. I expect I was
a good deal distraught and inattentive that morning, recalling what I
could of the beautiful strange people I should presently see again. Oddly
enough I had no doubt in my mind that they would be glad to see me. . .
Yes, I must have thought of the garden that morning just as a jolly sort of
place to which one might resort in the interludes of a strenuous scholas-
tic career.

"I didn't go that day at all. The next day was a half holiday, and that may
have weighed with me. Perhaps, too, my state of inattention brought
down impositions upon me and docked the margin of time necessary for
the detour. I don't know. What I do know is that in the meantime the
enchanted garden was so much upon my mind that I could not keep it to
myself.

"I told—What was his name?—a ferrety-looking youngster we used to call Squiff.

"Young Hopkins," said I.

"Hopkins it was. I did not like telling him, I had a feeling that in some way it was against the rules to tell him, but I did. He was walking part of the way home with me; he was talkative, and if we had not talked about the enchanted garden we should have talked of something else, and it was intolerable to me to think about any other subject. So I blabbed.

"Well, he told my secret. The next day in the play interval I found myself surrounded by half a dozen bigger boys, half teasing and wholly curious to hear more of the enchanted garden. There was that big Fawcett—you remember him?—and Carnaby and Morley Reynolds. You weren't there by any chance? No, I think I should have remembered if you were. . . .

"A boy is a creature of odd feelings. I was, I really believe, in spite of my secret self-disgust, a little flattered to have the attention of these big fellows. I remember particularly a moment of pleasure caused by the praise of Crawshaw—you remember Crawshaw major, the son of Crawshaw the composer?—who said it was the best lie he had ever heard. But at the same time there was a really painful undertow of shame at telling what I felt was indeed a sacred secret. That beast Fawcett made a joke about the girl in green—."

Wallace's voice sank with the keen memory of that shame. "I pretended not to hear," he said. "Well, then Carnaby suddenly called me a young liar and disputed with me when I said the thing was true. I said I knew where to find the green door, could lead them all there in ten minutes. Carnaby became outrageously virtuous, and said I'd have to—and bear out my words or suffer. Did you ever have Carnaby twist your arm? Then perhaps you'll understand how it went with me. I swore my story was true. There was nobody in the school then to save a chap from Carnaby though Crawshaw put in a word or so. Carnaby had got his game. I grew excited and red-eared, and a little frightened, I behaved altogether like a silly little chap, and the outcome of it all was that instead of starting alone for my enchanted garden, I led the way presently—cheeks flushed, ears hot, eyes smarting, and my soul one burning misery and shame—for a party of six mocking, curious and threatening schoolfellows.

"We never found the white wall and the green door. . ."

"You mean?—"

"I mean I couldn't find it. I would have found it if I could.

"And afterwards when I could go alone I couldn't find it. I never found it. I seem now to have been always looking for it through my school-boy days, but I've never come upon it again."

"Did the fellows—make it disagreeable?"

"Beastly. . . . Carnaby held a council over me for wanton lying. I remember how I sneaked home and upstairs to hide the marks of my blubbering. But when I cried myself to sleep at last it wasn't for Carnaby, but for the garden, for the beautiful afternoon I had hoped for, for the sweet friendly women and the waiting playfellows and the game I had hoped to learn again, that beautiful forgotten game. . . .

"I believed firmly that if I had not told—. . . . I had bad times after that—crying at night and wool-gathering by day. For two terms I slackened and had bad reports. Do you remember? Of course you would! It was *you*—your beating me in mathematics that brought me back to the grind again."

III

For a time my friend stared silently into the red heart of the fire. Then he said: "I never saw it again until I was seventeen.

"It leapt upon me for the third time—as I was driving to Paddington on my way to Oxford and a scholarship. I had just one momentary glimpse. I was leaning over the apron of my hansom smoking a cigarette, and no doubt thinking myself no end of a man of the world, and suddenly there was the door, the wall, the dear sense of unforgettable and still attainable things.

"We clattered by—I too taken by surprise to stop my cab until we were well past and round a corner. Then I had a queer moment, a double and divergent movement of my will: I tapped the little door in the roof of the cab, and brought my arm down to pull out my watch. 'Yes, sir!' said the cabman, smartly. 'Er—well—it's nothing,' I cried. 'My mistake! We haven't much time! Go on!' and he went on. . .

"I got my scholarship. And the night after I was told of that I sat over my fire in my little upper room, my study, in my father's house, with his praise—his rare praise—and his sound counsels ringing in my ears, and I smoked my favourite pipe—the formidable bulldog of adolescence—and thought of that door in the long white wall. 'If I had stopped,' I thought, 'I should have missed my scholarship, I should have missed Oxford—muddled all the fine career before me! I begin to see things better!' I fell musing deeply, but I did not doubt then this career of mine was a thing that merited sacrifice.

"Those dear friends and that clear atmosphere seemed very sweet to me, very fine, but remote. My grip was fixing now upon the world. I saw another door opening—the door of my career."

He stared again into the fire. Its red lights picked out a stubborn strength in his face for just one flickering moment, and then it vanished again.

"Well," he said and sighed, "I have served that career. I have done— much work, much hard work. But I have dreamt of the enchanted garden a thousand dreams, and seen its door, or at least glimpsed its door, four times since then. Yes—four times. For a while this world was so bright and interesting, seemed so full of meaning and opportunity that the half-effaced charm of the garden was by comparison gentle and remote. Who wants to pat panthers on the way to dinner with pretty women and distinguished men? I came down to London from Oxford, a man of bold promise that I have done something to redeem. Something—and yet there have been disappointments. . . .

"Twice I have been in love—I will not dwell on that—but once, as I went to someone who, I know, doubted whether I dared to come, I took a short cut at a venture through an unfrequented road near Earl's Court, and so happened on a white wall and a familiar green door. 'Odd!' said I to myself, 'but I thought this place was on Campden Hill. It's the place I never could find somehow—like counting Stonehenge—the place of that queer day dream of mine.' And I went by it intent upon my purpose. It had no appeal to me that afternoon.

"I had just a moment's impulse to try the door, three steps aside were needed at the most—though I was sure enough in my heart that it would open to me—and then I thought that doing so might delay me on the way to that appointment in which I thought my honour was involved. Afterwards I was sorry for my punctuality—I might at least have peeped in, I thought, and waved a hand to those panthers, but I knew enough by this time not to seek again belatedly that which is not found by seeking. Yes, that time made me very sorry. . . .

"Years of hard work after that and never a sight of the door. It's only recently it has come back to me. With it there has come a sense as though some thin tarnish had spread itself over my world. I began to think of it as a sorrowful and bitter thing that I should never see that door again. Perhaps I was suffering a little from overwork—perhaps it was what I've heard spoken of as the feeling of forty. I don't know. But certainly the keen brightness that makes effort easy has gone out of things recently, and that just at a time with all these new political developments—when I ought to be working. Odd, isn't it? But I do begin to find life toilsome, its rewards, as I come near them, cheap. I began a little while ago to want the garden quite badly. Yes—and I've seen it three times."

"The garden?"

"No—the door! And I haven't gone in!"

He leaned over the table to me, with an enormous sorrow in his voice as he spoke. "Thrice I had my chance—*thrice!* If ever that door offers itself to me again, I swore, I will go in out of this dust and heat, out of this dry glitter of vanity, out of these toilsome futilities. I will go and never return. This time I will stay. . . . I swore it and when the time came—*I didn't go*.

"Three times in one year have I passed that door and failed to enter. Three times in the last year.

"The first time was on the night of the snatch division on the Tenants' Redemption Bill, on which the Government was saved by a majority of three. You remember? No one on our side—perhaps very few on the opposite side—expected the end that night. Then the debate collapsed like eggshells. I and Hotchkiss were dining with his cousin at Brentford, we were both unpaired, and we were called up by telephone, and set off at once in his cousin's motor. We got in barely in time, and on the way we passed my wall and door—livid in the moonlight, blotched with hot yellow as the glare of our lamps lit it, but unmistakable. 'My God!' cried I. 'What?' said Hotchkiss. 'Nothing!' I answered, and the moment passed.

" 'I've made a great sacrifice,' I told the whip as I got in. 'They all have,' he said, and hurried by.

"I do not see how I could have done otherwise then. And the next occasion was as I rushed to my father's bedside to bid that stern old man farewell. Then, too, the claims of life were imperative. But the third time was different; it happened a week ago. It fills me with hot remorse to recall it. I was with Gurker and Ralphs—it's no secret now you know that I've had my talk with Gurker. We had been dining at Frobisher's, and the talk had become intimate between us. The question of my place in the reconstructed ministry lay always just over the boundary of the discussion. Yes—yes. That's all settled. It needn't be talked about yet, but there's no reason to keep a secret from you. . . . Yes—thanks! thanks! But let me tell you my story.

"Then, on that night things were very much in the air. My position was a very delicate one. I was keenly anxious to get some definite word from Gurker, but was hampered by Ralphs' presence. I was using the best power of my brain to keep that light and careless talk not too obviously directed to the point that concerns me. I had to. Ralphs' behaviour since has more than justified my caution. . . . Ralphs, I knew, would leave us beyond the Kensington High Street, and then I could surprise Gurker by a sudden frankness. One has sometimes to resort to these little devices. . . . And then it was that in the margin of my field of vision I became aware once more of the white wall, the green door before us down the road.

"We passed it talking. I passed it. I can still see the shadow of Gurker's marked profile, his opera hat tilted forward over his prominent nose, the many folds of his neck wrap going before my shadow and Ralphs' as we sauntered past.

"I passed within twenty inches of the door. 'If I say good-night to them, and go in,' I asked myself, 'what will happen?' And I was all a-tingle for that word with Gurker.

"I could not answer that question in the tangle of my other problems. 'They will think me mad,' I thought. 'And suppose I vanish now!—Amazing disappearance of a prominent politician!' That weighed with me. A thousand inconceivably petty worldlinesses weighed with me in that crisis."

Then he turned on me with a sorrowful smile, and, speaking slowly; "Here I am!" he said.

"Here I am!" he repeated, "and my chance has gone from me. Three times in one year the door has been offered me—the door that goes into peace, into delight, into a beauty beyond dreaming, a kindness no man on earth can know. And I have rejected it, Redmond, and it has gone—"

"How do you know?"

"I know. I know. I am left now to work it out, to stick to the tasks that held me so strongly when my moments came. You say, I have success—this vulgar, tawdry, irksome, envied thing. I have it." He had a walnut in his big hand. "If that was my success," he said, and crushed it, and held it out for me to see.

"Let me tell you something, Redmond. This loss is destroying me. For two months, for ten weeks nearly now, I have done no work at all, except the most necessary and urgent duties. My soul is full of inappeasable regrets. At nights—when it is less likely I shall be recognised—I go out. I wander. Yes. I wonder what people would think of that if they knew. A Cabinet Minister, the responsible head of that most vital of all departments, wandering alone—grieving—sometimes near audibly lamenting—for a door, for a garden!"

IV

I can see now his rather pallid face, and the unfamiliar sombre fire that had come into his eyes. I see him very vividly to-night. I sit recalling his words, his tones, and last evening's *Westminster Gazette* still lies on my sofa, containing the notice of his death. At lunch to-day the club was busy with him and the strange riddle of his fate.

They found his body very early yesterday morning in a deep excavation near East Kensington Station. It is one of two shafts that have been made in connection with an extension of the railway southward. It is protected from the intrusion of the public by a hoarding upon the high road, in which a small doorway has been cut for the convenience of some of the workmen who live in that direction. The doorway was left unfastened through a misunderstanding between two gangers, and through it he made his way. . . .

My mind is darkened with questions and riddles.

It would seem he walked all the way from the House that night—he has frequently walked home during the past Session—and so it is I figure his dark form coming along the late and empty streets, wrapped up, intent. And then did the pale electric lights near the station cheat the rough planking into a semblance of white? Did that fatal unfastened door awaken some memory?

Was there, after all, ever any green door in the wall at all?

I do not know. I have told his story as he told it to me. There are times when I believe that Wallace was no more than the victim of the coincidence between a rare but not unprecedented type of hallucination and a careless trap, but that indeed is not my profoundest belief. You may think me superstitious if you will, and foolish; but, indeed, I am more than half convinced that he had in truth, an abnormal gift, and a sense, something—I know not what—that in the guise of wall and door offered him an outlet, a secret and peculiar passage of escape into another and altogether more beautiful world. At any rate, you will say, it betrayed him in the end. But did it betray him? There you touch the inmost mystery of these dreamers, these men of vision and the imagination. We see our world fair and common, the hoarding and the pit. By our daylight standard he walked out of security into darkness, danger and death. But did he see like that?

The Magic Pillow

☆

Shen Chi-chi

In the seventh year of K'ai Yuan (719 A.D.) a Taoist priest by the name of Lü Weng, who had acquired the magic of the immortals, was traveling on the road to Hantan. He stopped at an inn and was sitting and resting with his back against his bag when he was joined in a very genial conversation by a young man named Lu Sheng, who wore a plain, short coat and rode a black colt and who had stopped at the inn on his way to the fields. After a while Lu Sheng suddenly sighed and said, looking at his shabby clothes, "It is because fate is against me that I have been such a failure in life!" "Why do you say that in the midst of such a pleasant conversation?" Lü Weng said, "For as far as I can see you suffer from nothing and appear to enjoy the best of health." "This is mere existence," Lu Sheng said. "I do not call this life." "What then do you call life?" asked the priest, whereupon the young man answered, "A man ought to achieve great things and make a name for himself; he should be a general at the head of an expedition or a great minister at court, preside over sumptuous banquets and order the orchestra to play what he likes, and cause his clan to prosper and his own family to wax rich—these things make what I call life. I have devoted myself to study and have enriched myself with travel; I used to think that rank and title were mine for the picking, but now at the prime of life I still have to labor in the fields. What do you call this if not failure?"

After he finished speaking he felt a sudden drowsiness. The innkeeper was steaming some millet at the time. Lü Weng reached into his bag and took out a pillow and gave it to Lu Sheng, "Rest your head on this pillow; it will enable you to fulfill your wishes." The pillow was made of green porcelain and had an opening at each end. Lu Sheng bent his head toward it and as he did so the opening grew large and bright, so that he was able to crawl into it. He found himself back home. A few months later he married the daughter of the Tsui family of Chingho, who was very beautiful and made him exceedingly happy. His wealth increased and the number of luxuries with which he surrounded himself multiplied day by day. The following year he passed the examinations and thus "discarded his hempen coat" and joined the ranks at court. He was made a member of the Imperial Secretariat and had the honor of composing occasional poems at the emperor's command. After serving a term as inspector of Weinan, he was promoted to the Censorate, and made secretary in attendance. In the latter capacity he took part in the drafting of important decrees.

Then followed a succession of provincial posts, in one of which, as the governor of Shensi, he built a canal eighty *li* in length, which brought so many benefits to the people of the region that they commemorated his achievement upon stone. Next he was made governor of the metropolitan district. In the same year the Emperor's campaigns against the encroaching barbarians reached a critical stage, and when the Turfan and Chulung hordes invaded Kuachou and Shachou and menaced the region of the Ho and the Huang, the Emperor, in his search for new talent, made Lu Sheng associate director of the Censorate and governor-general of the Hosi Circuit. Lu Sheng routed the barbarians, killing seven thousand men. He conquered nine hundred *li* of territory and built three cities to guard the frontier. The people of the frontier region built a monument on the Chuyen Mountain to commemorate his exploits, and when he returned to court he was received with triumphal honors and was made vice-president of the Board of Civil Service and then president of the Board of Revenue. No name carried so much prestige as his and he had the universal acclaim of popular sentiment, but these incurred the jealousy of the other ministers at court, and as a result of their slanderous attacks he was banished to a provincial post. Three years later, however, he was recalled to court and for more than ten years, with Hsiao Sung and P'ei Kuang-t'ing, he held the reins of government. Sometimes he received as many as three confidential messages from the Emperor in one day and was ever ready to assist His Majesty with his wise counsel.

Then again he fell victim to the jealousy of his colleagues. They charged him with conspiring with frontier generals to overthrow the dynasty and caused him to be thrown into prison. When the guards came to arrest him, he was stricken with terror and perplexity and said to his wife and sons: "Back in Shantung we have five hundred acres of good land, quite sufficient to keep us from cold and hunger. Why should I have sought rank and title, which in the end have only brought calamity? It is now too late to wish that I could again ride back and forth on the Hantan road as I once did, wearing my plain hempen coat!" Thereupon he drew his sword and attempted to kill himself, but was prevented from doing so by his wife. All those implicated in the plot were executed but Lu Sheng escaped death through the intercession of one of the eunuchs in the confidence of the Emperor. His sentence was commuted to exile to

Huanchou. In a few years the Emperor, having ascertained his innocence, recalled him, made him president of the Imperial Council, and gave him the title of Duke of Yenkuo.

He had five sons, all of whom were gifted and were admitted into official ranks. They all married daughters of influential families of the time and presented him with more than ten grandchildren. And so he lived for over fifty years, during which he was twice banished to the frontier wilds only to be recalled to court, vindicated, and given greater honors than before. He was given to extravagance and was addicted to pleasures. His inner apartments were filled with dancers and beautiful women, and innumerable were the gifts of fertile lands, mansions, fleet horses, and such treasures that the Emperor bestowed upon him.

When advanced age made him wish to retire from court life, his petitions were repeatedly refused. When at last he fell ill, emissaries sent by the Emperor to inquire after his condition followed upon one another's heels and there was nothing left undone that eminent physicians could do. But all was in vain and one night he died, whereupon he woke up with a start and found himself lying as before in the roadside inn, with Lü Weng sitting by his side and the millet that his host was cooking still not yet done. Everything was as it had been before he dozed off. "Could it be that I have been dreaming all this while?" he said, rising to his feet. "Life as you would have it is but like that," said Lü Weng. For a long while the young man reflected in silence, then he said, "I now know at last the way of honor and disgrace and the meaning of poverty and fortune, the reciprocity of gain and loss and the mystery of life and death, and I owe all this knowledge to you. Since you have thus deigned to instruct me in the vanity of ambition, dare I refuse to profit thereby?" With this he bowed profoundly to Lü Weng and went away.

Maps and Dreams

☆

Hugh Brody

The rivers of northeast British Columbia are at their most splendid in the early fall. The northern tributaries of the Peace achieve an extraordinary beauty; they, and their small feeder creeks and streams, are cold yet warm—perfect reflections of autumn. The banks are multicoloured and finely textured; clear water runs in smooth, shallow channels. The low water of late summer reveals gravel and sand beaches, textures and colours that are at other times of the year concealed. Such low water levels mean that all these streams are easily crossed, and so become the throughways along the valleys that have always been at the heart of the Indians' use of the land. In October those who know these creeks can find corners, holes, back eddies where rainbow trout and Dolly Varden abound.

The hunter of moose, deer, caribou (and in historic times, buffalo) does not pursue these large animals without regard to more abundant and predictable, if less satisfying, sources of food. The man who tracks and snares game, and whose success depends on his constant movement, cannot afford to fail for much more than two days running. On the third day of hunger he will find it hard to walk far or fast enough: hunger reduces the efficiency of the hunt. Hunger is inimical to effective hunting on foot; yet continuance of the hunt was, not long ago, the only means to avoid hunger. This potential source of insecurity for a hunter is resolved by his ability to combine two kinds of hunting: he pursues large ungulates in areas and with movements that bring him close to locations where he knows rabbits, grouse, or fish are to be found. These are security, but not staples. Hunting for large animals is the most efficient, the most rational activity for anyone who lives in the boreal forest. But such a hunter would be foolhardy indeed to hunt for the larger animals without a careful and strategic eye on the availability of the smaller ones.

In October, only a month after Joseph Patsah and his family first spoke to us about their lives, they suggested that I go hunting with them—and, of course, fishing. By now the rainbow trout would surely be plentiful and fat. Joseph said that he also hoped we could go far enough to see the cross. One evening, then, he proposed that we should all set out the next day for Bluestone Creek.

Between a proposal to go hunting and actual departure there is a large and perplexing divide. In the white man's world, whether urban or rural, after such a proposal there would be plans and planning; conversation about timing and practical details would also help to build enthusiasm. In Joseph's household, in all the Indian households of northeast British Columbia, and perhaps among hunters generally, planning is so muted as to seem nonexistent. Maybe it is better understood by a very different name, which is still to suppose that planning of some kind does in fact take place. . . .

Joseph and his family float possibilities. "Maybe we should go to Copper Creek. Bet you lots of moose up there." Or, "Could be caribou right now near Black Flats." Or, "I bet you no deer this time down on the Reserve..." Somehow a general area is selected from a gossamer of possibilities, and from an accumulation of remarks comes something rather like a consensus. No, that is not really it: rather, a sort of prediction, a combined sense of where we *might* go "tomorrow."...

The way to understand this kind of decision making as also to live by and even share it, is to recognize that some of the most important variables are subtle, elusive, and extremely hard or impossible to assess with finality. The Athapaskan hunter will move in a direction and at a time that are determined by a sense of weather (to indicate a variable that is easily grasped if all too easily oversimplified by the one word) and by a sense of rightness. He will also have ideas about animal movement, his own and others' patterns of land use...But already the nature of the hunter's decision making is being misrepresented by this kind of listing. To disconnect the variables, to compartmentalize the thinking, is to fail to acknowledge its sophistication and completeness. He considers variables as a composite, in parallel, and with the help of a blending of the metaphysical and the obviously pragmatic. To make a good, wise, sensible hunting choice is to accept the interconnection of all possible factors, and avoids the mistake of seeking rationally to focus on any one consideration that is held as primary. What is more, the decision is taken in the doing: there is no step or pause between theory and practice. As a consequence, the decision—like the action from which it is inseparable—is always alterable (and therefore may not properly even be termed a decision). The hunter moves in a chosen direction; but, highly sensitive to so many shifting considerations, he is always ready to change his directions.

Planning, as other cultures understand the notion, is at odds with this kind of sensitivity and would confound such flexibility. The hunter, alive to constant movements of nature, spirits, and human moods, maintains a way of doing things that repudiates a firm plan and any precise or specified understanding with others of what he is going to do. His course of action is not, must not be, a matter of predetermination. If a plan constitutes a decision about the right procedure or action, and the decision is congruent with the action, then there is no space left for a "plan," only for a bundle of open-ended and nonrational possibilities. Activity enters so far into this kind of planning as to undermine any so-called plans. . . .

"The next morning" came several times before we set out in the direction of Bluestone. Several individuals said they would come, but did not; others said they would not come, but did. Eventually, we drove in my rented pickup to a stretch of rolling forests, where hillsides and valley were covered by dense blankets of poplar, aspen, birch, and occasional stands of pine or spruce. After studied consideration of three places, Joseph and Atsin chose a campsite a short walk from a spring that created a narrow pool of good water in a setting of damp and frosted leaves.

There we camped, in a complex of shelters and one tent around a long central fire. It was a place the hunters had often used, and it had probably been an Indian campsite off and on for centuries. It was a clearing among thin-stemmed pine, a woodland tangled and in places made dense by a great number of deadfalls lying at all heights and angles to the ground. Night fell as we completed the camp. The fire was lit and was darkly reflected by these dead trees that crisscrossed against the forest.

Long before dawn (it cannot have been later than five o'clock), the men awoke. The fire rekindled, they sat around it and began the enormous and protracted breakfast that precedes every day's hunting: rabbit stew, boiled eggs, bannock, toasted sliced white bread, barbecued moose meat, whatever happens to be on hand, and cup after cup of strong, sweet tea. A little later, women and children joined the men at the fire and ate no less heartily.

As they ate, the light changed from a slight glimmer, the relief to predawn blackness, to the first brightness that falters without strength at the tops of the trees. As the light grew, the men speculated about where to go, sifting evidence they had accumulated from whatever nearby places they had visited since their arrival. Everyone had walked—to fetch water, cut wood, or simply to stretch the legs a little. Atsin, at the end of a short walk that morning, returned with a rabbit. He had taken it in a snare, evidently set as soon as we arrived the evening before. It was white already, its fur change a dangerously conspicuous anticipation of a winter yet to come. Conversation turned to rabbits. All the men had noticed a proliferation of runs and droppings. It was an excellent year for rabbit, the fifth or sixth in a cycle of seven improving years. It might be a good idea to hunt in some patches of young evergreens, along trails that led towards the river. There could be more rabbits there. Lots of rabbits. Always good to eat lots of rabbit stew. And there could be rainbow trout in that place, below the old cabin, and in other spots. Or maybe it would be good to go high up in the valley. . . This exchange of details and ideas continued off and on throughout the meal. When it had finally ended and everyone had reflected a good deal on the day's possibilities, the men set off. Perhaps it was clear to them where and why, but which possibilities represented a starting point was not easily understood by an outsider.

Atsin's younger brother Sam set off alone, at right angles to a trail that led to the river by way of a place said to be particularly good for rabbits. Two others, Jimmy Wolf and Charlie Fellow — both relations of Joseph's wife Liza — also set off at an angle, but in the opposite direction. I followed Atsin along another, more winding trail: Liza and her oldest child, Tommy, together with two other women and their small children, made their own way behind the men on the main trail; Atsin's son David attached himself to Brian Akattah and his ten-year-old nephew Peter. The choice of partner and trail was, if possible, less obviously planned than direction or hunting objective. Everyone was plainly free to go where and with whom he or she liked. As I became more familiar with this kind of hunt, though, I found that some individuals nearly always hunted alone, whereas others liked a companion, at least at the outset. A sense of great personal freedom was evident from the first. No one gives orders; everyone is, in some fundamental way, responsible to and for himself.

The distance between camp and the particular bend in the river that had been selected as the best possible fishing place was no more than a mile and a half. No time had been appointed for a rendezvous. Indeed clock time is of no significance here. (Only Joseph had a watch and it was never used for hunting purposes.) Everyone nonetheless appeared from the woods and converged on the fishing spot within minutes of one another. This co-ordination of activities is not easily understood, although it testified to the absence of big game, of moose, deer, or bear. If any of the hunters had located fresh tracks, he would have been long gone into the woods. Atsin, who seemed to be an expert at the job, appeared with two rabbits he had shot after glimpsing their helpless whiteness in the dun-coloured undergrowth. But fishing was going to supply the next meal. . . .

The trout were plentiful, as Joseph had said they would be, and fat. One after the other they came flying through the air into someone's hands, then to shore, where Atsin and Liza gutted them. A dozen or more, fish of one or two pounds each, every one of them with a brilliant red patch on its gills and red stripe along its sides—rainbow trout at their most spectacular. Then the fishing slowed down. Enough had been caught. Joseph, Brian, and David climbed back to the bank. We sat around the fires to eat rabbit stew and cook some of the fish. . . .

Moments, minutes, even hours of complete stillness: this was not time that could be measured. Hunters at rest, at ease, in wait, are able to discover and enjoy a special form of relaxation. There is a minimum of movement—a hand reaches out for a mug, an adjustment is made to the fire—and whatever is said hardly interrupts the silence, as if words and thoughts can be harmonized without any of the tensions of dialogue. Yet the hunters are a long way from sleep; not even the atmosphere is soporific. They wait, watch, consider. Above all they are still and receptive, prepared for whatever insight or realization may come to them, and ready for whatever stimulus to action might arise. This state of attentive waiting is perhaps as close as people can come to the falcon's suspended flight, when the bird, seemingly motionless, is ready to plummet in decisive action. To the outsider, who has followed along and tried to join in, it looks for all the world as if the hunters have forgotten why they are there. In this restful way hunters can spend many hours, sometimes days, eating, waiting, thinking.

The quality of this resting by the fire can be seen and felt when it is very suddenly changed, just as the nature of the falcon's hover becomes clear when it dives. Among hunters the emergence from repose may be slow or abrupt. But in either case a particular state of mind, a special way of being, has come to an end. One or two individuals move faster and more purposively, someone begins to prepare meat to cook, someone fetches a gun to work on, and conversation resumes its ordinary mode. This transformation took place that afternoon around the fire on the pebbled beach at just the time Sam gave up his fishing and began to walk back toward us. Atsin, Jimmy, and Robert all moved to new positions. Robert stood with his back to us, watching Sam's approach, while Atsin and Jimmy squatted where they could look directly at me.

In retrospect it seems clear that they felt the right time had come for something. Everyone seemed to give the few moments it took for this change to occur some special importance. Plainly the men had something to say and, in their own time, in their own way, they were going to say it. Signs and movements suggested that the flow of events that had begun in Joseph's home and Atsin's cabin, and continued with the fishing at Bluestone Creek, was about to be augmented. Something of significance to the men here was going to happen. I suddenly realized that everyone was watching me. Sam joined the group, but said nothing. Perhaps he, as a younger man, was now leaving events to his elders, to

Atsin, Jimmy, and Robert. There was a brief silence made awkward by expectancy, though an awkward pause is a very rare thing among people who accept that there is no need to escape from silence, no need to use words as a way to avoid one another, no need to obscure the real.

Atsin broke this silence. He spoke at first of the research: "I bet some guys make big maps. Lots of work, these maps. Joseph, he sure is happy to see maps."

Silence again. Then Robert continued: "Yeah, lots of maps. All over this country we hunt. Fish too. Trapping places. Nobody knows that. White men don't know that."

Then Jimmy spoke: "Indian guys, old-timers, they make maps too."

With these words, the men introduced their theme. The tone was friendly, but the words were spoken with intensity and firmness. The men seemed apprehensive, as if anxious to be very clearly understood—though nothing said so far required such concern. Once again, it is impossible to render verbatim all that they eventually said. I had no tape recorder and memory is imperfect. But even a verbatim account would fail to do justice to their meaning. Here, then, in summaries and glimpses, is what the men had in mind to say.

Some old-timers, men who became famous for their powers and skills, had been great dreamers. Hunters and dreamers. They did not hunt as most people now do. They did not seek uncertainly for the trails of animals whose movements we can only guess at. No, they located their prey in dreams, found their trails, and made dream-kills. Then, the next day, or a few days later, whenever it seemed auspicious to do so, they could go out, find the trail, re-encounter the animal, and collect the kill.

Maybe, said Atsin, you think this is all nonsense, just so much bullshit. Maybe you don't think this power is possible. Few people understand. The old-timers who were strong dreamers knew many things that are not easy to understand. People—white people, young people—yes, they laugh at such skills. But they do not know. The Indians around this country know a lot about power. In fact, everyone has had some experience of it. The fact that dream-hunting works has been proved many times.

A few years ago a hunter dreamed a cow moose kill. A fine, fat cow. He was so pleased with the animal, so delighted to make this dream-kill, that he marked the animal's hooves. Now he would be sure to recognize it when he went on the coming hunt. The next day, when he went out into the bush, he quickly found the dream-trail. He followed it, and came to a large cow moose. Sure enough, the hooves bore his marks. Everyone saw them. All the men around the fire had been told about the marks, and everyone on the Reserve had come to look at those hooves when the animal was butchered and brought into the people's homes.

And not only that fat cow moose—many such instances are known to the people, whose marks on the animal or other indications show that there was no mistaking, no doubts about the efficacy of such dreams. Do you think this is all lies? No, this is power they had, something they knew how to use. This was their way of doing things, the right way. They understood, those old-timers, just where all the animals came from. The trails converge, and if you were a very strong dreamer you could discover this, and see the source of trails, the origin of game. Dreaming revealed them. Good hunting depended upon such knowledge.

Today it is hard to find men who can dream this way. There are too many problems. Too much drinking. Too little respect. People are not good enough now. Maybe there will again be strong dreamers when these problems are overcome. Then more maps will be made. New maps.

Oh yes, Indians made maps. You would not take any notice of them. You might say such maps are crazy. But maybe the Indians would say that is what your maps are: the same thing. Different maps from different people—different *ways*. Old-timers made maps of trails, ornamented them with lots of fancy. The good people.

None of this is easy to understand. But good men, the really good men, could dream of more than animals. Sometimes they saw heaven and its trails. Those trails are hard to see, and few men have had such dreams. Even if they could see dream-trails to heaven, it is hard to explain them. You draw maps of the land, show everyone where to go. You explain the hills, the rivers, the trails from here to Hudson Hope, the roads. Maybe you make maps of where the hunters go and where the fish can be caught. That is not easy. But easier, for sure, than drawing out the trails to heaven. You may laugh at these maps of the trails to heaven, but they were done by the good men who had the heaven dream, who wanted to tell the truth. They worked hard on their truth.

Atsin had done most of the talking this far. The others interjected a few words and comments, agreeing or elaborating a little. Jimmy told about the cow moose with marked hooves. All of them offered some comparisons between their own and others' maps. And the men's eyes never ceased to remain fixed on me: were they being understood? Disregarded? Thought ridiculous? They had chosen this moment forthese explanations, yet no one was entirely secure in it. Several times, Atsin paused and waited, perhaps to give him a chance to sense or absorb the reaction to his words were intense but not tense hiatuses. Everyone was reassuring himself his seriousness was being recognized. That was all they needed to continue.

The longest of these pauses might have lasted as much as five minutes. During it the fire was rebuilt. It seemed possible, for a few moments, that they had finished, and that their attention was now returning to trout, camp, and the hunt. But the atmosphere hardly altered, and Jimmy quite abruptly took over where Atsin had left off.

The few good men who had the heaven dream were like the Fathers, Catholic priests, men who devoted themselves to helping others with that essential knowledge to which ordinary men and women have limited access. (Roman Catholic priests have drifted in and out of the lives of all the region's Indians, leaving behind fragments of their knowledge and somewhat rarefied and idealized versions of what they had to preach.) Most important of all, a strong dreamer can tell others how to get to heaven. We all have need of the trail, or a complex of trails, but, unlike other important trails, the way to heaven will have been seen in dreams that only a few, special individuals have had. Maps of heaven are thus important. And they must be good, complete maps. Heaven is reached only by careful avoidance of the wrong trails. These must also be shown so that the traveller can recognize and avoid them.

How can we know the general direction we should follow? How can anyone who has not dreamed the whole route begin to locate himself on such a map? When Joseph, or any of the other men, began to draw a hunting map, he had first to find his way. He did this by recognizing features, by fixing points of reference, and then, once he was oriented to the familiar and to the scale or manner in which the familiar was reproduced, he could begin to add his own layers of detailed information. But how can anyone begin to find a way on a map of trails to heaven, across a terrain that ordinary hunters do not experience in everyday activities or even in their dream-hunts?

The route to heaven is not wholly unfamiliar, however. As it happens, heaven is to one side of, and at the same level as, the point where the trails to animals all meet. Many men know where this point is, or at least some of its approach trails, from their own hunting dreams. Hunters can in this way find a basic reference, and once they realize that heaven is in a particular relation to this far more familiar centre, the map as a whole can be read. If this is not enough, a person can take a map with him; some old-timers who made or who were given maps of the trails to heaven choose to have a map buried with them. They can thus remind themselves which ways to travel if the actual experience of the trail proves to be too confusing. Others are given a corner of a map that will help reveal the trail to them. And even those who do not have any powerful dreams are shown the best maps of the route to heaven. The discoveries of the very few most powerful dreamers—and some of the dreamers have been women—are periodically made available to everyone.

The person who wishes to dream must take great care, even if he dreams only of the hunt. He must lie in the correct orientation, with his head towards the rising sun. There should be no ordinary trails, no human pathways, between his pillow and the bush. These would be confusing to the self that travels in dreams towards important and unfamiliar trails which can lead to a kill. Not much of this can be mapped—only the trail to heaven has been drawn up. There has been no equivalent need to make maps to share other important information.

Sometime, said Jimmy Wolf, you will see one of these maps. There are some of them around. Then the competence and strength of the old-timers who drew them will be unquestioned. Different trails can be explained, and heaven can be located on them. Yes, they were pretty smart, the men who drew them. Smarter than any white man in these parts and smarter than Indians of today. Perhaps, said Atsin, in the future there will be men good enough to make new maps of heaven—but not just now. There will be changes, he added, and the people will come once again to understand the things that Atsin's father had tried to teach him. In any case, he said, the older men are now trying to explain the powers and dreams of old-timers to the young, indeed to all those who have not been raised with these spiritual riches. For those who do not understand, hunting and life itself are restricted and difficult. So the people must be told everything, and taught all that they need, in order to withstand the incursions presently being made into their way of life, their land, and into their very dreams.

Los Caprichos: The Sleep of Reason Produces Monsters

☆

Francisco Goya

Dreams

☆

Timothy Findley

Doctor Menlo was having a problem: he could not sleep and his wife—
the other Doctor Menlo—was secretly staying awake in order to keep an
eye on him. The trouble was that, in spite of her concern and in spite of
all her efforts, Doctor Menlo—whose name was Mimi—was always
nodding off because of her exhaustion.

She had tried drinking coffee, but this had no effect. She detested
coffee and her system had a built-in rejection mechanism. She also
prescribed herself a week's worth of Dexedrine to see if that would do the
trick. *Five mg at bedtime* — all to no avail. And even though she put the
plastic bottle of small orange hearts beneath her pillow and kept aug-
menting her intake, she would wake half an hour later with a dreadful
start to discover the night was moving on to morning.

Everett Menlo had not yet declared the source of his problem. His
restless condition had begun about ten days ago and had barely raised his
interest. Soon, however, the time spent lying awake had increased from
one to several hours and then, on Monday last, to all-night sessions. Now
he lay in a state of rigid apprehension—eyes wide open, arms above his
head, his hands in fists—like a man in pain unable to shut it out. His
neck, his back and his shoulders constantly harried him with cramps and
spasms. Everett Menlo had become a full-blown insomniac.

Clearly, Mimi Menlo concluded, her husband was refusing to sleep
because he believed something dreadful was going to happen the
moment he closed his eyes. She had encountered this sort of fear in one
or two of her patients. Everett, on the other hand, would not discuss the
subject. If the problem had been hers, he would have said *such things
cannot occur if you have gained control of yourself*.

Mimi began to watch for the dawn. She would calculate its approach
by listening for the increase of traffic down below the bedroom window.
The Menlos' home was across the road from The Manulife Centre—
corner of Bloor and Bay streets. Mimi's first sight of daylight always
revealed the high, white shape of its terraced storeys. Their own apartment building was of a modest height and colour—twenty floors of

smoky glass and polished brick. The shadow of the Manulife would crawl across the bedroom floor and climb the wall behind her, grey with fatigue and cold.

The Menlo beds were an arm's length apart, and lying like a rug between them was the shape of a large, black dog of unknown breed. All night long, in the dark of his well, the dog would dream and he would tell the content of his dreams the way that victims in a trance will tell of being pursued by posses of their nameless fears. He whimpered, he cried and sometimes he howled. His legs and his paws would jerk and flail and his claws would scrabble desperately against the parquet floor. Mimi—who loved this dog—would lay her hand against his side and let her fingers dabble in his coat in vain attempts to soothe him. Sometimes, she had to call his name in order to rouse him from his dreams because his heart would be racing. Other times, she smiled and thought: *at least there's one of us getting some sleep*. The dog's name was Thurber and he dreamed in beige and white.

Everett and Mimi Menlo were both psychiatrists. His field was schizophrenia; hers was autistic children. Mimi's venue was the Parkin Institute at the University of Toronto; Everett's was the Queen Street Mental Health Centre. Early in their marriage they had decided never to work as a team and not—unless it was a matter of financial life and death—to accept employment in the same institution. Both had always worked with the kind of physical intensity that kills, and yet they gave the impression this was the only tolerable way in which to function. It meant there was always a sense of peril in what they did, but the peril— according to Everett—made their lives worth living. This, at least, had been his theory twenty years ago when they were young.

Now, for whatever unnamed reason, peril had become his enemy and Everett Menlo had begun to look and behave and lose his sleep like a haunted man. But he refused to comment when Mimi asked him what was wrong. Instead, he gave the worst of all possible answers a psychiatrist can hear who seeks an explanation of a patient's silence: he said there was *absolutely nothing wrong*.

"You're sure you're not coming down with something?"

"Yes."

"And you wouldn't like a massage?"

"I've already told you: no."

"Can I get you anything?"

"No."

"And you don't want to talk?"

"That's right."

"Okay, Everett. . ."

"Okay, what?"

"Okay, nothing. I only hope you get some sleep tonight."

Everett stood up. "Have you been spying on me, Mimi?"

"What do you mean by *spying*?"

"Watching me all night long."

"Well, Everett, I don't see how I can fail to be aware you aren't asleep when we share this bedroom. I mean—I can hear you grinding your teeth. I can see you lying there wide awake."

"When?"

"All the time. You're staring at the ceiling."

"I've never stared at the ceiling in my whole life. I sleep on my stomach."

"You sleep on your stomach *if* you sleep. But you have not been sleeping. Period. No argument."

Everett Menlo went to his dresser and got out a pair of clean pyjamas. Turning his back on Mimi, he put them on.

Somewhat amused at the coyness of this gesture, Mimi asked what he was hiding.

"Nothing!" he shouted at her.

Mimi's mouth fell open. Everett never yelled. His anger wasn't like that; it manifested itself in other ways, in silence and withdrawal, never shouts.

Everett was staring at her defiantly. He had slammed the bottom drawer of his dresser. Now he was fumbling with the wrapper of a pack of cigarettes.

Mimi's stomach tied a knot.

Everett hadn't touched a cigarette for weeks.

"Please don't smoke those," she said. "You'll only be sorry if you do."

"And you," he said, "will be sorry if I don't."

"But, dear. . ." said Mimi.

"Leave me for Christ's sake alone!" Everett yelled.

Mimi gave up and sighed and then she said: "all right. Thurber and I will go and sleep in the living-room. Goodnight."

Everett sat on the edge of his bed. His hands were shaking.

"Please," he said—apparently addressing the floor. "Don't leave me here alone. I couldn't bear that."

This was perhaps the most chilling thing he could have said to her. Mimi was alarmed; her husband was genuinely terrified of something and he would not say what it was. If she had not been who she was—if she had not known what she knew—if her years of training had not prepared her to watch for signs like this, she might have been better off.

As it was, she had to face the possibility the strongest, most sensible man on earth was having a nervous breakdown of major proportions. Lots of people have breakdowns, of course; but not, she had thought, the gods of reason.

"All right," she said—her voice maintaining the kind of calm she knew a child afraid of the dark would appreciate. "In a minute I'll get us something to drink. But first, I'll go and change. . . ."

Mimi went into the sanctum of the bathroom, where her nightgown waited for her—a portable hiding-place hanging on the back of the door. "You stay there," she said to Thurber, who had padded after her. "Mama will be out in just a moment."

Even in the dark, she could gauge Everett's tension. His shadow— all she could see of him—twitched from time to time and the twitching took on a kind of lurching rhythm, something like the broken clock in their living-room.

Mimi lay on her side and tried to close her eyes. But her eyes were tied to a will of their own and would not obey her. Now she, too, was caught in the same irreversible tide of sleeplessness that bore her husband backward through the night. Four or five times she watched him lighting cigarettes—blowing out the matches, courting disaster in the bed-clothes—conjuring the worst of deaths for the three of them: a flaming pyre on the twentieth floor.

All this behaviour was utterly unlike him; foreign to his code of disciplines and ethics; alien to everything he said and believed. *Openness, directness, sharing of ideas, encouraging imaginative response to every problem. Never hide troubles. Never allow despair* . . . These were his direc-tives in everything he did. Now, he had thrown them over.

One thing was certain. She was not the cause of his sleeplessness. She didn't have affairs and neither did he. He might be ill—but whenever he'd been ill before, there had been no trauma; never a trauma like this one, at any rate. Perhaps it was something about a patient—one of his tougher cases; a wall in the patient's condition they could not break through; some circumstance of someone's lack of progress—a sudden veering towards a catatonic state, for instance—something that Everett had not foreseen that had stymied him and was slowly. . .what? Destroy-ing his sense of professional control? His self-esteem? His scientific certainty? If only he would speak.

Mimi thought about her own worst case: a child whose obstinate refusal to communicate was currently breaking her heart and, thus, her ability to help. If ever she had needed Everett to talk to, it was now. All her fellow doctors were locked in a battle over this child; they wanted to take him away from her. Mimi refused to give him up; he might as well have been her own flesh and blood. Everything had been done—from gentle holding sessions to violent bouts of manufactured anger—in her attempt to make the child react. She was staying with him every day from the moment he was roused to the moment he was induced to sleep with drugs.

His name was Brian Bassett and he was eight years old. He sat on the floor in the furthest corner he could achieve in one of the observation-isolation rooms where all the autistic children were placed when nothing else in their treatment— nothing of love or expertise—had managed to break their silence. Mostly, this was a signal they were coming to the end of life.

There in his four-square, glass-box room, surrounded by all that can tempt a child if a child can be tempted—toys and food and story-book companions—Brian Bassett was in the process, now, of fading away. His eyes were never closed and his arms were restrained. He was attached to three machines that nurtured him with all that science can offer. But of course, the spirit and the will to live cannot be fed by force to those who do not want to feed.

Now, in the light of Brian Bassett's utter lack of willing contact with the world around him—his utter refusal to communicate—Mimi watched her husband through the night. Everett stared at the ceiling, lit by the Manulife building's distant lamps, borne on his back further and further out to sea. She had lost him, she was certain.

When, at last, he saw that Mimi had drifted into her own and welcome sleep, Everett rose from his bed and went out into the hall, past the simulated jungle of the solarium, until he reached the dining-room. There, all the way till dawn, he amused himself with two decks of cards and endless games of Dead Man's Solitaire.

Thurber rose and shuffled after him. The dining-room was one of Thurber's favourite places in all his confined but privileged world, for it was here—as in the kitchen—that from time to time a hand descended filled with the miracle of food. But whatever it was that his master was doing up there above him on the tabletop, it wasn't anything to do with feeding or with being fed. The playing cards had an old and dusty dryness to their scent and they held no appeal for the dog. So he once again lay down and he took up his dreams, which at least gave his paws some exercise. This way, he failed to hear the advent of a new dimension to his master's problem. This occurred precisely at 5:45 A.M. when the telephone rang and Everett Menlo, having rushed to answer it, waited breathless for a minute while he listened and then said: "yes" in a curious, strangulated fashion. Thurber—had he been awake—would have recognized in his master's voice the signal for disaster.

For weeks now, Everett had been working with a patient who was severely and uniquely schizophrenic. This patient's name was Kenneth Albright, and while he was deeply suspicious, he was also oddly caring. Kenneth Albright loved the detritus of life, such as bits of woolly dust and wads of discarded paper. He loved all dried-up leaves that had drifted from their parent trees and he loved the dead bees that had curled up to die along the window-sills of his ward. He also loved the spiderwebs seen high up in the corners of the rooms where he sat on plastic chairs and ate with plastic spoons.

Kenneth Albright talked a lot about his dreams. But his dreams had become, of late, a major stumbling block in the process of his recovery. Back in the days when Kenneth had first become Doctor Menlo's patient, the dreams had been overburdened with detail: "over-cast," as he would say, "with characters" and over-produced, again in Kenneth's phrase, "as if I were dreaming the dreams of Cecil B. de Mille."

Then he had said: "but a person can't really dream someone else's dreams. Or can they, Doctor Menlo?"

"No" had been Everett's answer—definite and certain.

Everett Menlo had been delighted, at first, with Kenneth Albright's dreams. They had been immensely entertaining—complex and filled with intriguing detail. Kenneth himself was at a loss to explain the meaning of these dreams, but as Everett had said, it wasn't Kenneth's job to explain. That was Everett's job. His job and his pleasure. For quite a long while, during these early sessions, Everett had written out the dreams, taken them home and recounted them to Mimi.

Kenneth Albright was a paranoid schizophrenic. Four times now, he had attempted suicide. He was a fiercely angry man at times—and at other times as gentle and as pleasant as a docile child. He had suffered so greatly, in the very worst moments of his disease, that he could no longer work. His job—it was almost an incidental detail in his life and had no importance for him, so it seemed—was returning reference books, in the Metro Library, to their places in the stacks. Sometimes—mostly late of an afternoon—he might begin a psychotic episode of such profound dimensions that he would attempt his suicide right behind the counter and even once, in the full view of everyone, while riding in the glass-walled elevator. It was after this last occasion that he was brought, in restraints, to be a resident patient at the Queen Street Mental Health Centre. He had slashed his wrists with a razor—but not before he had also slashed and destroyed an antique copy of *Don Quixote*, the pages of which he pasted to the walls with blood.

For a week thereafter, Kenneth Albright—just like Brian Bassett—had refused to speak or to move. Everett had him kept in an isolation cell, force-fed and drugged. Slowly, by dint of patience, encouragement and caring even Kenneth could recognize as genuine, Everett Menlo had broken through the barrier. Kenneth was removed from isolation, pampered with food and cigarettes, and he began relating his dreams.

At first there seemed to be only the dreams and nothing else in Kenneth's memory. Broken pencils, discarded toys and the telephone directory all had roles to play in these dreams but there were never any people. All the weather was bleak and all the landscapes were empty. Houses, motor cars and office buildings never made an appearance. Sounds and smells had some importance; the wind would blow, the scent of unseen fires was often described. Stairwells were plentiful, leading nowhere, all of them rising from a subterranean world that Kenneth either did not dare to visit or would not describe.

The dreams had little variation, one from another. The themes had mostly to do with loss and with being lost. The broken pencils were all given names and the discarded toys were given to one another as companions. The telephone books were the sources of recitations— hours and hours of repeated names and numbers, some of which— Everett had noted with surprise—were absolutely accurate.

All of this held fast until an incident occurred one morning that changed the face of Kenneth Albright's schizophrenia forever; an incident that stemmed—so it seemed—from something he had dreamed the night before.

Bearing in mind his previous attempts at suicide, it will be obvious that Kenneth Albright was never far from sight at the Queen Street Mental Health Centre. He was, in fact, under constant observation; constant, that is, as human beings and modern technology can manage. In the ward to which he was ultimately consigned, for instance, the toilet cabinets had no doors and the shower-rooms had no locks. Therefore, a person could not ever be alone with water, glass or shaving utensils. (All the razors were cordless automatics.) Scissors and knives were banned, as were pieces of string and rubber bands. A person could not even kill his feet and hands by binding up his wrists or ankles. Nothing poisonous was anywhere available. All the windows were barred. All the double doors between this ward and the corridors beyond were doors with triple locks and a guard was always near at hand.

Still, if people want to die, they will find a way. Mimi Menlo would discover this to her everlasting sorrow with Brian Bassett. Everett Menlo would discover this to his everlasting horror with Kenneth Albright.

On the morning of April 19th, a Tuesday, Everett Menlo, in the best of health, had welcomed a brand-new patient into his office. This was Anne

Marie Wilson, a young and brilliant pianist whose promising career had been halted mid-flight by a schizophrenic incident involving her ambition. She was, it seemed, no longer able to play and all her dreams were shattered. The cause was simple, to all appearances: Anne Marie had a sense of how, precisely, the music should be and she had not been able to master it accordingly. "Everything I attempt is terrible," she had said—in spite of all her critical accolades and all her professional success. Other doctors had tried and failed to break the barriers in Anne Marie, whose hands had taken on a life of their own, refusing altogether to work for her. Now it was Menlo's turn and hope was high.

Everett had been looking forward to his session with this prodigy. He loved all music and had thought to find some means within its discipline to reach her. She seemed so fragile, sitting there in the sunlight, and he had just begun to take his first notes when the door flew open and Louise, his secretary, had said: "I'm sorry, Doctor Menlo. There's a problem. Can you come with me at once?"

Everett excused himself.

Anne Marie was left in the sunlight to bide her time. Her fingers were moving around in her lap and she put them in her mouth to make them quiet.

Even as he'd heard his secretary speak, Everett had known the problem would be Kenneth Albright. Something in Kenneth's eyes had warned him there was trouble on the way: a certain wariness that indicated all was not as placid as it should have been, given his regimen of drugs. He had stayed long hours in one position, moving his fingers over his thighs as if to dry them on his trousers; watching his fellow patients come and go with abnormal interest—never, however, rising from his chair. An incident was on the horizon and Everett had been waiting for it, hoping it would not come.

Louise had said that Doctor Menlo was to go at once to Kenneth Albright's ward. Everett had run the whole way. Only after the attendant had let him in past the double doors, did he slow his pace to a hurried walk and wipe his brow. He didn't want Kenneth to know how alarmed he had been.

Coming to the appointed place, he paused before he entered, closing his eyes, preparing himself for whatever he might have to see. *Other people have killed themselves. I've seen it often enough*, he was thinking. *I simply won't let it affect me*. Then he went in.

The room was small and white—a dining-room—and Kenneth was sitting down in a corner, his back pressed out against the walls on either side of him. His head was bowed and his legs drawn up and he was obviously trying to hide without much success. An intern was standing above him and a nurse was kneeling down beside him. Several pieces of bandaging with blood on them were scattered near Kenneth's feet and there was a white enamel basin filled with pinkish water on the floor beside the nurse.

"Morowetz," Everett said to the intern. "Tell me what has happened here." He said this just the way he posed such questions when he took the interns through the wards at examination time, quizzing them on symptoms and prognoses.

But Morowetz the intern had no answer. He was puzzled. What had happened had no sane explanation.

Everett turned to Charterhouse, the nurse.

"On the morning of April 19th, at roughly ten-fifteen, I found Kenneth Albright covered with blood," Ms Charterhouse was to write in her report. "His hands, his arms, his face and his neck were stained. I would say the blood was fresh and the patient's clothing—mostly his shirt— was wet with it. Some—a very small amount of it—had dried on his forehead. The rest was uniformly the kind of blood you expect to find free-flowing from a wound. I called for assistance and meanwhile attempted to ascertain where Mister Albright might have been injured. I performed this examination without success. I could find no source of bleeding anywhere on Mister Albright's body."

Morowetz concurred.

The blood was someone else's.

"Was there a weapon of any kind?" Doctor Menlo had wanted to know.

"No, sir. Nothing," said Charterhouse.

"And was he alone when you found him?"

"Yes, sir. Just like this in the corner."

"And the others?"

"All the patients in the ward were examined," Morowetz told him.

"And?"

"Not one of them was bleeding."

Everett said: "I see."

He looked down at Kenneth.

"This is Doctor Menlo, Kenneth. Have you anything to tell me?"

Kenneth did not reply.

Everett said: "When you've got him back in his room and tranquillized, will you call me, please?"

Morowetz nodded.

The call never came. Kenneth had fallen asleep. Either the drugs he was given had knocked him out cold, or he had opted for silence. Either way, he was incommunicado.

No one was discovered bleeding. Nothing was found to indicate an accident, a violent attack, an epileptic seizure. A weapon was not located. Kenneth Albright had not a single scratch on his flesh from stem, as Everett put it, to gudgeon. The blood, it seemed, had fallen like the rain from heaven: unexplained and inexplicable.

Later, as the day was ending, Everett Menlo left the Queen Street Mental Health Centre. He made his way home on the Queen streetcar and the Bay bus. When he reached the apartment, Thurber was waiting for him. Mimi was at a goddamned meeting.

That was the night Everett Menlo suffered the first of his failures to sleep. It was occasioned by the fact that, when he wakened sometime after three, he had just been dreaming. This, of course, was not unusual—but the dream itself was perturbing. There was someone lying there, in the bright white landscape of a hospital dining-room. Whether it was a man or a woman could not be told, it was just a human body, lying down in a pool of blood.

Kenneth Albright was kneeling beside this body, pulling it open the way a child will pull a Christmas present open—yanking at its strings and ribbons, wanting only to see the contents. Everett saw this scene from several angles, never speaking, never being spoken to. In all the time he watched—the usual dream eternity—the silence was broken only by the sound of water dripping from an unseen tap. Then, Kenneth Albright rose and was covered with blood, the way he had been that morning. He stared at Doctor Menlo, looked right through him and departed. Nothing remained in the dining-room but plastic tables and plastic chairs and the bright red thing on the floor that once had been a person. Everett Menlo did not know and could not guess who this person might have been. He only knew that Kenneth Albright had left this person's body in Everett Menlo's dream.

Three nights running, the corpse remained in its place and every time that Everett entered the dining-room in the nightmare he was certain he would find out who it was. On the fourth night, fully expecting to discover he himself was the victim, he beheld the face and saw it was a stranger.

But there are no strangers in dreams; he knew that now after twenty years of practice. *There are no strangers; there are only people in disguise.*

Mimi made one final attempt in Brian Bassett's behalf to turn away the fate to which his other doctors—both medical and psychiatric—had consigned him. Not that, as a group, they had failed to expend the full weight of all they knew and all they could do to save him. One of his medical doctors—a woman whose name was Juliet Bateman—had moved a cot into his isolation room and stayed with him twenty-four hours a day for over a week. But her health had been undermined by this and when she succumbed to the Shanghai flu she removed herself for fear of infecting Brian Bassett.

The parents had come and gone on a daily basis for months in a killing routine of visits. But parents, their presence and their loving, are not the answer when a child has fallen into an autistic state. They might as well have been strangers. And so they had been advised to stay away.

Brian Bassett was eight years old—*unlucky eight*, as one of his therapists had said—and in every other way, in terms of physical development and mental capability, he had always been a perfectly normal child. Now, in the final moments of his life, he weighed a scant thirty pounds, when he should have weighed twice that much.

Brian had not been heard to speak a single word in over a year of constant observation. Earlier—long ago as seven months—a few expressions would visit his face from time to time. Never a smile—but often a kind of sneer, a passing judgement, terrifying in its intensity. Other times, a pinched expression would appear—a signal of the shyness peculiar to autistic children, who think of light as being unfriendly.

Mimi's militant efforts in behalf of Brian had been exemplary. Her fellow doctors thought of her as *Bassett's crazy guardian angel*. They begged her to remove herself in order to preserve her health. Being wise, being practical, they saw that all her efforts would not save him. But Mimi's version of being a guardian angel was more like being a surrogate warrior: a hired gun or a samurai. Her cool determination to thwart the enemies of silence, stillness and starvation gave her strength that even she had been unaware were hers to command.

Brian Bassett, seated in his corner on the floor, maintained a solemn composure that lent his features a kind of unearthly beauty. His back was straight, his hands were poised, his hair was so fine he looked the very picture of a spirit waiting to enter a newborn creature. Sometimes Mimi wondered if this creature Brian Bassett waited to inhabit could be human. She thought of all the animals she had ever seen in all her travels and she fell upon the image of a newborn fawn as being the most tranquil and the most in need of stillness in order to survive. If only all the natural energy and curiosity of a newborn beast could have entered into Brian Bassett, surely, they would have transformed the boy in the corner into a vibrant, joyous human being. But it was not to be.

On the 29th of April—one week and three days after Everett had entered into his crisis of insomnia—Mimi sat on the floor in Brian Bassett's isolation room, gently massaging his arms and legs as she held him in her lap.

His weight, by now, was shocking—and his skin had become translucent. His eyes had not been closed for days—for weeks—and their expression might have been carved in stone.

"Speak to me. Speak," she whispered to him as she cradled his head beneath her chin. "Please at least speak before you die."

Nothing happened. Only silence.

Juliet Bateman—wrapped in a blanket—was watching through the observation glass as Mimi lifted up Brian Bassett and placed him in his cot. The cot had metal sides—and the sides were raised. Juliet Bateman could see Brian Bassett's eyes and his hands as Mimi stepped away.

Mimi looked at Juliet and shook her head. Juliet closed her eyes and pulled her blanket tighter like a skin that might protect her from the next five minutes.

Mimi went around the cot to the other side and dragged the IV stand in closer to the head. She fumbled for a moment with the long plastic lifelines—anti-dehydrants, nutrients—and she adjusted the needles and brought them down inside the nest of the cot where Brian Bassett lay and she lifted up his arm in order to insert the tubes and bind them into place with tape.

This was when it happened—just as Mimi Menlo was preparing to insert the second tube.

Brian Bassett looked at her and spoke.

"No," he said. "Don't."

Don't meant death.

Mimi paused—considered—and set the tube aside. Then she withdrew the tube already in place and she hung them both on the IV stand.

All right, she said to Brian Bassett in her mind, *you win*.

She looked down then with her arm along the side of the cot—and one hand trailing down so Brian Bassett could touch it if he wanted to. She smiled at him and said to him: "not to worry. Not to worry. None of us is ever going to trouble you again." He watched her carefully. "Goodbye, Brian," she said. "I love you."

Juliet Bateman saw Mimi Menlo say all this and was fairly sure she had read the words on Mimi's lips just as they had been spoken.

Mimi started out of the room. She was determined now there was no turning back and that Brian Bassett was free to go his way. But just as she was turning the handle and pressing her weight against the door—she heard Brian Bassett speak again.

"Goodbye," he said.

And died.

Mimi went back and Juliet Bateman, too, and they stayed with him another hour before they turned out his lights. "Someone else can cover his face," said Mimi. "I'm not going to do it." Juliet agreed and they came back out to tell the nurse on duty that their ward had died and their work with him was over.

On the 30th of April—a Saturday—Mimi stayed home and made her notes and she wondered if and when she would weep for Brian Bassett. Her hand, as she wrote, was steady and her throat was not constricted and her eyes had no sensation beyond the burning itch of fatigue. She wondered what she looked like in the mirror, but resisted that discovery. Some things could wait. Outside it rained. Thurber dreamed in the corner. Bay Street rumbled in the basement.

Everett, in the meantime, had reached his own crisis and because of his desperate straits a part of Mimi Menlo's mind was on her husband. Now he had not slept for almost ten days. *We really ought to consign ourselves to hospital beds*, she thought. Somehow, the idea held no persuasion. It occurred to her that laughter might do a better job, if only they could find it. The brain, when over-extended, gives us the most surprisingly simple propositions, she concluded. *Stop*, it says to us. *Lie down and sleep.*

Five minutes later, Mimi found herself still sitting at the desk, with her fountain pen capped and her fingers raised to her lips in an attitude of gentle prayer. It required some effort to re-adjust her gaze and re-establish her focus on the surface of the window glass beyond which her mind had wandered. Sitting up, she had been asleep.

Thurber muttered something and stretched his legs and yawned, still asleep. Mimi glanced in his direction. *We've both been dreaming*, she thought, *but his dream continues*.

Somewhere behind her, the broken clock was attempting to strike the hour of three. Its voice was dull and rusty, needing oil.

Looking down, she saw the words BRIAN BASSETT written on the page before her and it occurred to her that, without this person, the words were nothing more than extrapolations from the alphabet—something fanciful we call a "name" in the hope that, one day, it will take on meaning.

She thought of Brian Bassett with his building blocks—pushing the letters around on the floor and coming up with more acceptable arrangements. *TINA STERABBS...IAN BRETT BASS...BEST STAB the RAIN:* a sentence. He had known all along, of course, that *BRIAN BASSETT* wasn't what he wanted because it wasn't what he was. He had come here against his will, was held here against his better judgement, fought against his captors and finally escaped.

But where was here to Ian Brett Bass? Where was here to Tina Sterabbs? Like Brian Bassett, they had all been here in someone else's dreams, and had to wait for someone else to wake before they could make their getaway.

Slowly, Mimi uncapped her fountain pen and drew a firm, black line through Brian Bassett's name. *We dreamed him*, she wrote, *that's all. And then we let him go.*

Seeing Everett standing in the doorway, knowing he had just returned from another Kenneth Albright crisis, she had no sense of apprehension. All this was only as it should be. Given the way that everything was going, it stood to reason Kenneth Albright's crisis had to come in this moment. If he managed, at last, to kill himself then at least her husband might begin to sleep again.

Far in the back of her mind a carping, critical voice remarked that any such thoughts were *deeply unfeeling and verging on the barbaric*. But Mimi dismissed this voice and another part of her brain stepped forward in her defence. *I will weep for Kenneth Albright*, she thought, *when I can weep for Brian Bassett. Now, all that matters is that Everett and I survive*.

Then she strode forward and put out her hand for Everett's briefcase, set the briefcase down and helped him out of his topcoat. She was playing wife. It seemed to be the thing to do.

For the next twenty minutes Everett had nothing to say, and after he had poured himself a drink and after Mimi had done the same, they sat in their chairs and waited for Everett to catch his breath.

The first thing he said when he finally spoke was: "finish your notes?"

"Just about," Mimi told him. "I've written everything I can for now." She did not elaborate. "You're home early," she said, hoping to goad him into saying something new about Kenneth Albright.

"Yes," he said. "I am." But that was all.

Then he stood up—threw back the last of his drink and poured another. He lighted a cigarette and Mimi didn't even wince. He had been smoking now three days. The atmosphere between them had been, since then, enlivened with a magnetic kind of tension. But it was a moribund tension, slowly beginning to dissipate.

Mimi watched her husband's silent torment now with a kind of clinical detachment. This was the result, she liked to tell herself, of her training and her discipline. The lover in her could regard Everett warmly and with concern, but the psychiatrist in her could also watch him as someone suffering a nervous breakdown, someone who could not be helped until the symptoms had multiplied and declared themselves more openly.

Everett went into the darkest corner of the room and sat down hard in one of Mimi's straight-back chairs: the ones inherited from her mother.

He sat, prim, like a patient in a doctor's office, totally unrelaxed and nervy; expressionless. Either he had come to receive a deadly diagnosis, or he would get a clean bill of health.

Mimi glided over to the sofa in the window, plush and red and deeply comfortable; a place to recuperate. The view—if she chose to turn only slightly sideways—was one of the gentle rain that was falling onto Bay Street. Sopping-wet pigeons huddled on the window-sill; people across the street in the Manulife building were turning on their lights.

A renegade robin, nesting in their eaves, began to sing.

Everett Menlo began to talk.

"Please don't interrupt," he said at first.

"You know I won't," said Mimi. It was a rule that neither one should interrupt the telling of a case until they had been invited to do so.

Mimi put her fingers into her glass so the ice-cubes wouldn't click. She waited.

Everett spoke—but he spoke as if in someone else's voice, perhaps the voice of Kenneth Albright. This was not entirely unusual. Often, both Mimi and Everett Menlo spoke in the voices of their patients. What was unusual, this time, was that, speaking in Kenneth's voice, Everett began to sweat profusely—so profusely that Mimi was able to watch his shirt front darkening with perspiration.

"As you know," he said, "I have not been sleeping."

This was the understatement of the year. Mimi was silent.

"I have not been sleeping because—to put it in a nutshell— I have been afraid to dream."

Mimi was somewhat startled by this. Not by the fact that Everett was afraid to dream, but only because she had just been thinking of dreams herself.

"I have been afraid to dream, because in all my dreams there have been bodies. Corpses. Murder victims."

Mimi—not really listening—idly wondered if she had been one of them.

"In all my dreams, there have been corpses," Everett repeated. "But I am not the murderer. Kenneth Albright is the murderer, and, up to this moment, he has left behind him fifteen bodies: none of them people I recognize."

Mimi nodded. The ice-cubes in her drink were beginning to freeze her fingers. Any minute now, she prayed, they would surely melt.

"I gave up dreaming almost a week ago," said Everett, "thinking that if I did, the killing pattern might be altered; broken." Then he said tersely, "it was not. The killings have continued. . . ."

"How do you know the killings have continued, Everett, if you've given up your dreaming? Wouldn't this mean he had no place to hide the bodies?"

In spite of the fact she had disobeyed their rule abut not speaking, Everett answered her.

"I know they are being continued because I have seen the blood."

"Ah, yes. I see."

"No, Mimi. No. You do not see. The blood is not a figment of my imagination. The blood, in fact, is the only thing not dreamed." He explained the stains on Kenneth Albright's hands and arms and clothes and he said: "It happens every day. We have searched his person for signs of cuts and gashes—even for internal and rectal bleeding. Nothing. We have searched his quarters and all the other quarters in his ward. His ward is locked. His ward is isolated in the extreme. None of his fellow patients was ever found bleeding—never had cause to bleed. There were no injuries—no self-inflicted wounds. We thought of animals. Perhaps a mouse—a rat. But nothing. Nothing. Nothing . . . We also went so far as to strip-search all the members of the staff who entered that ward and I, too, offered myself for this experiment. Still nothing. Nothing. No one had bled."

Everett was now beginning to perspire so heavily he removed his jacket and threw it on the floor. Thurber woke and stared at it, startled. At first, it appeared to be the beast that had just pursued him through the woods and down the road. But, then, it sighed and settled and was just a coat; a rumpled jacket lying down on the rug.

Everett said: "we had taken samples of the blood on the patient's hands—on Kenneth Albright's hands and on his clothing and we had these samples analysed. No. It was not his own blood. No, it was not the blood of an animal. No, it was not the blood of a fellow patient. No, it was not the blood of any member of the staff. . . ."

Everett's voice had risen.

"Whose blood was it?" he almost cried. "Whose the hell was it?"

Mimi waited.

Everett Menlo lighted another cigarette. He took a great gulp of his drink.

"Well. . ." He was calmer now; calmer of necessity. He had to marshall the evidence. He had to put it all in order—bring it into line with reason. "Did this mean that—somehow—the patient had managed to leave the premises—do some bloody deed and return without our knowledge of it? That is, after all, the only possible explanation. Isn't it?"

Mimi waited.

"Isn't it?" he repeated.

"Yes," she said. "It's the only possible explanation."

"Except there is no way out of that place. There is absolutely no way out."

Now, there was a pause.

"But one," he added—his voice, again, a whisper.

Mimi was silent. Fearful—watching his twisted face.

"Tell me," Everett Menlo said—the perfect innocent, almost the perfect child in quest of forbidden knowledge. "Answer me this—be honest: is there blood in dreams?"

Mimi could not respond. She felt herself go pale. Her husband—after all, the sanest man alive—had just suggested something so completely mad he might as well have handed over his reason in a paper bag and said to her, *burn this*.

"The only place that Kenneth Albright goes, I tell you, is into dreams," Everett said. "That is the only place beyond the ward into which the patient can or does escape."

Another—briefer—pause.

"It is real blood, Mimi. Real. And he gets it all from dreams. *My dreams*."

They waited for this to settle.

Everett said: "I'm tired. I cannot bear this any more. I'm tired...."

Mimi thought, *good. No matter what else happens, he will sleep tonight*. He did. And so, at last did she.

Mimi's dreams were rarely of the kind that engender fear. She dreamt more gentle scenes with open spaces that did not intimidate. She would dream quite often of water and of animals. Always, she was nothing more than an observer; roles were not assigned her; often, this was sad. Somehow, she seemed at times locked out, unable to participate. These were the dreams she endured when Brian Bassett died: field trips to see him in some desert setting; underwater excursions to watch him floating amongst the seaweed. He never spoke, and, indeed, he never appeared to be aware of her presence.

That night, when Everett fell into his bed exhausted and she did likewise, Mimi's dream of Brian Bassett was the last she would ever have of him and somehow, in the dream, she knew this. What she saw was what, in magical terms, would be called a disappearing act. Brian Bassett vanished. Gone.

Sometime after midnight on May Day morning, Mimi Menlo awoke from her dream of Brian to the sound of Thurber thumping the floor in a dream of his own.

Everett was not in his bed and Mimi cursed. She put on her wrapper and her slippers and went beyond the bedroom into the hall.

No lights were shining but the street lamps far below and the windows gave no sign of stars.

Mimi made her way past the jungle, searching for Everett in the living-room. He was not there. She would dream of this one day; it was a certainty.

"Everett?"

He did not reply.

Mimi turned and went back through the bedroom.

"Everett?"

She heard him. He was in the bathroom and she went in through the door.

"Oh," she said, when she saw him. "Oh, my God."

Everett Menlo was standing in the bathtub, removing his pyjamas. They were soaking wet, but not with perspiration. They were soaking wet with blood.

For a moment, holding his jacket, letting its arms hang down across his belly and his groin, Everett stared at Mimi, blank-eyed from his nightmare.

Mimi raised her hands to her mouth. She felt as one must feel, if helpless, watching someone burn alive.

Everett threw the jacket down and started to remove his trousers. His pyjamas, made of cotton, had been green. His eyes were blinded now with blood and his hands reached out to find the shower taps.

"Please don't look at me," he said. "I. . .Please go away."

Mimi said: "no." She sat on the toilet seat. "I'm waiting here," she told him, "until we both wake up."

Theme Questions

✡

✡ "Imagination deserted by reason produces impossible monsters; united with it, imagination is the mother of the arts and the source of all its marvels." Think about how this quotation from Goya applies to other selections in this section and elsewhere in the book.

✡ How important is the garden image in tales and stories of dreams? What other images, symbols, and metaphors are significant?

✡ Are the most important passages in life those "which we do not take"? Discuss in relation to any two selections in this section.

✡ Timothy Findley has one of his characters say: "There are no strangers [in dreams]; there are only people in disguise." Do you agree? Why or why not?

Time

About time. In time. On time. Out of time. Time out. On the edge of time.

Time is everywhere. It is in minutes on our wrists and on the wall. It is in seasons in the trees and in the skies. And it is in aeons in the sun and in the stars. Time is measured on our bodies and even in our voices. And time is always the victor, for we know that we must succumb to it someday.

We organize our world according to time; we think of it as precise and predictably regular. Yet, there are occasions in our lives when something special occurs, when, in an instant, we are transformed forever. At such moments, we may gain an insight or a vision which gives new meaning and direction to our lives. Similarly, while many people think of time as linear, it is also a cycle, of history, of nature, and of life. We may like to think of time as orderly and rational, but there are occasions where it also seems to rush, stand still, or even bend.

Time is limitless, for we not only live in the present and reflect on our past, but also contemplate the future. We can even imagine the possibility that many times and many realities may exist simultaneously, somewhere, somehow. Through art and literature, we can explore the edges of time, and play in safety with the possibilities and ideas we find there.

Finding Time

✩

David S. Landes

The question to ask is: Why clocks? Who needs them? After all, nature is the great time-giver (*Zeitgeber*), and all of us, without exception, live by nature's clock. Night follows day; day, night; and each year brings its succession of seasons. These cycles are imprinted on just about every living thing in what are called circadian ("about a day") and circannual biological rhythms. They are stamped in our flesh and blood; they persist even when we are cut off from time cues; they mark us as earthlings.

These biological rhythms are matched by societal work patterns: day is for labor, night for repose, and the round of seasons is a sequence of warmth and cold, planting and harvest, life and death.

Into this natural cycle, which all peoples have experienced as a divine providence, the artificial clock enters as an intruder. For example, in ancient Rome:

> The gods confound the man who first found out
> How to distinguish hours. Confound him, too,
> Who in this place set up a sundial,
> To cut and hack my days so wretchedly
> Into small pieces! When I was a boy,
> My belly was my sundial—one surer,
> Truer, and more exact than any of them.
> This dial told me when 'twas proper time
> To go to dinner, when I ought to eat;
> But nowadays, why even when I have,
> I can't fall to unless the sun gives leave.
> The town's so full of these confounded dials...
>
> *Plautus*

And yet the sundial is the most natural of clocks, for it simply registers the movement of nature's prime timepiece. In essence, it is a schematization of the tree that casts a shadow and thus tracks the passing day. Since our unhappy Roman thought sundials a plague, what would he have said about mechanical clocks, going night and day, sky cloudy or clear, keeping an equal beat and beating equal hours in all seasons? "By its essential nature," wrote Lewis Mumford, the clock "dissociated time from human events." To which I would add: and human events from nature. The clock is a *machine*, a work of artifice, a man-made device with no model in nature—the kind of invention that needed planning, thinking, trying, and then more of each. No one could have stumbled on it or dreamed it up. But someone, or rather some people, wanted very much to track the time—not merely to know it, but to use it. Where and how did so strange, so *unnatural* a need develop?

A Mad Tea-Party

☆

Lewis Carroll

[Alice] had not gone much farther before she came in sight of the house of the March Hare: she thought it must be the right house, because the chimneys were shaped like ears and the roof was thatched with fur. It was so large a house, that she did not like to go nearer till she had nibbled some more of the left-hand bit of mushroom, and raised herself to about two feet high: even then she walked up towards it rather timidly, saying to herself "Suppose it should be raving mad after all! I almost wish I'd gone to see the Hatter instead!"

There was a table set out under a tree in front of the house, and the March Hare and the Hatter were having tea at it: a Dormouse was sitting between them, fast asleep, and the other two were using it as a cushion, resting their elbows on it, and talking over its head. "Very uncomfortable for the Dormouse," thought Alice; "only as it's asleep, I suppose it doesn't mind."

The table was a large one, but the three were all crowded together at one corner of it. "No room! No room!" they cried out when they saw Alice coming. "There's *plenty* of room!" said Alice indignantly, and she sat down in a large arm-chair at one end of the table.

"Have some wine," the March Hare said in an encouraging tone.

Alice looked all round the table, but there was nothing on it but tea. "I don't see any wine," she remarked.

"There isn't any," said the March Hare.

"Then it wasn't very civil of you to offer it," said Alice angrily.

"It wasn't very civil of you to sit down without being invited," said the March Hare.

"I didn't know it was *your* table," said Alice: "it's laid for a great many more than three."

"Your hair wants cutting," said the Hatter. He had been looking at Alice for some time with great curiosity, and this was his first speech.

"You should learn not to make personal remarks," Alice said with some severity: "it's very rude."

The Hatter opened his eyes very wide on hearing this; but all he *said* was "Why is a raven like a writing-desk?"

"Come, we shall have some fun now!" thought Alice. "I'm glad they've begun asking riddles—I believe I can guess that," she added aloud.

"Do you mean that you think you can find out the answer to it?" said the March Hare.

"Exactly so," said Alice.

"Then you should say what you mean," the March Hare went on.

"I do," Alice hastily replied; "at least—at least I mean what I say—that's the same thing, you know."

"Not the same thing a bit!" said the Hatter. "Why, you might just as well say that 'I see what I eat' is the same thing as 'I eat what I see'!"

"You might just as well say," added the March Hare, "That 'I like what I get' is the same thing as 'I get what I like'!"

"You might just as well say," added the Dormouse, which seemed to be talking in its sleep, "That 'I breathe when I sleep' is the same thing as 'I sleep when I breathe'!"

"It *is* the same thing with you," said the Hatter, and here the conversation dropped, and the party sat silent for a minute, while Alice thought over all she could remember about ravens and writing-desks, which wasn't much.

The Hatter was the first to break the silence. "What day of the month is it?" he said, turning to Alice: he had taken his watch out of his pocket, and was looking at it uneasily, shaking it every now and then, and holding it to his ear.

Alice considered a little, and then said "The fourth."

"Two days wrong!" sighed the Hatter. "I told you butter wouldn't suit the works!" he added, looking angrily at the March Hare.

"It was the *best* butter," the March Hare meekly replied.

"Yes, but some crumbs must have got in as well," the Hatter grumbled: "you shouldn't have put it in with the bread-knife."

The March Hare took the watch and looked at it gloomily: then he dipped it into his cup of tea, and looked at it again: but he could think of nothing better to say than his first remark, "It was the *best* butter, you know."

Alice had been looking over his shoulder with some curiosity. "What a funny watch!" she remarked. "It tells the day of the month, and doesn't tell what o'clock it is!"

"Why should it?" muttered the Hatter. "Does *your* watch tell you what year it is?"

"Of course not," Alice replied very readily: "but that's because it stays the same year for such a long time together."

"Which is just the case with *mine*," said the Hatter.

Alice felt dreadfully puzzled. The Hatter's remark seemed to her to have no sort of meaning in it, and yet it was certainly English. "I don't quite understand you," she said, as politely as she could.

"The Dormouse is asleep again," said the Hatter, and he poured a little hot tea upon its nose.

The Dormouse shook its head impatiently, and said, without opening its eyes, "Of course, of course: just what I was going to remark myself."

"Have you guessed the riddle yet?" the Hatter said, turning to Alice again.

"No, I give it up," Alice replied. "What's the answer?"

"I haven't the slightest idea," said the Hatter.

"Nor I," said the March Hare.

Alice sighed wearily. "I think you might do something better with the time," she said, "than wasting it in asking riddles that have no answers."

"If you knew Time as well as I do," said the Hatter, "you wouldn't talk about wasting *it*. It's *him*."

"I don't know what you mean," said Alice.

"Of course you don't!" the Hatter said, tossing his head contemptuously. "I dare say you never even spoke to Time!"

"Perhaps not," Alice cautiously replied; "but I know I have to beat time when I learn music."

"Ah! That accounts for it," said the Hatter. "He wo'n't stand beating. Now, if you only kept on good terms with him, he'd do almost anything you liked with the clock. For instance, suppose it were nine o'clock in the morning, just time to begin lessons: you'd only have to whisper a hint to Time, and round goes the clock in a twinkling! Half-past one, time for dinner!"

("I only wish it was," the March Hare said to itself in a whisper.)

"That would be grand, certainly," said Alice thoughtfully; "but then—I shouldn't be hungry for it, you know."

"Not at first, perhaps," said the Hatter: "But you could keep it to half-past one as long as you liked."

"Is that the way *you* manage?" Alice asked.

The Hatter shook his head mournfully. "Not I!" he replied. "We quarreled last March—just before *he* went mad, you know——" (pointing his teaspoon at the March Hare,) "——it was at the great concert given by the Queen of Hearts, and I had to sing

'*Twinkle, twinkle, little bat!*
How I wonder what you're at!'

You know the song, perhaps?"

"I've heard something like it," said Alice.

"It goes on, you know," the Hatter continued, "in this way:

'*Up above the world you fly,*
Like a tea-tray in the sky.
Twinkle, twinkle—'"

Here the Dormouse shook itself, and began singing in its sleep "*Twinkle, twinkle, twinkle, twinkle* ——" and went on so long that they had to pinch it to make it stop.

"Well, I'd hardly finished the first verse," said the Hatter, "when the Queen bawled out 'He's murdering the time! Off with his head!'"

"How dreadfully savage!" exclaimed Alice.

"And ever since that," the Hatter went on in a mournful tone, "he wo'n't do a thing I ask! It's always six o'clock now."

A bright idea came into Alice's head. "Is that the reason so many tea-things are put out here?" she asked.

"Yes, that's it," said the Hatter with a sigh: "it's always tea-time, and we've no time to wash the things between whiles."

"Then you keep moving round, I suppose?" said Alice.

"Exactly so," said the Hatter: "as the things get used up."

"But what happens when you come to the beginning again?" Alice ventured to ask.

"Suppose we change the subject," the March Hare interrupted, yawning. "I'm getting tired of this. I vote the young lady tells us a story."

"I'm afraid I don't know one," said Alice, rather alarmed at the proposal.

"Then the Dormouse shall!" they both cried. "Wake up, Dormouse!" And they pinched it on both sides at once.

The Dormouse slowly opened its eyes. "I wasn't asleep," it said in a hoarse, feeble voice, "I heard every word you fellows were saying."

"Tell us a story!" said the March Hare.

"Yes, please do!" pleaded Alice.

"And be quick about it," added the Hatter, "or you'll be asleep again before it's done."

"Once upon a time there were three little sisters," the Dormouse began in a great hurry; "And their names were Elsie, Lacie, and Tillie; and they lived at the bottom of a well ——"

"What did they live on?" said Alice, who always took a great interest in questions of eating and drinking.

"They lived on treacle," said the Dormouse, after thinking a minute or two.

"They couldn't have done that, you know," Alice gently remarked. "They'd have been ill."

"So they were," said the Dormouse; "*very* ill."

Alice tried a little to fancy to herself what such an extraordinary way of living would be like, but it puzzled her too much: so she went on: "But why did they live at the bottom of a well?"

"Take some more tea," the March Hare said to Alice, very earnestly.

"I've had nothing yet," Alice replied in an offended tone: "so I ca'n't take more."

"You mean you ca'n't take *less*," said the Hatter: "it's very easy to take *more* than nothing."

"Nobody asked *your* opinion," said Alice.

"Who's making personal remarks now?" the Hatter asked triumphantly.

Alice did not quite know what to say to this: so she helped herself to some tea and bread-and-butter, and then turned to the Dormouse, and repeated her question. "Why did they live at the bottom of a well?"

The Dormouse again took a minute or two to think about it, and then said "It was a treacle-well."

"There's no such thing!" Alice was beginning very angrily, but the Hatter and the March Hare went "Sh! Sh!" and the Dormouse sulkily remarked "If you ca'n't be civil, you'd better finish the story for yourself."

"No, please go on!" Alice said very humbly. "I wo'n't interrupt you again. I dare say there may be *one*."

"One, indeed!" said the Dormouse indignantly. However, he consented to go on. "And so these three little sisters—they were learning to draw, you know——"

"What did they draw?" said Alice, quite forgetting her promise.

"Treacle," said the Dormouse, without considering at all, this time.

"I want a clean cup," interrupted the Hatter: "let's all move one place on."

He moved on as he spoke, and the Dormouse followed him: the March Hare moved into the Dormouse's place, and Alice rather unwillingly took the place of the March Hare. The Hatter was the only one who got any advantage from the change; and Alice was a good deal worse off than before, as the March Hare had just upset the milk-jug into his plate.

Alice did not wish to offend the Dormouse again, so she began very cautiously: "But I don't understand. Where did they draw the treacle from?"

"You can draw water out of a water-well," said the Hatter; "so I should think you could draw treacle out of a treacle-well—eh, stupid?"

"But they were *in* the well," Alice said to the Dormouse, not choosing to notice this last remark.

"Of course they were," said the Dormouse: "well in."

This answer so confused poor Alice, that she let the Dormouse go on for some time without interrupting it.

"They were learning to draw," the Dormouse went on, yawning and rubbing its eyes, for it was getting very sleepy; "and they drew all manner of things—everything that begins with an M——"

"Why with an M?" said Alice.

"Why not?" said the March Hare.

Alice was silent.

The Dormouse had closed its eyes by this time, and was going off into a doze; but, on being pinched by the Hatter, it woke up again with a little shriek, and went on: "— —that begins with an M, such as mouse-traps, and the moon, and memory, and muchness—you know you say things are 'much of a muchness'—did you ever see such a thing as a drawing of a muchness!"

"Really, now you ask me," said Alice, very much confused, "I don't think— —"

"Then you shouldn't talk," said the Hatter.

This piece of rudeness was more than Alice could bear: she got up in great disgust, and walked off: the Dormouse fell asleep instantly, and neither of the others took the least notice of her going, though she looked back once or twice, half hoping that they would call after her: the last time she saw them, they were trying to put the Dormouse into the teapot.

"At any rate I'll never go *there* again!" said Alice, as she picked her way through the wood. "It's the stupidest tea-party I ever was at in all my life!"

Just as she said this, she noticed that one of the trees had a door leading right into it. "That's very curious!" she thought. "But everything's curious to-day. I think I may as well go in at once." And in she went.

Once more she found herself in the long hall, and close to the little glass table. "Now, I'll manage better this time," she said to herself, and began by taking the little golden key, and unlocking the door that led to the garden. Then she set to work nibbling at the mushroom (she had kept a piece of it in her pocket) till she was about a foot high; then she walked down the little passage: and *then*—she found herself at last in the beautiful garden, among the bright flower-beds and the cool fountains.

Pythagoras

☆

Ovid

                   Full sail, I voyage
Over the boundless ocean, and I tell you
Nothing is permanent in all the world.
All things are fluent; every image forms,
Wandering through change. Time is itself a river
In constant movement, and the hours flow by
Like water, wave on wave, pursued, pursuing,
Forever fugitive, forever new.
That which has been, is not; that which was not,
Begins to be; motion and moment always
In process of renewal. Look, the night,
Worn out, aims toward the brightness, and sun's glory
Succeeds the dark. The color of the sky
Is different at midnight, when tired things
Lie all at rest, from what it is at morning
When Lucifer rides his snowy horse, before
Aurora paints the sky for Phoebus' coming.
The shield of the god reddens at early morning,
Reddens at evening, but is white at noonday
In purer air, farther from earth's contagion.
And the Moon-goddess changes in the nighttime,
Lesser today than yesterday, if waning,
Greater tomorrow than today, when crescent.

Notice the year's four seasons: they resemble
Our lives. Spring is a nursling, a young child,
Tender and young, and the grass shines and buds
Swell with new life, not yet full-grown nor hardy,
But promising much to husbandman, with blossom
Bright in the fertile fields. And then comes summer
When the year is a strong young man, no better time
Than this, no richer, no more passionate vigor.
Then comes the prime of Autumn, a little sober,
But ripe and mellow, moderate of mood,
Halfway from youth to age, with just a showing
Of gray around the temples. And then Winter,
Tottering, shivering, bald or gray, and agèd.

Our bodies also change. What we have been,
What we now are, we shall not be tomorrow.
There was a time when we were only seed,
Only the hope of men, housed in the womb,
Where Nature shaped us, brought us forth, exposed us
To the void air, and there in light we lay,
Feeble and infant, and were quadrupeds
Before too long, and after a little wobbled
And pulled ourselves upright, holding a chair,
The side of the crib, and strength grew into us,
And swiftness; youth and middle age went swiftly
Down the long hill toward age, and all our vigor
Came to decline, so Milon, the old wrestler,
Weeps when he sees his arms whose bulging muscles
Were once like Hercules', and Helen weeps
To see her wrinkles in the looking glass:
Could this old woman ever have been ravished,
Taken twice over? Time devours all things
With envious Age, together. The slow gnawing
Consumes all things, and very, very slowly.

Not even the so-called elements are constant.
Listen, and I will tell you of their changes.
There are four of them, and two, the earth and water,
Are heavy, and their own weight bears them downward,
And two, the air and fire (and fire is purer
Even than air) are light, rise upward
If nothing holds them down. These elements
Are separate in space, yet all things come
From them and into them, and they can change
Into each other. Earth can be dissolved
To flowing water, water can thin to air,
And air can thin to fire, and fire can thicken
To air again, and air condense to water,
And water be compressed to solid earth.
Nothing remains the same: the great renewer,
Nature, makes form from form, and, oh, believe me
That nothing ever dies. What we call birth
Is the beginning of a difference,
No more than that, and death is only ceasing
Of what had been before. The parts may vary,
Shifting from here to there, hither and yon,
And back again, but the great sum is constant.

The Persistence of Memory

✡

Salvador Dali

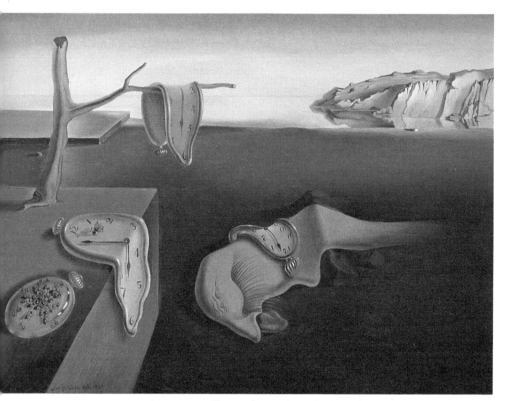

The Granger Collection, New York. ©Salvador Dali 1993/VIS*ART Copyright Inc.

The Secret Miracle

✡

Jorge Luis Borges

And God had him die for a hundred
years and then revived him and said:
"How long have you been here?"
"A day or a part of a day," he answered.
Koran, II, 261

The night of March 14, 1943, in an apartment in the Zeltnergasse of
Prague, Jaromir Hladik, the author of the unfinished drama entitled *The
Enemies, of Vindication of Eternity*, and of a study of the indirect Jewish
sources of Jakob Böhme, had a dream of a long game of chess. The players
were not two persons, but two illustrious families; the game had been
going on for centuries. Nobody could remember what the stakes were,
but it was rumored that they were enormous, perhaps infinite; the
chessmen and the board were in a secret tower. Jaromir (in his dream)
was the first-born of one of the contending families. The clock struck the
hour for the game, which could not be postponed. The dreamer raced
over the sands of a rainy desert, and was unable to recall either the pieces
or the rules of chess. At that moment he awoke. The clangor of the rain
and of the terrible clocks ceased. A rhythmic, unanimous noise, punctu-
ated by shouts of command, arose from the Zeltnergasse. It was dawn,
and the armored vanguard of the Third Reich was entering Prague.

On the nineteenth the authorities received a denunciation; that same
nineteenth, toward evening, Jaromir Hladik was arrested. He was taken
to an aseptic, white barracks on the opposite bank of the Moldau. He was
unable to refute a single one of the Gestapo's charges; his mother's family
name was Jaroslavski, he was of Jewish blood, his study on Böhme had a
marked Jewish emphasis, his signature had been one more on the protest
against the *Anschluss*. In 1928 he had translated the *Sepher Yezirah* for
the publishing house of Hermann Barsdorf. The fulsome catalogue of the
firm had exaggerated, for publicity purposes, the translator's reputation,
and the catalogue had been examined by Julius Rothe, one of the officials
who held Hladik's fate in his hands. There is not a person who, except in

the field of his own specialization, is not credulous; two or three adjectives in Gothic type were enough to persuade Julius Rothe of Hladik's importance, and he ordered him sentenced to death *pour encourager les autres*. The execution was set for March 29th, at 9:00 A.M. This delay (whose importance the reader will grasp later) was owing to the desire on the authorities' part to proceed impersonally and slowly, after the manner of vegetables and plants.

Hladik's first reaction was mere terror. He felt he would not have shrunk from the gallows, the block, or the knife, but that death by a firing squad was unbearable. In vain he tried to convince himself that the plain, unvarnished fact of dying was the fearsome thing, not the attendant circumstances. He never wearied of conjuring up these circumstances, senselessly trying to exhaust all their possible variations. He infinitely anticipated the process of his dying, from the sleepless dawn to the mysterious volley. Before the day set by Julius Rothe he died hundreds of deaths in courtyards whose forms and angles strained geometrical probabilities, machine-gunned by variable soldiers in changing numbers, who at times killed him from a distance, at others from close by. He faced these imaginary executions with real terror (perhaps with real bravery); each simulacrum lasted a few seconds. When the circle was closed, Jaromir returned once more and interminably to the tremulous vespers of his death. Then he reflected that reality does not usually coincide with our anticipation of it; with a logic of his own he inferred that to foresee a circumstantial detail is to prevent its happening. Trusting in this weak magic, he invented, *so that they would not happen*, the most gruesome details. Finally, as was natural, he came to fear that they were prophetic. Miserable in the night, he endeavored to find some way to hold fast to the fleeting substance of time. He knew that it was rushing headlong toward the dawn of the twenty-ninth. He reasoned aloud: "I am now in the night of the twenty-second; while this night lasts (and for six nights more), I am invulnerable, immortal." The nights of sleep seemed to him deep, dark pools in which he could submerge himself. There were moments when he longed impatiently for the final burst of fire that would free him, for better or for worse, from the vain compulsion of his imaginings. On the twenty-eighth, as the last sunset was reverberating from the high barred windows, the thought of his drama, *The Enemies*, deflected him from these abject considerations.

Hladik had rounded forty. Aside from a few friendships and many habits, the problematic exercise of literature constituted his life. Like all writers, he measured the achievements of others by what they had accomplished, asking them that they measure him by what he envisaged or planned. All the books he had published had left him with a complex feeling of repentance. His studies of the work of Böhme, of Ibn Ezra, and of Fludd had been characterized essentially by mere applications; his translation of the *Sepher Yezirah*, by carelessness, fatigue, and conjecture. *Vindication of Eternity* perhaps had fewer shortcomings. The first volume gave a history of man's various concepts of eternity, from the immutable Being of Parmenides to the modifiable Past of Hinton. The second denied (with Francis Bradley) that all the events of the universe make up a temporal series, arguing that the number of man's possible experiences is not infinite, and that a single "repetition" suffices to prove that time is a fallacy . . . Unfortunately, the arguments that demonstrate this fallacy are equally fallacious. Hladik was in the habit of going over them with a kind of contemptuous perplexity. He had also composed a series of Expressionist poems; to the poet's chagrin they had been included in an anthology published in 1924, and no subsequent anthology but inherited them. From all this equivocal, uninspired past Hladik had hoped to redeem himself with his drama in verse, *The Enemies*. (Hladik felt the verse form to be essential because it makes it impossible for the spectators to lose sight of irreality, one of art's requisites.)

The drama observed the unities of time, place, and action. The scene was laid in Hradčany, in the library of Baron von Roemerstadt, on one of the last afternoons of the nineteenth century. In the first scene of the first act a strange man visits Roemerstadt. (A clock was striking seven, the vehemence of the setting sun's rays glorified the windows, a passionate, familiar Hungarian music floated in the air.) This visit is followed by others; Roemerstadt does not know the people who are importuning him, but he has the uncomfortable feeling that he has seen them somewhere, perhaps in a dream. They all fawn upon him, but it is apparent—first to the audience and then to the Baron—that they are secret enemies, in league to ruin him. Roemerstadt succeeds in checking or evading their involved schemings. In the dialogue mention is made of his sweetheart, Julia von Weidenau, and a certain Jaroslav Kubin, who at one time pressed his attentions on her. Kubin has now lost his mind, and believes himself to be Roemerstadt. The dangers increase; Roemerstadt, at the end of the second act, is forced to kill one of the conspirators. The third and final act opens. The incoherencies gradually increase; actors who had seemed out of the play reappear; the man Roemerstadt killed returns for a moment. Someone points out that evening has not fallen; the clock strikes seven, the high windows reverberate in the western sun, the air carries an impassioned Hungarian melody. The first actor comes on and repeats the lines he had spoken in the first scene of the first act. Roemerstadt speaks to him without surprise; the audience understands that Roemerstadt is the miserable Jaroslav Kubin. The drama has never taken place; it is the circular delirium that Kubin lives and relives endlessly.

Hladik had never asked himself whether this tragicomedy of errors was preposterous or admirable, well thought out or slipshod. He felt that the plot I have just sketched was best contrived to cover up his defects and point up his abilities and held the possibility of allowing him to redeem (symbolically) the meaning of his life. He had finished the first act and one or two scenes of the third; the metrical nature of the work made it possible for him to keep working it over, changing the hexameters, without the manuscript in front of him. He thought how he still had two acts to do, and that he was going to die very soon. He spoke with God in the darkness: "If in some fashion I exist, if I am not one of Your repetitions and mistakes, I exist as the author of *The Enemies*. To finish this drama, which can justify me and justify You, I need another year. Grant me these days, You to whom the centuries and time belong." This was the last night, the most dreadful of all, but ten minutes later sleep flooded over him like a dark water.

Toward dawn he dreamed that he had concealed himself in one of the naves of the Clementine Library. A librarian wearing dark glasses asked him: "What are you looking for?" Hladik answered: "I am looking for God." The librarian said to him: "God is in one of the letters on one of the pages of one of the four hundred thousand volumes of the Clementine. My fathers and the fathers of my fathers have searched for this letter; I have grown blind seeking it." He removed his glasses, and Hladik saw his eyes, which were dead. A reader came in to return an atlas. "This atlas is worthless," he said, and handed it to Hladik, who opened it at random. He saw a map of India as in a daze. Suddenly sure of himself, he touched one of the tiniest letters. A ubiquitous voice said to him: "The time of your labor has been granted." At this point Hladik awoke.

He remembered that men's dreams belong to God, and that Maimonides had written that the words heard in a dream are divine when they are distinct and clear and the person uttering them cannot be seen. He dressed: two soldiers came into the cell and ordered him to follow them.

From behind the door, Hladik had envisaged a labyrinth of passageways, stairs, and separate buildings. The reality was less spectacular: they descended to an inner court by a narrow iron stairway. Several soldiers—some with uniform unbuttoned—were examining a motorcycle and discussing it. The sergeant looked at the clock; it was 8:44. They had to wait until it struck nine. Hladik, more insignificant than pitiable, sat down on a pile of wood. He noticed that the soldiers' eyes avoided his. To ease his wait, the sergeant handed him a cigarette. Hladik did not smoke; he accepted it out of politeness or humility. As he lighted it, he noticed that his hands were shaking. The day was clouding over; the soldiers spoke in a low voice as though he were already dead. Vainly he tried to recall the woman of whom Julia von Weidenau was the symbol.

The squad formed and stood at attention. Hladik, standing against the barracks wall, waited for the volley. Someone pointed out that the wall was going to be stained with blood; the victim was ordered to step forward a few paces. Incongruously, this reminded Hladik of the fumbling preparations of photographers. A big drop of rain struck one of Hladik's temples and rolled slowly down his cheek; the sergeant shouted the final order.

The physical universe came to a halt.

The guns converged on Hladik, but the men who were to kill him stood motionless. The sergeant's arm eternized an unfinished gesture. On a paving stone of the courtyard a bee cast an unchanging shadow. The wind had ceased, as in a picture. Hladik attempted a cry, a word, a movement of the hand. He realized that he was paralyzed. Not a sound reached him from the halted world. He thought: "I am in hell, I am dead." He thought: "I am mad." He thought: "Time has stopped." Then he reflected that if that was the case, his mind would have stopped too. He wanted to test this; he repeated (without moving his lips) Vergil's mysterious fourth Eclogue. He imagined that the now remote soldiers must be sharing his anxiety; he longed to be able to communicate with them. It astonished him not to feel the least fatigue, not even the numbness of his protracted immobility. After an indeterminate time he fell asleep. When he awoke the world continued motionless and mute. The drop of water still clung to his cheek, the shadow of the bee to the stone. The smoke from the cigarette he had thrown away had not dispersed. Another "day" went by before Hladik understood.

He had asked God for a whole year to finish his work; His omnipotence had granted it. God had worked a secret miracle for him; German lead would kill him at the set hour, but in his mind a year would go by between the order and its execution. From perplexity he passed to stupor, from stupor to resignation, from resignation to sudden gratitude.

He had no document but his memory; the training he had acquired with each added hexameter gave him a discipline unsuspected by those who set down and forget temporary, incomplete paragraphs. He was not working for posterity or even for God, whose literary tastes were unknown to him. Meticulously, motionlessly, secretly, he wrought in time his lofty, invisible labyrinth. He worked the third act over twice. He eliminated certain symbols as over-obvious, such as the repeated striking of the clock, the music. Nothing hurried him. He omitted, he condensed, he amplified. In certain instances he came back to the original version.

He came to feel an affection for the courtyard, the barracks; one of the faces before him modified his conception of Roemerstadt's character. He discovered that the wearying cacophonies that bothered Flaubert so much are mere visual superstitions, weakness and limitation of the written word, not the spoken...He concluded his drama. He had only the problem of a single phrase. He found it. The drop of water slid down his cheek. He opened his mouth in a maddened cry, moved his face, dropped under the quadruple blast.

Jaromir Hladik died on March 29, at 9:02 A.M.

Theme Questions

✿

✿ Two examples of the way we order time are the clock and the "belly." What other ways do we use?

✿ Writers often describe time by comparing it to other experiences. How do such metaphors enlarge our understanding of time?

✿ Compare the first paragraph of "The Secret Miracle," page 86, with "The Persistence of Memory," page 85. What are the similarities? What are the differences?

✿ Why would a story about time begin with a dream? How are the two connected? What is the difference between dream-time and waking-time?

Heritage: Turn and Face the Stranger

I am...where I came from? where I am? who my parents are? what my traditions say I should be?

Our heritage helps us to know who we are, where we come from, and what we value. Our past gives birth to our present and our future. Yet, what happens when our heritage and our lives no longer coincide, when the relationship between who we were and what we are is no longer clear? We can be bound by our heritage and feel ambivalent towards it at the same time. In our world, continuities are constantly being broken, leaving the past feeling odd and unfamiliar.

Discovery and appreciation of our heritage often arise in the midst of feeling like an outsider in a society with a different history, language, and culture. At such times, home can be more an idea than a place, a paradise of our minds which never existed in reality.

We want to be in all places at once—in the country of our mind as well as the country of our place. Heritage poses dilemmas, even contradictions, that art and literature can help us to explore. It speaks to the importance of reconciling our past with our future, and our identity with that of others.

Raven and the First Humans

☆

Bill Reid

Courtesy of the UBC Museum of Anthropology, photo credit Bill McLennan.

West Coast Indian

✩

George Clutesi

In the beginning he merely marked
Then he incised on rock.
Later he carved on wood to paint and color with rock and roe.
He believed in a God; he aspired to a generous heart.
Asked for strength of arm, a true aim for his bow,
To provide and share with his fellow man.

He did his work at summertime.
He waxed strong; his possessions increased with his toil.
With the thunderdrum he sang at wintertime,
Great feasts he gave because his heart was full,
He sang of deeds and glories won by his house and his clan.
He was at peace with his God; his life indeed was full.

He chose the timber wolf for his symbol,
The killer whale was lord of the salt-chuck,
The thunderbird meant power and might
Like the wind, rain and the thunder.
The lightning snake was its ally.
Mah-uk, leviathan of the sea, represented abundance.

Inspired thus, on great cedar planks he drew
The symbols of his tribe.
Earth and rock, the root and bark, the salmon roe,
Lent their colors, bold and true;
Indeed great men from far off lands marvelled to see
Art forms, shown nowhere else but here.

Allied to the Nootkas, the Tse-shahts
Belonged to the clan of the wolf.
With all the powers at hand,
A great potlatch he would now command.
To bid you: "Come, enter and share with me."
A rich cultural inheritance is his indeed.

Exiled from Paradise

✡

Eva Hoffman

It is April 1959, I'm standing at the railing of the *Batory's* upper deck, and I feel that my life is ending. I'm looking out at the crowd that has gathered on the shore to see the ship's departure from Gdynia—a crowd that, all of a sudden, is irrevocably on the other side—and I want to break out, run back, run toward the familiar excitement, the waving hands, the exclamations. We can't be leaving all this behind—but we are. I am thirteen years old, and we are emigrating. It's a notion of such crushing, definitive finality that to me it might as well mean the end of the world.

My sister, four years younger than I, is clutching my hand wordlessly; she hardly understands where we are, or what is happening to us. My parents are highly agitated; they had just been put through a body search by the customs police, probably as the farewell gesture of anti-Jewish harassment. Still, the officials weren't clever enough, or suspicious enough, to check my sister and me—lucky for us, since we are both carrying some silverware we were not allowed to take out of Poland in large pockets sewn into our skirts especially for this purpose, and hidden under capacious sweaters.

When the brass band on the shore strikes up the jaunty mazurka rhythms of the Polish anthem, I am pierced by a youthful sorrow so powerful that I suddenly stop crying and try to hold still against the pain. I desperately want time to stop, to hold the ship still with the force of my will. I am suffering my first, severe attack of nostalgia, or *tesknota*—a word that adds to nostalgia the tonalities of sadness and longing. It is a feeling whose shades and degrees I'm destined to know intimately, but at this hovering moment, it comes upon me like a visitation from a whole new geography of emotions, an annunciation of how much an absence can hurt. Or a premonition of absence, because at this divide, I'm filled to the brim with what I'm about to lose—images of Cracow, which I loved as one loves a person, of the sun-baked villages where we had taken summer vacations, of the hours I spent poring over passages of music with my piano teacher, of conversations and escapades with friends. Looking ahead, I come across an enormous, cold blankness—a darkening, an erasure, of the imagination, as if a camera eye has snapped shut, or as if a heavy curtain has been pulled over the future. Of the place where we're going—Canada—I know nothing. There are vague outlines of half a continent, a sense of vast spaces and little habitation. When my parents were hiding in a branch-covered forest bunker during the war, my father had a book with him called *Canada Fragrant with Resin* which, in his horrible confinement, spoke to him of majestic wilderness, of animals roaming without being pursued, of freedom. That is partly why we are going there, rather than to Israel, where most of our Jewish friends have gone. But to me, the word "Canada" has ominous echoes of the "Sahara." No, my mind rejects the idea of being taken there, I don't want to be pried out of my childhood, my pleasures, my safety, my hopes for becoming a pianist. The *Batory* pulls away, the foghorn emits its lowing, shofar sound, but my being is engaged in a stubborn refusal to move. My parents put their hands on my shoulders consolingly; for a moment, they allow themselves to acknowledge that there's pain in this departure, much as they wanted it.

Many years later, at a stylish party in New York, I met a woman who told me that she had had an enchanted childhood. Her father was a highly positioned diplomat in an Asian country, and she had lived surrounded by sumptuous elegance, the courtesy of servants, and the delicate advances of older men. No wonder, she said, that when this part of her life came to an end, at age thirteen, she felt she had been exiled from paradise, and had been searching for it ever since.

No wonder. But the wonder is what you can make a paradise out of. I told her that I grew up in a lumpen apartment in Cracow, squeezed into three rudimentary rooms with four other people, surrounded by squabbles, dark political rumblings, memories of wartime suffering and daily struggle for existence. And yet, when it came time to leave I, too, felt I was being pushed out of the happy, safe enclosures of Eden.

equal opportunity

✿

Jim Wong-Chu

in early canada
when railways were highways

each stop brought new opportunities

there was a rule

    the chinese could only ride
    the last two cars
    of the trains

that is

until a train derailed
killing all those
in front

(the chinese erected an altar and thanked buddha)

a new rule was made
    the chinese must ride
    the front two cars
    of the trains

that is

until another accident
claimed everyone
in the back

(the chinese erected an altar and thanked buddha)

after much debate
common sense prevailed

the chinese are now allowed
to sit anywhere
on any train

A Proper Goodbye

☆

Katherine Alexander

Eleni was on her knees in the garden when the phone started ringing. She was kneading the earth around the freshly-planted eggplant seeds and trying to decide whether to cook chicken for the dinner on Sunday or a nice leg of lamb. The grandchildren always asked for chicken, but Costa liked lamb on a festive occasion. Her sons would want to cook outdoors on that contraption they'd bought her the summer before. They'd thought she was being difficult when she'd refused to go near the thing. Would they have understood if she'd told them that in Greece they'd have no choice but to cook in an outdoor oven that had to be watched every minute because in the summer it heated so quickly the food burned, while in winter it needed to be fed a continual supply of twigs so the heat wouldn't give out, and that having her own lovely indoor stove which could be regulated by the switch of a knob meant a sort of freedom to her?

Costa understood. As well as the stove, he'd bought her a huge refrigerator that made its own ice and needed to be defrosted only once a week, and a washing machine that rumbled quietly in the corner as it filled and emptied itself and even wrung the clothes out so all she had to do was hang them up to dry. He was a good man, her Costa. She'd make the lamb. After all, the family dinner was for his birthday. They'd already had his annual Name Day party for family and friends, but the children liked the Canadian custom of celebrating birthdays.

Her Stephano would've been thirty-four now. And the baby, the one she barely remembered—there hadn't even been time to photograph her before God took her away—would've been thirty-five. It was hard to mourn an infant she'd known for only a few months so long ago, but with Stephano it was different. She'd asked Costa over and over to find out where their son was so they could visit, take flowers, but all he'd say was it was better left alone.

The feeling that she'd let her children down wouldn't leave Eleni, not with two of them gone and Angela over thirty and still unmarried. It was something she could never put into words. All she could do was pray to the Virgin, asking forgiveness for she knew not what. Yet even with all her prayers, the deaths of two children continued to hang like a cloud over the happiness her others gave her, and the goodness of her husband.

The phone was still ringing. Didn't Angela realize it might be her Papa? He liked to go to the store every day—to keep an eye on things, he'd say—but he'd often tire quickly and call Angela to pick him up.

Eleni sighed, rocked back on her knees. She'd better go in and see what was going on. Anyway, there was nothing more to be done in the garden for now. The eggplant was being stubborn as usual. Unlike the zucchini that blossomed beautifully year after year, nothing seemed to work with the eggplant. She'd tried different mixes of soils, different patches of garden for a little more sunlight or a little less, but the result was always the same: leathery lumps the size of walnuts. The worst thing was they seemed to lie there, contentedly nestling among the dark green leaves, mocking her.

The phone finally stopped ringing as she got up off her knees. She rubbed the loose dirt from her hands, went to the side of the house, turned on the hose and washed her hands. When she came around the corner, shaking her dripping hands, Angela was standing on the porch steps.

"Who was on the phone?"

Angela reached out to her mother.

"Did you answer?"

Angela took her mother's hands.

"You'll get all wet." Eleni was getting impatient.

Angela put her arms around her mother, drew her close.

Eleni stiffened, then quickly pulled away, saw her daughter's eyes brimming with tears. "Your Papa?" she whispered.

Angela nodded. "I'll take you, Mama."

Eleni rushed into the house, grabbed a light coat to cover her old housedress and ran out the front door. Angela was waiting for her in the car.

They drove in silence. Eleni pulled her coat tight around her. She shouldn't have let Costa go this morning. Some days, when he seemed more tired than others, she would get after him to stay home. Not that he would. But she'd try. This morning though, he had seemed almost his old self, joking with her as she'd helped him pick out a tie. He'd probably done too much at the store, tried to help out when he should've just sat quietly and let his sons do the work.

"Why didn't you answer the phone right away?"

"I was taking the *koulourákia* out of the oven—I was afraid they'd burn if I left them to answer the phone."

"Burnt cookies are more important than your Papa!"

"I'm sorry, Mama."

"I didn't. . .oh, never mind." She couldn't sit still, couldn't move, it was taking forever. Costa had never been sick, apart from the recent tiredness, and that had only started after the trip to Greece.

Visiting their homeland after so many years had been difficult for both of them. Their parents had been dead for years, and the relatives and friends they'd met after so long had been unrecognizable. The stern middle-aged women who'd said they were her sisters had nothing in common with the laughing children she'd left behind. For Costa it had been worse; he'd found one of his brothers dying, another a sickly old man, and three of his aging sisters swathed in widow's black.

After a few days, Eleni had grown accustomed to her adult sisters and to being back in Greece, but Costa had been on edge no matter what they did or who they saw. When he'd suggested she take her sisters on a holiday to Rhodes, she hadn't wanted to leave him, but he'd insisted, saying it would give him a chance to visit some of the people and places from his youth that would have no meaning for her. Whatever past he'd relived while she was gone had done nothing but bring him sorrow, and she'd always regretted leaving him alone that time.

"Can't you go faster?" Eleni said. Angela was always so careful.

"We'll be there in a minute, Mama."

Eleni smoothed down her hair. She had to look nice for Costa. "Why are you going this way?"

"He's not at the store, Mama." When Eleni saw they were turning into the entrance of the Miseracordia, her breath caught in her throat. She'd only been to the hospital to visit others, never for anyone in her family, except the grandchildren, but childbirth was different. Her sons were walking quickly toward the car. Why weren't they with their papa?

Paul held the car door open and Tim helped her out. They huddled around her on the sidewalk in front of the entrance, but neither one spoke. Then she looked at their faces. She clutched at the lapels of her coat, pulling it even tighter around her throat. She knew what they couldn't tell her. "I want to see him."

"Mama, he's. . ."

"I know. I want to see him."

They led her to a room and she saw her husband lying on a cot, his head turned to one side, his mouth slightly open as if he was asleep. His tie had been pulled away, and his shirt collar unbuttoned. In their bedroom that morning, he'd held out two ties to Eleni, and she'd picked the grey striped one, teasing him about how distinguished he looked in his new light-grey summer suit. They never talked about how tired he seemed so much of the time, how haggard. He didn't look haggard any longer, lying as though asleep, the care finally gone from his face.

Eleni had never seen death before. She'd known it, but she'd never seen it. Her Stephano had died far away in a strange place. As for the baby, one day she was there, sick and crying, and the next she was gone. She used to think sometimes that if only she'd known some English she might have been able to find out where they'd taken her dead baby and where her son had been buried. But Costa had always said it wasn't necessary for her to know more than a few words of English to do the shopping. He looked after everything else, didn't he? He did. He had. He'd looked after her from the time she'd come to him as a bride of sixteen.

She reached a hand to him. Her sons tried to hold her back, but she pushed them away. His cheek was warm, soft; he'd shaved in the morning before Angela had driven him downtown. She'd had his usual cornflakes with sliced peaches ready for him in the kitchen when he'd come downstairs and a second cup of coffee for Eleni. He hadn't seemed tired at all. They'd talked about the dinner on Sunday and how he was looking forward to seeing the grandchildren. Eleni stroked his face, rearranged his tie so that it was resting nicely on his shirt, leaned over and kissed his brow. Then she sat down beside him. She began to whisper. Soon strong hands lifted her and led her away.

After, at home, a glass of brandy in her hand, at her lips, the worried looks and hushed voices of family, friends, Priest, drew in closer and closer until she gasped out in suffocation. Even Matina, who'd been her first friend when she'd come to Canada, and was still the person she felt closest to, could say nothing to appease her. She ran out of the room, upstairs, threw off her clothes. Her old chenille bathrobe felt good. She started for the bathroom. Angela was waiting in the hall. "Let me help, Mama, please."

"I'm going to have a bath."

"Don't lock the door, Mama." Angela was clenching her hands, a habit she'd acquired lately.

"I'm going to have a bath!"

"In case you need anything." Angela never raised her voice from that whining tone. It was enough to drive a person crazy.

"Fine. I'll leave the door wide open so you can all come and watch!"

She slammed the door shut, locked it, and turned the faucets on full force. She poured a handful of bath salts into the water and tossed in some bubble bath capsules—gifts from tiny grandchildren at Christmas—lowered herself into the water, let the tub fill, turned off the faucets, lay back and closed her eyes.

People came and went, walking up to the casket, crossing themselves, whispering words to Eleni sitting stiffly between her two sons in the dark-panelled room.

Costa was laid out in ivory satin inside a dark mahogany box, baskets of white lilies on either side. His hair was neatly combed. He had on his good black suit and black tie. She'd wanted to dress him herself, but her sons had said it wasn't allowed. And so strangers had tended to his final needs, the way they had for her son. She closed her eyes to the image of Stephano and tried to focus on Costa as she'd seen him earlier on that last day, helping him on with his tie, or at breakfast. She shouldn't have let him go out, he was tired, but she'd been thinking about her gardening, and so had paid him little attention. She liked her garden, liked the feel of the house when the men were gone, only she and Angela quietly going about their work, sometimes not talking for hours.

"We should go now, Mama." Paul, sombre, like his father, squeezed her hand. Tim, on the other side, had his arm linked through hers. Their wives sat across from them.

"Where's your sister?"

"Right here, Mama." Angela leaned across Tim.

"Go now, all of you. I want to talk to your Papa."

Ignoring the whispers, nudges, looks of concern, Eleni insisted on her time alone with her husband. Matina paused on her way out. "I'll be fine," Eleni assured her.

The Priest grasped her hands. "Think of your children now, *Kyría Eléni*," he said. "*Zoí se más*, life to the living."

The living, always the living. But the dead lingered on. She would have liked to have explained to the Priest that she'd never properly said her goodbyes to the dead—her parents in Greece, her infant child buried in an unknown cemetery right here in this city, her son somewhere in Europe—but he'd only murmur men's words of faith that meant nothing to her. It was to the Virgin she prayed nightly, the Virgin who offered her comfort.

"I'd like to stay here with Costa a little longer, *Páter*."

He left her finally to join the others. They would all wait for her so they could go to the house together. Once there, Paul and Tim would preside over bottles of liquor and their wives would be in the kitchen with Angela preparing coffee and filling plates with *paxi-mádia*, the crisp biscuits always served at times like these. Eleni knew she was holding everyone up, but she couldn't leave, not yet. She needed to say a proper goodbye to Costa and this was their last chance to be alone.

She tried looking down at him, at the stiff, white figure in the casket, surrounded by floral tributes from family and friends, the prayers of the Priest still fresh in the air, but all Eleni could see was her son, her Stephano, dead, alone in a foreign land with no one to mourn him, no one to take flowers to his grave, no one to brush away the leaves in autumn, the snow in winter. "Not even a headstone," she whispered, "nothing to mark the place."

She started to cry. "It's not right. Those people who sent him to war should've been able to find him for us." She wiped her eyes with the back of her hand. "It's not right, Costa, not right." She fumbled in her pocket for a handkerchief, blew her nose. "Remember how tall he was, Costa, how handsome? He had your eyes, always smiling. Remember his letters, the way he described the places he visited? Such beautiful words, Costa. Like poems."

The room was getting very warm. Eleni took off her coat, pushed the veiled hat off her head. She searched in her purse for a clean handkerchief. "Forgive me, Costa. I shouldn't be telling you these things, upsetting you." She wiped her eyes, paused to collect her thoughts. "You were a good husband, Costa. That's what I started to say. My prayers go with you." She crossed herself. "Keep his soul safe, *Panagía*. Amen."

Eleni sat quietly, letting the silent tears flow, not knowing any more whether she was crying for a lost son or a dead husband. For a moment, she wished someone was with her, someone who would help her understand. But who? Even Matina could do nothing now. For all her kindness, she hadn't been able to help when Stephano had been taken from her, or the first tiny baby. Like everyone else, she'd hover, shush her when she'd try to speak, murmur condolences, talk about God's will. It was better this way, at least for a little while.

She sat for a long time; then, when she couldn't bear either the silence or her own thoughts any longer and was getting ready to face the others, a voice intruded. "Oh, Eleni, Eleni." Both the voice and the ample body that almost covered hers in an embrace were instantly recognizable. Tasia was one of the oldest of what the children called the old-timers. Since her own husband had been dead for years and she'd had no children of her own, everyone else's life was Tasia's concern. Out of respect, no one excluded her from any occasion, be it wedding, christening, name-day celebration, even funeral.

"*Paidí mou*, my child," old Tasia cried. "My dear, my child," she crooned. "Such a loss. Such a fine man."

As wearisome as Tasia was even at the best of times, Eleni was relieved to see her now, for the old woman's lament would force Eleni to concentrate on mourning Costa instead of indulging her own confused thoughts.

"Ah," Tasia wailed. "Such a loss, such a terrible loss...a fine man...a good man." Eleni let herself drift away from the words, searching her cluttered mind for memories, happy memories, while Tasia droned on— "good man...well-loved...pillar of the community"—but all her memories were shrouded in pain. She tried to think about Costa and the way he'd been before he'd taken her to Greece and had begun looking ill, but that always took her to Stephano and the awful day the first telegram arrived.

She didn't want to think about Stephano any more today. It wasn't fair to Costa. She needed to grieve for Costa, pray for his soul. "So brave...at his age...honour his son." Tasia's words were slowly coming into focus. "Poor boy...taken so young...honour his son...brave man...travel so far...honour his son."

Eleni grabbed the old woman, stared her full in the face.

"My dear, you mustn't blame yourself," Tasia said. "It was right of him to go. Take comfort, my child, take comfort. Costa did the right thing."

"Right?" Eleni echoed.

"At his age, and ill, to travel so far to honour his son." Tasia was patting her hand, smiling through tears. "Stephano will rest now."

Eleni jerked away. "Leave me. Go now. Please. Go."

She heard the soft intake of breath, the abrupt closing of a door, and she was alone with the cruel words the old woman had thrown in her face. Unbelievable words. They horrified her. Costa had known where Stephano was; worse, he'd gone there without her. No. He wouldn't have done that. It was a mistake. Tasia was wrong, she'd misunderstood, was repeating malicious gossip.

Eleni shivered. She huddled back into her coat. Costa had never been a cruel man. He would not have denied her a final goodbye to her son. But the seed the old woman had planted wouldn't be rooted out, and Eleni's thoughts flew to the early years when their first baby had died and Costa had taken her away in the night. Perhaps Costa had been right to try and protect her then; she had been a very young bride and the baby a mere infant. But Stephano? She'd raised him to manhood. Surely Costa would've seen the difference!

Suddenly her children were surrounding her. "Tell me the truth," she cried. Pavlo bowed his head. "You can't look me in the face," she accused.

"Papa didn't want you to know," he mumbled.

Eleni grasped her son's lapels. "It's true? You mean it's true? Everyone knew? Even that old crone?" She clutched at him, gasping in anger. "Your

Papa went to the grave? Did you go too? Did you? And me? What about me?"

"Mama, don't." Tim was holding her arms. "It's not Paul's fault. Papa made us promise."

She pushed them both away. "Why?" she screamed at them. "Why?" She turned on her husband. "Why?" She tore her hands through her hair. "Why?"

"He didn't want to upset you," Paul said.

"Like you are now," Tim added.

"He wanted to spare you, Mama, to protect you," Paul added.

"Protect? Upset? How could you, Costa! How could you!" She screamed and cried and Matina came, tried to hold her, shush her, but she wouldn't be stopped. Propriety meant nothing to her now. Neither the words nor the feelings of others mattered any longer. Nothing mattered except this betrayal. She clutched Matina's arm. "Did you know?" she demanded.

Matina shook her head.

"I want to talk to your Papa," she cried to her sons.

"But, Mama..."

"Now."

"Mama, please..."

"Alone."

"Eleni..."

"I have to."

Whispers, nudges, looks of concern; all of them smugly thinking they knew what was best for her. Like Costa. But she'd have it out with him when the others were gone. She took the glass of water someone handed her, but refused the tiny pills probably meant to calm her down. She wouldn't be calm. She waved everyone away, shaking her head, refusing to speak or to listen to any of them, children, friends, relatives, even the Priest.

When they finally left, she crossed herself, begged forgiveness of the Virgin for what she was about to say, and turned on her husband.

"What I said before, about you being a good husband, I always thought you were, even when I didn't agree with everything you said but now I'm not so sure." Eleni's voice was low. "You gave me many things, Costa, a nice house, there were no other women—at least I don't think so—and you never gambled or came home drunk, so I should be grateful. But you did other things I didn't like and I never spoke out. Well, I'm going to speak now."

She paused, swallowed, took off her coat and laid it on the bench. Her hat was there too; when did it come off? She would have liked to have got rid of the black dress as well. She yearned to be back home, in her floral housedress, a scarf around her head, digging in the earth in her backyard, tending to her flowers, struggling with the eggplant. But she wasn't. She was here, and there were things that had to be said. She crossed herself once more. "Forgive me, *Panagía*," she said again.

She stood up, leaned her hands on the arms of the bench next to her. "You kept me in darkness, Costa. Yes, in darkness. I came to you a young girl and it was your duty to teach me about this new country. When I'd tell you I wanted to learn English, you'd say we were Greek, what did I need to know English for? So I could speak properly to people at stores when I went shopping, or to the neighbours, or read about what was happening in the world, that was why, Costa!"

"I don't know what's going on so much of the time, Costa, because you kept me in darkness. When the children were young, I didn't notice so much because we all spoke Greek, but once the boys grew up and went into business with you, it was different. After supper you'd send me into the kitchen with Angela so you could talk with your sons, and it was always English, English, English! Why, Costa? So I wouldn't know what you were talking about? And you wanted Angela like me. I was so proud, Costa, when you praised me to our daughter and told her you wanted her to grow up to be as wonderful a woman as her mother. Proud! That's how stupid I was. And what did Angela learn? All the things I knew, things any fool can do, cook, and clean and sew. And now our daughter's growing old, with no husband, heaven knows why, and no life outside the house because you wouldn't allow it. When she started growing up you said she mustn't go out with Canadian boys because they weren't like us and wouldn't respect her. Maybe you were right, I don't know; I would've felt strange with a *xéno* son-in-law, it's true. But, Costa, there weren't many Greek boys to choose from, and she's getting old now, what's to become of her?

"Something else, Costa. Do you know how I feel when my little grandchildren come up to me, hold out an English book and say "*giagía* read" and I have to pretend I can't find my glasses, or they're broken, or my head hurts."

"Even the little babies can read the language of this country, but not their ignorant *giagía*. Remember when those papers and medals and letters came about Stephano? You said they were expressions of condolence. They were more though, Costa. They told you where our son was, but you wouldn't tell me. Paul and Tim say this was to protect me. Was I so delicate, Costa? I gave birth to five children and never mind how many I lost that you never knew about. Did you know how hard that was, Costa, one baby after another, and no machines then for the piles of washing day after day? How could I have done all that if I was so weak? And what about crossing the ocean all by myself to come to you when I was only sixteen?"

"Did you never wonder how a delicate flower could carry loads of washing up and down stairs and go for days without sleep because of sick children? I was strong, Costa, couldn't you see how strong? But I was stupid, wasn't I? Yet you said you respected me. How could you respect a stupid woman who can't read and write like everyone else? And how can I respect you now, Costa, and keep your memory pure, when you've left me with this bitterness?"

Eleni turned and stood silently until she was composed again. "All those years I told myself I was lucky to have such a good husband," she said quietly, her back still to him. She took a deep breath. "I can forgive you for keeping me stupid and in darkness, Costa. I can even forgive you for taking my baby away from me, but may the Virgin excuse me, I will, never, ever forgive you for keeping the truth from me about my son."

She turned to him, her fists clenched by her sides. "You paid your final respects to him, Costa, but you would not allow me to do that. You did not have that right, Costa, do you hear? Do you hear me? *You did not have that right!*"

She slumped on the bench, closed her eyes for a moment. "Forgive me, *Panagía*," she whispered, crossing herself, "but I had to tell him."

She picked up her coat, hat, gloves and purse, got up, and without looking toward the coffin, walked steadily out of the room.

Later that evening, after the others had done with their whispering and staring and hovering and had gone home, Eleni called Angela to sit on the couch with her.

"Did you know about Stephano?"

"No, Mama. Truly. No one said anything."

"Your Papa wanted to protect you as well, it seems," Eleni said, her mouth dry.

"It's all right, Mama. I understand."

"I raised you well, didn't I, daughter?"

Eleni pushed off her black shoes, loosened her belt. She removed the rings from her fingers, the diamond Costa had given her on their twenty-fifth wedding anniversary—it was wartime; Stephano had just left for overseas and Paul was in training school—and the cocktail ring for her fiftieth birthday two years ago, but she left the plain gold wedding band in its place. She lay her head on the back of the couch, soft blue brocade to pick up the blue in the Persian carpet Tim's wife had suggested when she'd asked for help in picking out fabric.

She had much to be thankful for. She ought, like a good woman, to dwell on that. For it seemed, from all she'd heard from her sons in the past few hours, anything their papa had done, or not done, had always been with her best interests at heart. And so he'd flown to visit Stephano's grave that week he'd sent her to Rhodes with her sisters. They'd all known, of course. And for a long time before that there had been a stone to mark her son's grave, and a foreign woman paid to keep it clean and covered in flowers. Her sons seemed to think she'd take comfort in the knowledge that another woman had been looking after her child's grave these many years. What strange creatures these men she'd been living with, how distorted their ideas.

Eleni looked over at her daughter. Something had to be done, at least for her. It wasn't clear to Eleni how, or what, but she knew she had to try. But first she needed one final gesture from her daughter.

"Would you go with me to visit your brother's grave?"

"Go to France?" Angela seemed surprised. "On our own?"

"Yes," Eleni said. "On our own."

Africa

☆

David Diop

Africa my Africa
Africa of proud warriors in ancestral savannahs
Africa of whom my grandmother sings
On the banks of the distant river
I have never known you
But your blood flows in my veins
Your beautiful black blood that irrigates the fields
The blood of your sweat
The sweat of your work
The work of your slavery
The slavery of your children
Africa tell me Africa
Is this you this back that is bent
This back that breaks under the weight of humiliation
This back trembling with red scars
And saying yes to the whip under the midday sun
But a grave voice answers me
Impetuous son that tree young and strong
That tree there
In splendid loneliness amidst white and faded flowers
That is Africa your Africa
That grows again patiently obstinately
And its fruit gradually acquires
The bitter taste of liberty.

Ancestors—The Genetic Source

☆

David Suzuki

My grandparents emigrated from Japan to this country at the turn of the century. Like so many immigrants, they left their homeland reluctantly. But they came from a poverty so profound that they were prepared to take the risk and deal with the terrifying unknown of a totally alien culture and language. Their children, my parents, were born in Vancouver over seventy-five years ago. They were Canadians by birth. By culture, they were genuine hybrids, fluently bilingual but fiercely loyal to the only country they had ever known—Canada.

On December 7, 1941, an event took place that had nothing to do with me or my family and yet which had devastating consequences for all of us—Japan bombed Pearl Harbor in a surprise attack. With that event began one of the shoddiest chapters in the tortuous history of democracy in North America. More than twenty thousand people, mostly Canadians by birth, were uprooted, their tenuous foothold on the West Coast destroyed, and their lives shattered to an extent still far from fully assessed. Their only crime was the possession of a common genetic heritage with the enemy.

Although I have little recollection of that time, Pearl Harbor was the single most important event shaping my life; years later in reassessing my life during a personal trauma, I realized that virtually every one of my emotional problems went right back to it.

Throughout the entire ordeal of those war years, my parents acted with a dignity, courage, and loyalty that this young country did not deserve. Today, my mother is dead, never having known the symbolic acknowledgement that a wrong was committed against her. But if there is anything worthwhile to be salvaged from those years, it is that her story and my father's, through me, will not be forgotten and will serve as a legacy to all Canadians, a reminder of the difficulty of living up to the ideals of democracy. The stories of how my parents and their parents fared in Canada are both a tribute to their strength of character and a record of the enormous changes that have occurred in this country. Whatever I am has been profoundly shaped by these two facts.

My genes can be traced in a direct line to Japan. I am a pure-blooded member of the Japanese race. And whenever I go there, I am always astonished to see the power of that biological connection. In subways in Tokyo, I catch familiar glimpses of the eyes, hairline, or smile of my Japanese relatives. Yet when those same people open their mouths to communicate, the vast cultural gulf that separates them from me becomes obvious: English is my language, Shakespeare is my literature, British history is what I learned, and Beethoven is my music.

For those who believe that in people, just as in animals, genes are the primary determinant of behaviour, a look at second- and third-genera-tion immigrants to Canada gives powerful evidence to the contrary. The overriding influence is environmental. We make a great mistake by associating the inheritance of physical characteristics with far more complex traits of human personality and behaviour.

Each time I visit Japan, I am reminded of how Canadian I am and how little the racial connection matters. I first visited Japan in 1968 to attend the International Congress of Genetics in Tokyo. For the first time in my life, I was surrounded by people who all looked like me. While sitting in a train and looking at the reflections in the window, I found that it was hard to pick out my own image in the crowd. I had grown up in a Caucasian society in which I was a minority member. My whole sense of self had developed with that perspective of looking different. All my life I had wanted large eyes and brown hair so I could be like everyone else. Yet on that train, where I did fit in, I didn't like it.

On this first visit to Japan I had asked my grandparents to contact relatives and let them know I was coming. I was the first in the Suzuki clan in Canada to visit them. The closest relative on my father's side was my grandmother's younger brother, and we arranged to meet in a seaside resort near his home. He came to my hotel room with two of his daughters. None of them spoke any English, while my Japanese was so primitive as to be useless. In typical Japanese fashion, they showered me with gifts, the most important being a package of what looked like wood carved in the shape of bananas! I had no idea what it was. (Later I learned the package contained dried tuna fish from which slivers are shaved off to flavour soup. This is considered a highly prized gift.) We sat in stiff silence and embarrassment, each of us struggling to dredge up a common word or two to break the quiet. It was excruciating! My great uncle later wrote my grandmother to tell her how painful it had been to sit with her grandson and yet be unable to communicate a word.

To people in Japan, all non-Japanese—black, white, or yellow—are *gaijin* or foreigners. While *gaijin* is not derogatory, I find that its use is harsh because I sense doors clanging shut on me when I'm called one. The Japanese do have a hell of a time with me because I look like them and can say in perfect Japanese, "I'm a foreigner and I can't speak Japanese." Their reactions are usually complete incomprehension followed by a sputtering, "What do you mean? You're speaking Japanese." And finally a pejorative, "Oh, a *gaijin*!"

Once when my wife, Tara, who is English, and I went to Japan, we asked a man at the travel bureau at the airport to book a *ryokan*—a traditional Japanese inn—for us in Tokyo. He found one and booked it for us "*Suzuki-san*" and off we went. When we arrived at the inn and I entered the foyer, the owner was confused by my terrible Japanese. When Tara entered, the shock was obvious in his face. Because of my name, they had expected a "real" Japanese. Instead, I was a *gaijin* and the owner told us he wouldn't take us. I was furious and we stomped off to a phone booth where I called the agent at the airport. He was astonished and came all the way into town to plead our case with the innkeeper. But the innkeeper stood firm and denied us a room. Apparently he had accepted *gaijin* in the past with terrible consequences.

As an example of the problem, Japanese always take their shoes off when entering a *ryokan* because the straw mats (*tatami*) are quickly frayed. To a Japanese, clomping into a room with shoes on would be comparable to someone entering our homes and spitting on the floor. Similarly, the *ofuro*, or traditional tub, has hot clean water that all bathers use. So one must first enter the bathroom, wash carefully, and rinse off *before* entering the tub. Time in the *ofuro* is for relaxing and soaking. Again, Westerners who lather up in the tub are committing a terrible desecration.

To many Canadians today, the word "Jap" seems like a natural abbreviation for Japanese. Certainly for newspaper headlines it would seem to make sense. So people are often shocked to see me bristle when they have used the word Jap innocently. To Japanese-Canadians, Jap or Nip (from "*Nippon*") were epithets used generously during the pre-war and war years. They conjure up all of the hatred and bigotry of those times. While a person using the term today may be unaware of its past use, every Japanese-Canadian remembers.

The thin thread of Japanese culture that does link me to Japan was spun out of the poverty and desperation of my ancestors. My grandparents came to a Canadian province openly hostile to their strange appearance and different ways. There were severe restrictions on how much and where they could buy property. Their children, who were born and raised in Canada, couldn't vote until 1948 and encountered many barriers to professional training and property ownership. Asians, regardless of birthplace, were third-class citizens. That is the reality of the Japanese-Canadian experience and the historical cultural legacy that came down to the third and fourth generations—to me and my children.

The first Japanese immigrants came to Canada to make their fortunes so they could return to Japan as people of wealth. The vast majority was uneducated and impoverished. But in the century spanning my grandparents' births and the present, Japan has leapt from an agrarian society to a technological and economic giant.

Now, the Japanese I meet in Japan or as recent immigrants to Canada come with far different cultural roots. Present-day Japanese are highly educated, upper-middle class, and proud of their heritage. In Canada they encounter respect, envy, and curiosity in sharp contrast to the hostility and bigotry met by my grandparents.

Japanese immigrants to North America have names that signify the number of generations in the new land (or just as significantly, that count the generational distance *away* from Japan). My grandparents are *Issei*, meaning the first generation in Canada. Most *Issei* never learned more than a rudimentary knowledge of English. *Nisei*, like my parents, are the second generation here and the first native-born group. While growing up they first spoke Japanese in the home and then learned English from playmates and teachers. Before the Second World War, many *Issei* sent their children to be educated in Japan. When they returned to Canada, they were called *Kika-nisei* (or *Kibei* in the United States). Most have remained bilingual, but many of the younger *Nisei* now speak Japanese with difficulty because English is their native tongue. My sisters and I are *Sansei* (third generation); our children are *Yonsei*. These generations, and especially *Yonsei*, are growing up in homes where English is the only spoken language, so they are far more likely to speak school-taught French as their second language than Japanese.

Most *Sansei*, like me, do not speak Japanese. To us, the *Issei* are mysteries. They came from a cultural tradition that is a hundred years old. Unlike people in present-day Japan, the *Issei* clung tightly to the culture they remembered and froze that culture into a static museum piece like a relic of the past. Not being able to speak each other's language, *Issei* and *Sansei* were cut off from each other. My parents dutifully visited my grandparents and we children would be trotted out to be lectured at or displayed. These visits were excruciating, because we children didn't understand the old culture, and didn't have the slightest interest—we were Canadians.

My father's mother died in 1978 at the age of ninety-one. She was the last of the *Issei* in our family. The final months of her life, after a left-hemisphere stroke, were spent in that terrible twilight—crippled, still aware, but unable to communicate. She lived the terminal months of her life, comprehending but mute, in a ward with Caucasian strangers. For over thirty years I had listened to her psychologically blackmailing my father by warning him of her imminent death. Yet in the end, she hung on long after there was reason to. When she died, I was astonished at my own reaction, a great sense of sadness and regret at the cleavage of my last link with the source of my genes. I had never been able to ask what made her and others of her generation come to Canada, what they felt when they arrived, what their hopes and dreams had been, and whether it was worth it. And I wanted to thank her, to show her that I was grateful that, through them, I was born a Canadian.

Theme Questions

✪

✪ What is the importance of origin myths and depictions of them in art? Are other kinds of myths important to people? In what ways?

✪ Diop's poem reveals the depth of his feeling for Africa, though he says "I have never known you." How can the idea of the place of one's heritage be so powerful, without having been there? How has the author acquired knowledge of Africa?

✪ Nostalgia is an emotion that arises from the relationship between memory and reality. What feelings and senses evoke nostalgic memories for you (e.g., the smell of a particular flower or food, or a sound that you associate with a particular place or time)? Why are these memories of our senses so important to our personal histories and to our feeling of well being?

✪ What acts of discrimination have you witnessed or experienced? What distinctions can you make between social and political discrimination? "While we are all equal under the law, we are not all treated equally in society." Do you agree or disagree? Explain.

✪ What kinds of tensions arise between one's traditional life before emigration and one's life in a new country?

Self – and Other

"Know thyself"—probably the most difficult command imaginable. In fact, the quest for self-knowledge is a life-long process. We are always in the making. Part of the search for self-understanding lies in our awareness of others; part of it lies within ourselves. Sometimes we learn about ourselves by seeing aspects of who we are in others. At other times, others force us to recognize ourselves for who we really are.

Family, history, nation, tradition—the self is a part of others' lives. How do we acknowledge our past and our ties to others and still assert our own identity? We cannot escape our families or our history, so we must somehow reconcile their demands with our needs. We must accept the limitations they impose on our lives without allowing them to define our lives.

As human beings, we are uniquely capable of being both self and other simultaneously; our imaginations allow us to stand outside ourselves, watching our own actions. Ultimately, we can begin to know ourselves by observing our behaviour, by learning our stories, or by affirming our past and recapturing our lost identity.

Martha and Elvira

☆

Diana Braithwaite

A one-act play (edited from the original)

Martha and Elvira includes portions of stories as told by ex-slaves:
Mary Reynolds
Katie Rowe
Nicey Kinney
Other men and women whose stories are told with no name attached.

BACKGROUND

1867. The Civil War in the United States is over and slavery has been abolished. Thousands of Blacks who have previously arrived in Canada via the Underground Railroad are now leaving and returning to the United States in hopes of reuniting with their lost loved ones and families.

Martha and Elvira is the story of two women who in order to realize their individual dreams must lose each other and the companionship they have shared for many years.

CHARACTERS

Martha

A small wiry woman, always moving, fussing, adjusting things as she talks. Occasionally lapses into spells where she becomes disoriented. She has been unable to handle the losses of her children and her husband, and desperately clings to what she has now—Elvira, her home, son, and family. There is no going back for Martha.

Elvira

Larger in build, slower, more rooted, Elvira is less committed to the country in which she now lives, and more committed to finding her daughter Hannah and telling her what little she knows about her own past. Elvira is the rock and foundation for Martha.

Setting

The play is set on a small farm somewhere in southern Ontario. It is early evening. Martha and Elvira are sitting on the back porch, just after a soldier has brought the news that Elvira's daughter is still alive in the south.

. . .

The stage is set with two chairs (one should be a rocking chair, which Martha uses), and a low wooden table in the middle. Elvira has a shawl loosely draped over the back of her chair and her shoes should be set underneath it. If desired, there could be a stack of corn, carrots, and other farm-related paraphernalia around the area which is to be the porch. Crickets are heard in the background. Elvira enters (in black) with a bowl of snapping beans and sits in her chair, singing softly to herself.

She sits quietly rocking herself and nodding. She has a slight smile on her face. Martha bustles in holding a tray with tea and biscuits.

Martha

Elvira, Elvira! Who was that man that was just here? Looked like a soldier. *(She notices Elvira, who appears to be sleeping.)*

Elvira?! Well look at you! Crickets singing, moon comin' up, and you sitting here noddin', like it all don't mean nothin'. Those snapping beans finished yet?

Well, I brought you some tea to drink, thought you'd be thirsty. And some biscuits, 'cause I know how you like your food. Vira! Are you hearing anything I'm saying?

Elvira

I got two ears in my head don't I? And you is reaching both of 'em just fine. I was just here listenin' to you and the Lord at the same time, that's all.

(Martha pours two cups of tea, handing one to Elvira.)

Martha

Well I hope he was telling you something good. And how do I know if you don't answer? You have the strangest look on your face tonight sister!

(Martha walks towards the edge of the porch, breathing in the air.)

You smell that clover? Smell sweet, don't it? There's something in the air tonight Vira. Something. I don't quite know what it is.

Drink up your tea now, going to get cold! Nothin' worse than cold tea.

(Martha settles into her rocking chair.)

Crops comin' up good this year. Yes sir. Cabbage heads round and sweet as honey. Haven't known corn that tastes as sweet as what we raisin'. Bring a good price at the market. Ain't that right, Vi?

Elvira (absentmindedly) Mmm hmmm.

Martha
Yes, yes, it surely will. *(Reaches for a biscuit and pauses.)* These taste very good, if I do say so myself!

We got our own livin' now, you and me sister, come a long way together, and still here to tell the tale! You helped me and I helped you. Billy Junior got a good wife and three children. Yes ma'am, we have all what we need now. A good home, and our freedom. What more could we ask?

(Martha leans in to put butter and jam on the biscuit, and while doing so, notices that Elvira's eyes are closed again.)

. . .

(Lights fade slightly as song—BEEN IN THE STORM SO LONG—begins. Song plays for a few seconds and then fades as lights come back up.)

Elvira (quietly, still sitting)
Remember when we first left the south, Brother Thomas was our way out. He say. . .

Martha
Keep one on the north star, and the other on your path!

Elvira
Say, you won't see nobody, 'cause there won't be no moon lighting the way.

Martha
And that night was black. Brother Thomas say. . .

Elvira
Meet down under Yansee's tree. He said. I got this here rifle, and you got one another.

Martha
There is no turnin' back.

(They start to march together slowly, picking up speed as the song speeds up.)

Martha

I didn't know you before that, sister.

Elvira

You come up with some others from one of the houses down the way. Your man Bill was one of Brother Thomas' right hand men.

Martha

I was so proud of him. My man Billy.

Elvira

Brother Thomas say, "follow that star until you reach the Canaan land."

Martha

Say "people, owls are quiet unless there's danger around. Then they call out. You going to do the same."

Elvira *(standing)*

Whoo! Whoo!

Martha

Brother Thomas went ahead of us to guide the way. We walked along close to the bushes. Couldn't see to put one foot in front of the other. I started to get scared. And the baby started to fuss. "Billy, we got to go back. We ain't gonna make it. The baby ain't gonna make it."

Elvira

Billy say, "He ain't gonna make it if we stay here, we making a way for him now."

Martha

Billy take the baby from me and give the child oil of tincture, to make him sleep. There was a marsh we had to cross, which led to an open field.

(They sing together, walking on the spot.)

Walk together, sister,
don't you get weary
Walk together, brother
don't you get weary
Walk together sister

don't you get weary
There's a campground waitin'
in the promised land.

(*Martha claps her hands, they speed up their steps, still moving on the spot.*)

Elvira
Bounty hunter.

Martha
My baby cried out loud. There was no place to hide.

(*They both crouch down.*)

Elvira
Bounty hunter come up real close behind us. One of the children, Ben, I held his hand. "Run boy! Run!"

(*Elvira claps her hands.*)

Ben's hand slipped away. He was dead. The bounty hunter was getting closer to us.

Martha
The baby was crying loud now. I took the rifle from Billy.

Elvira
The bounty hunter started shooting. There wasn't nothing more we could do.

Martha
He aimed the gun at me. He would have killed me and the baby sister. I tried to stop him, but I wasn't fast enough. Bounty hunter cocked the gun. And Billy called out No! And he threw himself in front of me.

(*Elvira claps her hands.*)

Martha
And my man was dead. My man was dead. Billy Junior fall from his Daddy's arms.

Elvira
I picked up the baby and held him close.

Martha
Well, nothin' seemed to matter then. I aimed my rifle straight at that bounty hunter's heart. Why all I'm seeing is my man dead. . . . That hunter see the red in my eyes. I look at him straight, and pull the trigger.

Elvira
You killed him Martha.

Martha (*sitting down on her chair*)
I killed him dead. Never said nothin' to nobody. 'Ceptin' for you, Brother Thomas was the only one that knowed that. I killed for my Billy and for my freedom, sister. And I came too far to turn back now.

Elvira (*sitting down*)
We wrapped Little Ben, and Bill, in a blanket. And then we moved on.

Martha
Days and nights passed, we walked and walked. We were running out of food, and the days were getting colder. But when we reached to a place called Ohio, we knew we were close. Stopped at a house on the way. Some Church people were there dressed in big hats and the women had on those big bonnets. Gave us some food, I do believe it was boiled potatoes with ham, and gravy, you remember that, Vi?

Elvira
Unnh uh. It was rice and stew.

Martha
Huh?

Elvira
Said it was rice and stew. With a mess of biscuits on the side.

Martha
Well, I don't remember no rice and stew. I could have sworn it was potatoes with ham, and gravy. Well, whatever it was, it sure tasted good.

Elvira
I got long remembrance, Martha, long remembrance. No way for me to disremember, 'less I die. I remember some days clear as I remember this day right here.

. . .

[But] that was a long while ago sister. You and me ain't nobody's slaves no more. Only thing that's ruling us now is time.

Martha

We come a long way sister. You helped me, and I helped you. My son is a grown man now with his own children. I only wished his poppa could see what fine grandchildren that he got.

I had me eight children. Two dead, and five that were sold off to different plantations. And I never seen or heard about them again. Billy is my only child left now. All the rest gone.

Elvira

I was fourteen years old when the Massa told me to fix that cabin for living with Jumas. I never had no learnin'. I thought he meant for me to tend the cabin. That started the pestigation for me. Jumas weren't nothin' but a big bully, and thought that everybody should do what he say. First night I was there, I fixed up the cabin, and then crawled in my bunk. If that old Jumas didn't come a crawlin' in with me. I says, "What you meaning by this fool?" He said that this was his bunk too and he was ready to use it. I told him he was touched in the head! I put both my feet 'gainst him and shoved him out hard on the floor. That got that fool out. But he start back towards me like he ain't had enough. He looked just like a bear comin' out of the bushes! So I look around, and grab me a broomstick. It was about three feet long, with those strong bristles. I said "Nigger, come and get it," and I brought down that broom, wham, right over the head. Did that man stop in his tracks? I says he did. He just sat back and looked at me. He was lookin' like a bull. So I looked back at him. We must have stayed like that for a good while. Just watchin' each other's moves. After that he said, "Pretty girl, you think you smart don't you? But you ain't smart enough. The master, he's gonna show you who's in charge." Next day old man Hindley call me up to the house and say "Elvira, I pays big money for you to raise children. What you think I put you with Jumas for? Now if you don't want whuppen at the stake, then you better do what I say." So I yields. When my first baby was born, I named her Precious. 'Cause she was the most precious thing to me. She died three days later. Right in my arms. She just stopped breathing. After that, every child that I had was born dead. Everyone but Hannah.

When Hannah come along, and live, that was the time when I decided that this girl was special. She wasn't live no slave life. And I was going to give her a home somehow. After she was born, I just put on to everyone like she had died, just like the others. I wrapped her up in a blanket and said I was taking her out to the woods to bury her. Said it wasn't meant for me to have children. There was an old woman who lived not far from the plantation and I had heard that she helped people who were tryin' to run. So I went to her, and I begged her to take care of my child, until I was ready to leave and take her with me. She took Hannah, and every day I would go there and bring her what food I could, and sing to her. (*She mimes rocking the baby and singing.*) "Momma's baby is sweet like honey, Momma's baby is pretty like a flower" and then one day, I went there to see her, and wasn't nothin' there. They had found out 'bout old lady Jessie and burnt down her house. And I didn't know if my child was alive or dead. I didn't know what to do. I went there every day for weeks after, just waiting, just hoping for a sign. Then, when I found out I was going to be sold to another plantation, I went back the night before we was to leave, and I took a rock and carved my name on a tree should in case Hannah ever come back. Hoping maybe she would see that and come lookin' for me. That's why I got to go to her now. I got to tell her what little I know about my momma and my poppa, and what he told me 'bout his. She got to know. And I got to tell her that somebody was carin' 'bout her all this time. I got to let her know.

(*Martha nods silently.*)

Martha
Sometimes it feels like we keep walking down a road trying to get somewhere, and just when we almost reach there, the road takes you off somewhere again, and you got to stop and see which way it is that you really want to go. Seems like I found my road, sister, and you got to find yours now. Only thing is, they're going two different ways.

(*Martha is weary now, and stands up slowly.*)

Martha
Well, tomorrow comes early.

Elvira
You go on in. I won't be long.

Marta's Monologue *and*
Lucia's Monologue

☆

Mary di Michele

Marta's Monologue

All my life I've tried to please my father,
I live at home, teach school around the corner
at St. Mary's. I make a good salary
and help children to learn to read and write.
I have very little experience, that's true
but I know enough to risk nothing,
to live where it's safe,
to have a job that's secure,
to love those who love me, my parents,
and to offer the proper respect to our relatives
so that when my uncles gather with my father around the table
I listen very carefully to all their bull shit
as they split *lupini* and throw the shells
into the bowl I don't fail to provide for them.

My elder sister, Lucia, is not like me,
she's not good. She's the first born,
the stubborn one, who wears Italia
like a cheap necklace around her throat,
with a charm that makes her heart green
with tarnish, Lucia, the poet
who talks about us in obscure verses
nobody reads for sure,
Lucia, who claims that someone in the family,
her twin, committed suicide, but it's not true,
she has no twin, I'm the second born
and a full year younger than she is.
Lucia is *putane* because she doesn't live at home
and because she won't say hello

or pretend to like uncle Joe
whom she calls a macho pig.
Secretly I know she pretends to write
and the family is ashamed of that gypsy
daughter, the bohemian, the cuckoo's
egg in our nest.
Sometimes we wish she were dead.
Sometimes we wish she were married.

At every family gathering
I pull out the accordion.
I play like a full orchestra
overtures by Verdi and Rossini,
the music he loves,
the music I've learned by heart
as an act of love.
Out of my musical box
spring the burnished grapes in wicker baskets
of Italia, the Appennini breathe with lungs
that are the bellows of my accordion,
La Maiella scratches his snowy cap
in the Abruzzi, he's the grand old man
of mountains, I've never seen him
but I've watched my father's head
grow white and bald.
The roads,
the mountain roads,
winding up
the steep flanks,
the round shoulders of the hills,
the geography of hearts,
winding up
like a complex thought about someone you love,
how you can never understand them,
how loving them is an act of faith,
a way of choosing to live
or to die,
by instinct,
something that you can't just back out of.
You can't really love unless you realize
that a mortal life isn't time enough to love anyone,
not time enough to know yourself,

so I love my father, who is from the beginning,
who stood to make water
and lay down to make love to my mother,
who knew me from the beginning
as a vague stirring in his loins,
as a burst of ecstasy
on a Sunday morning.

Lucia has other notions about love.
About love she says she's an expert.
I don't know when she adopted the sacred heart
of eros. Five years after she left the church,
she was still a miracle worker of sorts.
I never could understand how she had the visions
and I had the faith,
except that she was the prodigal daughter
and I was the one who resented the fact
that she was not punished, but rewarded,
for doing whatever she wanted to do.

Lucia says that love is a labyrinth:
you approach a familiar doorway,
the door is wide open or barred shut,
the door is too small or too big for you
to reach the handle,
the door is the first hurdle,
then you enter the tunnel,
frescoes and graffiti blister on the walls,
the light you walk by never fails
to reveal a shadow,
you are searching for the one you think you love
through passageways that lead nowhere
back to the self.

What I really think about love is all mixed up
in my head with what I remember being taught as a child
in religion class at school, the lessons I parrot today
to another generation of squirming innocents.
The family is the first experience
and then what the priest has to say
is a kind of generalization,
the holy family being a prototype

for relationships sanctified by the church
and sanctioned by the state.
I remember how impatient this model of divine grace
working in the world made Lucia.
She was an artist and therefore a narcissist
and believed, when she believed anything at all
that a person's relationship with God
had more to do with the way you love yourself.
Yet we would pray in church,
light candles, and for her they flared,
for me they smoked. I couldn't understand it.
We were ten and eleven years old,
and she would talk about the old gods
as if they were related and equal,
mythology and religion,
a pagan temple and a catholic church,
and she would have her prayers answered,
(whatever she really wanted she seemed to get)
while my prayers, addressed properly to Jesus,
to God, the Father, in His name,
by which He was bound to answer,
were like conversations on a pay telephone,
He never rang back.

Every night I'm afraid I'll wake up
dead and find Lucia there before me,
that even my death will be a hand-me-down.
I know that I'm afraid of getting to the bottom
of the differences between us,
as if to really know her
would be to lose my soul,
and all the clothes she wore before me,
were gifts of shed skin
or cast off experience.
I made them my own and found the fit
gave me a form.
I didn't give a fig about fashion,
but second hand clothes from my sister
identified me as hers.

Lucia wanted to be smarter in her life than in her books
so she made me the butt of her poems.

She would experiment with herself that way,
by putting me in the pigeon box of her words
and watching to see what would happen,
that way she wasn't prepared to make any mistakes.
She demanded some clarity of purpose in her life,
she wanted to act with a vengeance,
not because she was mad at anything
but to clear up the confusion,
a dusty room would give her a headache,
a Marx brothers film on television would send her
running out of the room screaming.
In health class the film of a birth,
the untidy womb giving expression
to an anonymous morass of mucus and blood,
the human shape, a fish on a line,
made her sick and I heard her say:
"Never, never, never…"
in the darkened room,
and as the lights came on, I noticed she had
unbuttoned her shirt and was staring down
at her breasts. I think she feels
the same way about the family,
I think that by denying us
she thinks she can deny that she has legs,
that she's a woman, like any other woman,
servant to a dark blood she doesn't understand.

I'm not ambitious,
I find my art in the accordion
that entertains uncle Joe,
that makes my father hum
and my mother proud at weddings,
I always play and I don't mind,
in fact, I enjoy it,
but more when Lucia's not there
with her sulking face and rude
staccato laughter,
with that you're wasting yourself look,
half pity, more contempt.

But when a woman's life is so worthless,
I think she's got a perfect right

to do nothing,
to paint her nails,
to bake a cake,
and to wait for a man
to buy her shoes
so that she can go walking with him
on a Sunday afternoon
eating ice cream.
Not that I'm waiting for one,
but I like to be with friends
and to exchange tips on the latest
lipstick. I wear it thick and red,
the same shade I remember mother wearing.

Lucia and I would play when she wasn't looking
and paint big mouths with her rouge no. 5,
our lips quivering like blue gas flames
with excitement, as we prepared to be women.
A woman's always naked without her lipstick,
I remember mother saying.
One day I entered her bedroom alone
not prepared for the amazing transformation
I achieved by carefully drawing a cupid's
bow mouth with quick smooth strokes.
It stopped me for a moment as I looked up
from the lips I was defining
to see my skin, startling white,
my eyes, more intensely blue,
my hair, serenaded by the light
from the balcony,
and I saw that I was beautiful,
and I thought I must be rich,
and I thought there was nothing else
I needed to do. Then Lucia barged in,
grabbed the lipstick and painted her nose
bright red, ripped open her blouse,
her breasts like molted birds,
and shouted that a woman always seemed naked
without her lipstick on,
and her ironic laughter brought mother in
and a tanning for both of us.

Friday night when I'm going nowhere
and I'm alone, I play with my kohl
eye pencils and become Cleopatra.
Friday night and I know what it means to enter
a room with the sparkling white heart
of a refrigerator.
I paint my eyes like a cat's so that I can look at myself
in nine different ways,
Friday night and I watch the late show to learn
the Hollywood way to the nirvana of a stunning face
and celluloid figure
which tells me more about being female
than the poetry of Emily Dickinson
or the epistles of Saint Paul.

But I learn most about being a woman
from watching my mother, Alma.
I learn from her how a woman is made for love
and for cleaning house.
She's very fat with eating pasta and the insults
of my father who takes for granted her loyalty
and would love a divorce and a younger woman.
He'll never leave her though
because the family's a landscape
he doesn't want changed.

For me she's the ring of smoke the wind wears
on the left hand, on the fourth finger,
open and generous, if somewhat gratuitous,
like a house built for birds,
a house with an entrance, but no door,
a house with windows, but no panes,
a house, where the wind never begs at the front steps
for nothing.

I have to admit I'm happiest when Lucia's visiting
and we all work together as in the old days
preparing preserves of vegetables from the garden for
winter eating,
peeling the burnt skins back from roasted peppers,
pulling off the black ash that sticks
to the fingers in brittle chips,

pulling off the pepper tops,
watching the oil squirt then run
along our fingers, an orange sticky drool,
watching what I'm doing and doing it well.
I confess there was a time when I wanted to be like Lucia,
when I thought her incredibly wise,
when I thought it courage that made her leave home
and generosity that made her experiment with love.
I remember how she used to say
with what seemed such a special kind of knowledge:
"I love you, no matter who you are,
that's not logical, but the axiom
on which logic depends."
I guess it's something like the love we learned about in church
or from mother, it's so big and so perfect
it's like a circle drawn on the black board,
the imaginary lines of the imagined perfection
and then erased with an unthinking brush
by a monitor after class.
But Lucia couldn't leave home without coming back too,
whenever she claimed to be flat broke or in despair,
she couldn't stop being the center of attention.

Disappointed is the unthinking brush
bloated with chalk dust and the promise of a better life.
I only want my fair share.
I want what's mine and what Lucia kicks over.
I want father to stop mooning about her
and listen to my rendition of Mimosa.

Lucia's Monologue

So much of my life has been wasted feeling guilty
about disappointing my father and mother.
It makes me doubt myself.
It's impossible to live my life that way.
I know they've made their sacrifices,
they tell me often enough,
how they gave up their lives,
and now they need to live their lives through me.

If I give it to them, it won't make them young again,
it'll only make me fail along with them,
fail to discover a different, if mutant, possibility,
succeed only in perpetuating a species of despair.

Most of the time I can't even talk to my father.
I talk to mother and she tells him what she thinks
he can stand to hear.
She's always been the mediator of our quarrels.
He's always been the man and the judge.
And what I've come to understand about justice
in this world isn't pretty,
how often it's just an excuse to be mean or angry
or to hoard property,
a justice that washes away
the hands of the judge.

Nobody disputes the rights of pigeons to fly
on the blue crest of the air across the territory
of a garden, nobody can dispute that repetition
is the structure of despair and our common lives
and that the disease takes a turn for the worse
when we stop talking to each other.

I've stopped looking for my father in other men.
I've stopped living with the blond child that he loved
too well.
Now I'm looking for the man with the hands of a musician,
with hands that can make wood sing,
with the bare, splintered hands of a carpenter.
I want no auto mechanics with hands blind with grease
and the joints of a machine.
I want no engineers in my life,
no architects of cages.
I want to be with the welders of bridges
and the rivers whose needs inspired them.

I learned to be a woman in the arms of a man,
I didn't learn it from ads for lipstick
or watching myself in the mirror.
I learned more about love from watching my mother
wait on my father hand and foot

than from scorching novels on the best seller lists.
I didn't think I could be Anna Karenina or Camille,
I didn't think I could be Madame Bovary or Joan of Arc,
I didn't think that there was a myth I could wear
like a cloak of invisibility
to disguise my lack of self knowledge.

The sky is wearing his snow boots already.
I have to settle things with my father before the year is
dead.
It's about time we tried talking
person to person.

More than a tired man, my father is a such a lonely,
disappointed man.
He has learned through many years of keeping his mouth
shut
to say nothing,
but he still keeps thinking about
everything.

"If I had the language like you," he says to me,
"I would write poems too about what I think.
You younger generation aren't interested in history.
If you want people to listen to you
you got to tell them something new,
you got to know something about history to do that.
I'm a worker and I didn't go to school,
but I would have liked to be an educated man,
to think great thoughts, to write them,
and to have someone listen.
You younger generation don't care about anything in the
past,
about your parents,
the sacrifices they made for you,
you say: 'What did you do that for,
we didn't ask you!'
right,
is that right?
These are good poems you have here Lucia,
but what you think about Italy!
'a country of dark men full of violence and laughter,

a country that drives its women to dumb despair.'
That's not nice what you say,
you think it's very different here?
You got to tell the truth when you write,
like the bible. I'm your father, Lucia,
remember, I know you."

The truth is not nice,
the truth is that his life is almost over
and we don't have a common language any more.
He has lost a tooth in the middle of his upper plate,
the gap makes him seem boyish and very vulnerable.
It also makes me ashamed.

It's only when he's tired like this that he can
slip off his reserve, the roman stoicism,
the lips buttoned up against pain
and words of love.

I have his face, his eyes, his hands,
his anxious desire to know everything,
to think, to write everything,
his anxious desire to be heard,
and we love each other and say nothing,
we love each other in that country
we couldn't live in.

Heritage

✩

Neil Bissoondath

We are probably all familiar with the classic Canadian short story "The Hockey Sweater" by the Québécois writer Roch Carrier. It is a simple and effective tale that depicts, through the neatly captured voice of a child, life in a small Quebec town in the late forties. Life in this town is governed by the imperatives of school, church and hockey as the opening paragraph, which I would like to read to you, makes clear. The translation is by Sheila Fischman.

> The winters of my childhood were long, long seasons. We lived in three places—the school, the church and the skating rink—but our real life was on the skating rink. [. . S]chool was. . .a quiet place where we could prepare for the next hockey game, lay out our next strategies. As for church, we found there the tranquillity of God: there we forgot school and dreamed about the next hockey game. Through our daydreams it might happen that we would recite a prayer: we would ask God to help us play as well as Maurice Richard.

We all know what happens next. The boy—who, like his friends, worships the Montreal Canadiens—is accidentally sent a Toronto Maple Leafs sweater by the Eaton's mail-order department. Forced to wear it because his mother fears offending Monsieur Eaton, an *Anglais*, his anger flares on the ice after he is given what he thinks is an unfair penalty. He smashes his stick in frustration, only to be confronted by the young vicar.

> "My child," he said, "just because you're wearing a new Toronto Maple Leafs sweater unlike the others, it doesn't mean you're going to make the laws around here. A proper young man doesn't lose his temper. Now take off your skates and go to the church and ask God to forgive you."
>
> Wearing my Maple Leafs sweater I went to the church, where I prayed to God; I asked him to send, as quickly as possible, moths that would eat up my Toronto Maple Leafs sweater.

"The Hockey Sweater" is a charming story that reveals much about the sporting and religious life of Quebec as well as, more generally, about the mythology of hockey in Canada. One would not expect it to upset anyone.

But it may be that expectations exist in order to be demolished.

Some years after its initial appearance, the publishers received a letter requesting permission to include the story in a new anthology for schools. The letter read in part as follows: "Our authors. . .are requesting some minor changes. [. . .] they would like to delete the reference to God. . .As the program will be used by elementary school students from varying backgrounds and religions, we hope that you will grant these changes." It was accompanied by photocopies of the relevant pages with the offending references scratched out.

Censorship is nothing new in this world. It appears everywhere in one guise or another, for reasons that are not always ill-meaning but which are nearly always misguided. Think of the calls we have heard, among many, many others, for the banning of William Shakespeare's *The Merchant of Venice* for anti-Semitism, of Margaret Laurence's *The Diviners* for sexual content, or Alexander Solzhenitsyn's *One Day in the Life of Ivan Denisovich* for rough language. And I will just mention the name of Salman Rushdie—long may he thrive—who has experienced the most spectacular case of attempted censorship in modern times.

In the face of these cases, and of hundreds of others, the request to delete God from "The Hockey Sweater" seems minor. But the attitude implicit in the request—that literature must be sanitized in order to avoid all possibility of giving offence—is now making itself felt in ways that are exquisitely mind-boggling for writers. . . .

Let me give you an example. After the publication of my first book in 1985, I gave an interview, among many others, to a man who said he was a journalist from Trinidad, the place where I was born and which I had left twelve years before. We had a long chat over coffee, but it became clear as we talked that he had not taken the trouble to read my book. Some days later, after the publication of an interview I had done with *NOW* magazine, I received a phone call from this man. His first words to me were: "Neil, I'm disappointed in you." How so? I asked. He explained that I had written and said things that I should not have about corruption and racism and the dangers of life in the Caribbean. I realized then that he'd read the book, as well as the *NOW* interview. We talked for forty-five minutes, during which he admitted that he agreed with all that I had said—but, really, I should not be saying it here, in Canada. I finally brought the conversation to an end when I realized that we had irreconcilable views on the role of the writer: While I sought to reflect reality as faithfully as I could in my writing, he expected me to play the role of propagandist for the tourist industry back in the islands: why write about corruption when there were sandy beaches to describe? Why write about racism when Carnival was so much more colourful? I was pointing to the shadows when he wanted the sun.

Writer as propagandist, writer as salesperson, writer as spokesperson. The world offers a dizzying array of extra-literary possibilities for the writer—all of them attractive, all of them perilous. . . .

We have, in this country, accepted with little hesitation the psychology of separation. We have, through the practice of multiculturalism, created a kind of psychic apartheid, homelands of the mind: as our provinces, greedy for power, pull apart, so too do our communities, greedy for "rights," pull apart. Once the psychology of separation takes hold, no logical limits suggest themselves. . .so, as a country, we go on, seeking to narrow ourselves in every way possible and in many ways unimaginable, retreating behind the crenellated walls of self-imposed ghettoes.

The psychology of separation is an insidious one. Once you accept the institutional division of people by culture, it is easy to subdivide them in other ways too, by gender, for example, and by race.

This urge to segregate has made itself felt in the Canadian literary community. It first came to public attention some years ago when a nasty spat developed among the editors of the Women's Press. A proposed short-story anthology ran into trouble when objections were raised about certain of the stories already contracted for publication. The problem was simple: white female writers had written from the viewpoint of black female characters; they had "appropriated" the experiences of women already exploited in a society dominated by white males; they had, in telling their stories, practised a kind of cultural imperialism. The house, a vital and necessary publisher, split viciously over the issue.

But this was just the beginning. Soon other demands were made: not only must whites not write about blacks, but men must not write about women, non-natives about natives, and so on, all based on the claim that if you haven't lived the life, you don't have the right to write about it. And the writer who dares to explore territory deemed not his or her own becomes a thief, open to charges of racism and sexism from people who object to being portrayed in ways other than they would portray themselves—and self-portraits, let us face it, tend to be free of blemishes.

Well, I stand before you a sinner, the proof of my crimes in my books for all to see. I have written not only from the viewpoint of young, brown-skinned men of East Indian descent born in the Caribbean and living in Canada but also from the perspective of a young Japanese woman, a young black man, a young black woman, a young Central American girl, a middleaged Spanish man, an elderly Jewish man, a young white woman, a young white man, a Marxist revolutionary, a CIA agent. I have written about the left and right and the victims thereof. I have written about political oppressors and the politically oppressed.

It is no wonder, then, that [some reviewers] see in me a right-wing racist dedicated to the preservation of imperialist colonialism. It may come as a surprise, though, that I have also been called a communist for an article I did on Spanish fascism, a social-democrat for writing about the downtrodden of society, a feminist for exploring the treatment of women. There is, in fact, hardly a label that has not been tossed at me, each ill-fitting, each contradicted by something else I've written. It is the risk you take when your fiction arises from political concerns, more specifically from the effect of politics on the everyday lives of ordinary people. I am resigned to the fact that there will never be a shortage of those who will try to define me and my work in terms rarely favourable.

I have on the whole avoided responding to my detractors, preferring to let my work speak for itself. But there comes a time when, as ignorance gains ground and mindless shrillness claims its victims, certain things need to be said, certain points need to be stated without apology and without equivocation.

Let me put it as succinctly as I can: those who seek to subordinate literature, its functions and its freedoms, to sexual, racial or religious politics seek nothing less than to impose their own ideological visions on the imaginations of others. They claim rights for themselves that they would deny to those who do not share their view of the world. . . .

In this society, the charge of racism is a particularly virulent one. There are few who do not recognize it as an evil. It is, though, a charge too easily levelled by those who interpret the world through the colour of their skin. Declaring themselves anti-racists, they ironically share a racial vision of life with the architects and defenders of Apartheid. I put it to you that to define yourself by your colour is racist, just as to define yourself by your gender is sexist. I also put it to you that imposed political ideology distorts reality—and sharpened racial ideology distorts the soul. . . .

Ideological considerations have also led to calls for publishers to publish an imposed quota of "minority" writers—and this regardless of quality. Notions of quality, the argument goes, are nothing but the artificial inventions of white males who, seeking to prolong their control of society, use tools—such as ideas of excellence—to keep undesirables on the edges of the mainstream. I would suggest to you that such ideas are the products of the talentless who, grown sanctimonious, seek a kind of artistic welfare.

The academic world, too, is being severely affected. An idea now making the rounds in literature departments is that male professors should not be allowed to teach novels by women writers, since they are constitutionally incapable of grasping the female point of view. The pressures are such, I am told, that male professors worry about how they teach George Eliot or Charlotte Brontë or Virginia Woolf. And their worries, not literary but political, are beginning to affect the general quality of their teaching. It occurs to few, one professor said to me, that if men should not teach Atwood or Akhmatova, then—on the same grounds—women too should not teach Shakespeare or Chaucer. We are in danger of entering a terrifying circle. For just think what a loss it would be to diminish our perspectives on great, or even not so great, works of literature because of attitudes reminiscent of a spiteful child refusing to let others play with his baseball simply because, in his opinion, they play less well than he does.

It is no secret that ideology stringently applied has a way of eventually eating its own children. Last fall, while in Vancouver on a book promotion tour, I met a young woman with an interesting story to tell. It is important to know that she considers herself a dyed-in-the-wool feminist. She told me about an article she'd written about her favourite singer, a black American woman of great talent and renown. She submitted the piece to a feminist magazine which had published her work in the past. After some time, the editors informed her that while they very much liked the article they would not publish it. She had, they explained, quoted too many male critics. Her explanation that most music critics are male—and her suggestion that publishing women writers might help change that situation—made no impression. For their basic objection to the article was that while the singer was black, the writer was white—an intolerable situation, in their view. The article, on purely racial grounds, could never be good enough.

Such limitations on subject matter lead to chilling logical conclusions. For does this not mean that, say, *young* women must not write about *old* women, gay men about straight men, Protestants about Catholics? Does this not mean that physically handicapped writers must write only about the physically handicapped and native writers only about natives, indeed, a Cree writer only about Crees, a Mohawk writer only about Mohawks? In the end, then, does this view not say that fiction must give way to autobiography?

It is self-evident that a free society depends on a multiplicity of voices and visions, on an interplay of conflicting views. We would only diminish ourselves by diminishing that variety. The terms of this debate are altering perceptions of literature, and with that I have no argument. But I fear too that the tone of the debate is devaluing literature, its nature and its role—and to this I object. All perspectives are welcome—as citizens of this society, we will all be the richer for it—but no one has the right to try to suppress the voice of anyone else.

Any attempt to padlock the mind is a question of fundamental liberty. Any limitation on subject matter represents, for all writers but for the writer of fiction in particular, a severe restriction on the free play of the imagination. As Salman Rushdie has pointed out, you have to feel that you write in absolute freedom—and freedom of expression means nothing if it does not include the freedom to offend.

It is clear that those who accept the padlocking of the imagination are profoundly ignorant of the writing process.

In an interview Timothy Findley once said, "In the gay community they say, 'When are you going to write *the* gay novel?' But I don't define my life by my sexuality. I'm not a *gay* writer, I'm not a *male* writer, I'm just a writer."

Just a writer: those three words are at the heart of it. In a way, to be a writer of fiction is the simplest of jobs. It is to be a story-teller, nothing more, nothing less. But to tell a good story, and to tell it well, is a demanding, at times mysterious, process. To be *just a writer* is to be prey, to a great extent, to the demands and urges of the writing process itself.

Let me, first of all, tell you what I do *not* do. I do not sit at my computer and think: I will write a story today about a black woman or a Jewish man—for to do so would be to engage in journalism. I do not decide that I will write a story to score points about racism or socialism or capitalism—for to do so would be to engage in propaganda. I avoid at all costs playing the role of puppeteer, manipulating my characters, telling them what to think or how to act. For to do any of the above would be to kill all possibility of spinning credible fiction.

The most hackneyed advice to young writers is: Write what you know about. Describe, in other words, what you have experienced. It is good advice—so long as one remembers that there are many ways of experiencing an event. Writing what you know about does not mean writing only about what you have *lived*. It includes all that you have come to understand or appreciate through conversation, observation, reading, dreaming, films—the multifaceted channels that feed us as human beings. The brain is a remarkable instrument, it almost always knows things we are not consciously aware of. It constantly processes that information, adding, retrieving, shifting, connecting. It is in this way that originality occurs.

How my fiction comes about, then, is not easily explained for, although I am frequently asked where I get my ideas for stories, the truth is that I don't really know. What happens is this: I don't find the stories, they find me.

Characters emerge unbidden, often arising from stories or events that have etched themselves in my subconscious, their voices sometimes speaking at the most inconvenient of moments (such as when I'm in the shower or doing the dishes), and I do my best to capture on paper what they say or show to me. I follow them into their worlds, grateful for their generosity, constrained by their reticence. And it is in the writing that I discover who they are and what stories they have to relate. It is in the writing, sentence by sentence, that I discover their appearance and their lives, their joys and their pains. Nothing is planned, nothing is decided ahead of time. It is rare, when I begin working on a story, that I know what the outcome will be—and even when I do I never have any idea how we will get there. Frequently, in the doing, my own story will surprise me.

If the characters live, they will at times do and say things I dislike or with which I disagree but this, far from detracting from their validity, lends them a greater integrity, for literary characters are not the writers' playthings. They should be fully developed individuals with minds and lives of their own, existing in the imaginative world of the writer.

Literary characters must be true only to themselves and their circumstances. They owe allegiance—and this brings me to another point—to neither the writer nor the social group to which they belong. They are, if they truly live, individuals with their own psychology and their own biography, no more and no less representative or symbolic of a group than any one of us in this room. To oblige a character to adopt a preordained stance is to kill that character; it is to take away his individuality, to remove his freedom of choice. When ideological concerns are allowed precedence over artistic ones, the art—the short story, the novel, the film—emerges dull and lifeless, the literary achievement sacrificed to the political document, the role of fiction subverted.

Just as Timothy Findley does not define his writing by his gender or his sexuality, so I do not define my writing by my gender or my colour. One's concerns go far beyond these boxes, extending to a wider humanity. Nobel Prize winner Nadine Gordimer, a white female guilty of writing from perspectives neither white nor female, once explained it succinctly: "When it comes to their essential faculty as writers," Ms. Gordimer once wrote, "all writers are androgynous beings."

So what then is, or should be, the role of fiction?

As I've already said, my first aim is to tell a good story. To entertain. But it is, in part too, the challenge of capturing as precisely as language will allow a tiny slice of the human experience and sharing that feeling, that perception, with others. I also aim in my writing to question harsh realities and challenge accepted verities, to offer new angles on old truths.

But the urge to write goes beyond this, for one also hopes for a grander effect. And what could be grander than shedding light, to the best of one's ability, on the unknown? This is why I am attracted in my fiction to characters pointedly different from myself. For writing is, for me, neither autobiography nor therapy. It is, first and foremost, an act of discovery. I seek, through literary exploration, to understand lives very different from my own, pursuing what I would call the demystification of the other. It is only through the true understanding of others that we can ever hope to make real progress against racism, sexism and all the other evils that afflict us. Only by replacing ignorance with knowledge—not the rhetoric of politics but the intimate details of single lives—can we hope to move beyond them. *It is precisely because I have not lived the life that I seek to explore and, I hope, understand it—and, with luck, to help others understand it too. . . .*

In closing, I would like to quote from the letter sent by the publisher in response to the request I mentioned at the outset to remove the references to God from "The Hockey Sweater":

We will not agree to these changes. We certainly understand that the books will be used by elementary students from varying backgrounds and religions, and we feel that one of the purposes of education is to foster tolerance of the varying backgrounds and beliefs of others sharing this planet.

If the authors have so little faith in the good sense of teachers and pupils (even elementary ones), then I suggest they do one of two things: delete this story or add a note to the effect that the story is set in a small Quebec village shortly after World War II, and that the small boy who is the protagonist of the story is, as are all other members of the village, a Roman Catholic—and therefore believes in God.

However, we feel that adding such a note, while it points out the historical context of the story, and perhaps would elicit a discussion, is calling too much attention to details which probably would either be overlooked, or be dealt with very quickly in a classroom context.

We are not open to discussion on this point, and we hope that you will understand our reasons....

On that note, I will close. Thank you very much for your attention.

Blossom

Priestess of Oya, Goddess of winds, storms and waterfalls

✩

Dionne Brand

Blossom's was jumping tonight. Oya and Shango and God and spirit and ordinary people was chanting and singing and jumping the place down. Blossom's was a obeah house and speakeasy on Vaughan Road. People didn't come for the cheap liquor Blossom sell, though as night wear on, on any given night, Blossom, in she waters, would tilt the bottle a little in your favour. No, it wasn't the cheap liquor, even if you could drink it all night long till morning. It was the feel of the place. The cheap light revolving over the bar, the red shag covering the wall against which Blossom always sit, a line of beer, along the window-sill behind, as long as she ample arms spread out over the back of a wooden bench. And, the candles glowing bright on the shrine of Oya, Blossom's mother Goddess.

This was Blossom's most successful endeavour since coming to Canada. Every once in a while, under she breath, she curse the day she come to Toronto from Oropuche, Trinidad. But nothing, not even snarky white people, could keep Blossom under. When she first come it was to babysit some snot-nosed children on Oriole Parkway. She did meet a man, in a club on Henry Street in Port-of-Spain, who promise she to take care of she, if she ever was in Toronto. When Blossom reach, the man disappear and through the one other person she know in Toronto she get the work on Oriole.

Well Blossom decide long that she did never mean for this kinda work, steady cleaning up after white people, and that is when she decide to take a course in secretarial at night. Is there she meet Peg and Betty, who she did know from home, and Fancy Girl. And for two good years they all try to type; but their heart wasn't in it. So they switch to carpentry and upholstering. Fancy Girl swear that they could make a good business because she father was a joiner and white people was paying a lot of money for old-looking furniture. They all went along with this until Peg say she need to make some fast money because, where they was going to find white people who like old furniture, and who was going to buy old furniture from Black women anyway. That is when Fancy Girl come up with the pyramid scheme.

They was to put everybody name on a piece of paper, everybody was to find five people to put on the list and that five would find five and so on. Everybody on the list would send the first person one hundred dollars. In the end everybody was to get thousands of dollars in the mail and only invest one hundred, unless the pyramid break. Fancy Girl name was first and so the pyramid start. Lo and behold, Fancy Girl leave town saying she going to Montreal for a weekend and it was the last they ever see she. The pyramid bust up and they discover that Fancy Girl pick up ten thousand dollars clean. Blossom had to hide for months from people on the pyramid and she swear to Peg that, if she ever see Fancy Girl Munro again, dog eat she supper.

Well now is five years since Blossom in Canada and nothing ain't breaking. She leave the people on Oriole for some others on Balmoral. The white man boss-man was a doctor. Since the day she reach, he eyeing she, eyeing she. Blossom just mark this down in she head and making sure she ain't in no room alone with he. Now one day, it so happen that she in the basement doing the washing and who come down there but he, playing like he looking for something. She watching him from the corner of she eye and, sure as the day, he make a grab for she. Blossom know a few things, so she grab on to he little finger and start to squeeze it back till he face change all colour from white to black and he had to scream out. Blossom sheself start to scream like all hell, until the wife and children run downstairs too.

It ain't have cuss. Blossom ain't cuss that day. The wife face red and shame and then she start to watch Blossom cut eye. Well look at my cross nah Lord, Blossom think, here this dog trying to abuse me and she watching *me* cut eye! Me! a church-going woman! A craziness fly up in Blossom head and she start to go mad on them in the house. She flinging things left right and centre and cussing big word. Blossom fly right off the handle, until they send for the police for Blossom. She didn't care. They couldn't make she hush. It don't have no dignity in white man feeling you up! So she cuss out the police too, when they come, and tell them to serve and protect she, like they supposed to do and lock up the so-and-so. The doctor keep saying to the police, "Oh this is so embarrassing. She's crazy, she's crazy." And Blossom tell him, "You ain't see crazy yet." She run and dash all the people clothes in the swimming pool and shouting, "Make me a weapon in thine hand, oh Lord!" Blossom grab on to the doctor neck, dragging him, to drown him. It take two police to unlatch Blossom from the man red neck, yes. And how the police get Blossom to leave is a wonder; but she wouldn't leave without she pay, and in cash money too besides, she tell them. Anyhow, the police get Blossom to leave the house;

and they must be 'fraid Blossom too, so they let she off down the street and tell she to go home.

The next day Blossom show up on Balmoral with a placard saying the Dr So-and-So was a white rapist; and Peg and Betty bring a Black Power flag and the three of them parade in front of that man house whole day. Well is now this doctor know that he mess with the wrong woman, because when he reach home that evening, Blossom and Peg and Betty bang on he car, singing, "We Shall Not be Moved" and chanting, "Doctor So-and-So is a Rapist." They reach into the car and, well, rough up the doctor—grabbing he tie and threatening to cut off he balls. Not a soul ain't come outside, but you never see so much drapes and curtain moving and swaying up and down Balmoral. Police come again, but they tell Doctor So-and-So that the sidewalk is public property and as long as Blossom and them keep moving they wasn't committing no crime. Well, when they hear that, Blossom and them start to laugh and clap and sing "We Shall Overcome." That night, at Peg house, they laugh and they eat and they drink and dance and laugh more, remembering the doctor face when they was banging on he car. The next day Blossom hear from the Guyanese girl working next door that the whole family on Balmoral, Doctor, wife, children, cat, and dog, gone to Florida.

After that, Blossom decide to do day work here and day work there, so that no white man would be over she and she was figuring on a way to save money to do she own business.

Blossom start up with Victor one night in a dance. It ain't have no reason that she could say why she hook up with him except that in a dance one night, before Fancy Girl take off, when Peg and Betty and Fancy Girl was in they dance days, she suddenly look around and all three was jack up in a corner with some man. They was grinding down the Trinidad Club and there was Blossom, alone at the table, playing she was groovin' to the music.

Alone. Well, keeping up sheself, working, working and keeping the spirits up in this cold place all the time...Is not until all of a sudden one moment, you does see yourself. Something tell she to stop and witness the scene. And then Blossom decide to get a man. All she girl pals had one, and Blossom decide to get one too. It sadden she a little to see she riding partners all off to the side so. After all, every weekend they used to fête and insult man when they come to ask them to dance. They would fête all night in the middle of the floor and get tight on southern comfort. Then they would hobble down the steps out of the club on Church or "Room at the Top," high heels squeezing and waist in pain, and hail a taxi home to one house or the other. By the time the taxi reach wherever they was going, shoes would be in hand and stockings off and a lot of groaning and description of foot pain would hit the door. And comparing notes on which man look so good and which man had a hard on, they would cook, bake, and salt fish, in the morning and laugh about the night before. If is one thing with Blossom, Peg and Betty and Fancy Girl, they like to have a good time. The world didn't mean for sorrow; and suffering don't suit nobody face, Blossom say.

So when she see girl-days done and everybody else straighten up and get man, Blossom decide to get a man too. The first, first man that pass Blossom eyes after deciding was Victor and Blossom decide on him. It wasn't the first man Blossom had, but it was the first one she decide to keep. It ain't have no special reason either; is just when Victor appear, Blossom get a idea to fall in love. Well, then start a long line of misery the likes of which Blossom never see before and never intend to see again. The only reason that the misery last so long is because Blossom was a stubborn woman and when she decide something, she decide. It wasn't even that Blossom really like Victor because whenever she sit down to count he attributes, the man was really lacking in kindness and had a streak of meanness when it come to woman. But she figure like and love not the same thing. So Blossom married to Victor that same summer, in the Pentecostal Church. Victor wanted to live together, but Blossom say she wouldn't be able to go to church no more if she living in sin and if Victor want any honey from she, it have to be with God blessing.

The wedding night, Victor disappear. He show up in a dance, in he white wedding suit and Blossom ain't see him till Monday morning. So Blossom take a sign from this and start to watch Victor because she wasn't a hasty woman by nature. He come when he want, he go when he want and vex when she ain't there. He don't bring much money. Blossom still working day work and every night of the week Victor have friends over drinking Blossom liquor. But Blossom love Victor, so she put up with this type of behaviour for a good few years; because love supposed to be hard and if it ain't hard, it ain't sweet, they say. You have to bear with man, she mother used to say, and besides, Blossom couldn't grudge Victor he good time. Living wasn't just for slaving and it seem that in this society the harder you work, the less you have. Judge not lest ye be judged; this sermon Blossom would give to Peg and Betty anytime they contradict Victor. And anyway, Blossom have she desires and Victor have more than reputation between he legs.

So life go on as it supposed to go on, until Blossom decide not to go to work one day. That time, they was living on Vaughan Road and Blossom wake up feeling like a old woman. Just tired. Something tell she to stay home and figure out she life; because a thirty-six year old woman shouldn't feel so old and tired. She look at she face in the mirror and figure that she look like a old woman too. Ten years she here now, and nothing shaking, just getting older and older, watching white people live. She, sheself living underneath all the time. She didn't even feel like living with Victor anymore. All the sugar gone outa the thing. Victor had one scheme after another, poor thing. Everything gone a little sour.

She was looking out the window, toward the bus stop on Vaughan Road, thinking this. Looking at people going to work like they does do every morning. It make she even more tired to watch them. Today she was supposed to go to a house on Roselawn. Three bathrooms to clean, two living rooms, basement, laundry—God knows what else. Fifty dollars. She look at she short fingers, still water-laden from the day before, then she look at the bus stop again. No, no. Not today. Not this woman. In the bedroom, she watch Victor lying in the bed, face peaceful as ever, young like a baby. Passing into the kitchen shaking she head, she think, "Victor you ain't ready for the Lord yet."

Blossom must be was sitting at the kitchen table for a hour or so when Victor get up. She hear him bathe, dress and come out to the kitchen. "Ah, ah, you still here? Is ten o'clock you know!" She didn't answer. "Girl, you ain't going to work today, or what?" She didn't answer. "You is a happy woman yes, Blossom. Anyway," as he put he coat on, "I have to meet a fella." Something just fly up in Blossom head and she reach for the bread knife on the table. "Victor, just go and don't come back, you hear me?" waving the knife. "Girl you crazy or what?" Victor edged toward the door, "What happen to you this morning?"

Next thing Blossom know, she running Victor down Vaughan Road screaming and waving the bread knife. She hear somebody screaming loud, loud. At first she didn't know who it is, and is then she realize that the scream was coming from she and she couldn't stop it. She dress in she nightie alone and screaming in the middle of the road. So it went on and on and on until it turn into cry and Blossom just cry and cry and cry and then she start to walk. That day Blossom walk. And walk and cry, until she was so exhausted that she find she way home and went to sleep.

She wake up the next morning, feeling shaky and something like spiritual. She was frightened, in case the crying come back again. The apartment was empty. She had the feeling that she was holding she body around she heart, holding sheself together, tight, tight. She get dressed and went to the Pentecostal Church where she get married and sit there till evening.

For two weeks this is all Blossom do. As soon as she feel the crying welling up inside she and turning to a scream, she get dressed and go to the Pentecost. After two weeks, another feeling come; one as if Blossom dip she whole head in water and come up gasping. She heart would pump fast as if she going to die and then the feeling, washed and gasping. During these weeks she could drink nothing but water. When she try to eat bread, something reach inside of she throat and spit it out. Two weeks more and Blossom hair turn white all over. Then she start to speak in tongues that she didn't ever learn, but she understand. At night, in Blossom cry dreams, she feel sheself flying round the earth and raging around the world and then, not just this earth, but earth deep in the blackness beyond sky. There, sky become further than sky and further than dream. She dream so much farther than she ever go in a dream, that she was awake. Blossom see volcano erupt and mountain fall down two feet away and she ain't get touch. She come to the place where legahoo and lajabless is not even dog and where soucouyant, the fireball, burn up in the bigger fire of an infinite sun, where none of the ordinary spirit Blossom know is nothing. She come to the place where pestilence mount good, good heart and good heart bust for joy. The place bright one minute and dark the next. The place big one minute, so big Blossom standing in a hole and the blackness rising up like long shafts above she and widening out into a yellow and red desert as far as she could see; the place small, next minute, as a pin head and only Blossom heart what shrink small, small, small, could fit in the world of it. Then she feel as if she don't have no hand, no foot and she don't need them. Sometimes, she crawling like mapeepee snake; sometimes she walking tall, tall, like a moco jumbie through desert and darkness, desert and darkness, upside down and sideways.

In the mornings, Blossom feel she body beating up and breaking up on a hard mud ground and she, weeping as if she mourning and as if somebody borning. And talking in tongues, the tongues saying the name, Oya. The name sound through Blossom into every layer of she skin, she flesh—like sugar and seasoning. Blossom body come hard like steel and supple like water, when she say Oya. Oya. This Oya was a big spirit Blossom know from home.

One night, Oya hold Blossom and bring she through the most terrifying dream in she life. In the dream, Oya make Blossom look at Black people suffering. The face of Black people suffering was so old and hoary that Blossom nearly dead. And is so she vomit. She skin wither under Suffering look; and she feel hungry and thirsty as nobody ever feel before. Pain dry out Blossom soul, until it turn to nothing. Blossom so 'fraid she dead that she takes she last ball of spit, and stone Suffering. Suffering jump up so fast and grab the stone, Blossom shocked, because she did think Suffering was decrepit. Then Suffering head for Blossom with such a speed that Blossom fingernails and hairs fall out. Blossom start to dry away, and melt away, until it only had one grain of she left. And Suffering still descending. Blossom scream for Oya and Oya didn't come and Suffering keep coming. Blossom was never a woman to stop, even before she start to dream. So she roll and dance she grain-self into a hate so hard, she chisel sheself into a sharp hot prickle and fly in Suffering face. Suffering howl like a beast and back back. Blossom spin and chew on that nut of hate, right in Suffering eyeball. The more Blossom spin and dance, the more Suffering back back; the more Suffering back back, the bigger Blossom get, until Blossom was Oya with she warrior knife, advancing. In the cold light of Suffering, with Oya hot and advancing, Suffering slam a door and disappear. Blossom climb into Oya lovely womb of strength and fearlessness. Full of joy when Oya show she the warrior dance where heart and blood burst open. Freeness, Oya call that dance; and the colour of the dance was red and it was a dance to dance high up in the air. In this dance Oya had such a sweet laugh, it make she black skin shake and it full up Blossom and shake she too.

Each night Blossom grow more into Oya. Blossom singing, singing for Oya to come,

"Oya arriwo Oya, Oya arriwo Oya, Oya kauako arriwo, Arripiti O Oya."

Each night Blossom learn a new piece of Oya and finally, it come to she. She had the power to see and the power to fight; she had the power to feel pain and the power to heal. For life was nothing as it could be taken away any minute; what was earthly was fleeting; what could be done was joy and it have no beauty in suffering.

"Oya O Ologbo O de, Ma yak ba Ma Who! leh, Oya O Ologo O de, Ma yak ba Ma Who! leh, Oya Oh de arriwo, Oya Oh de cumale."

From that day, Blossom dress in yellow and red from head to foot, the colour of joy and the colour of war against suffering. She head wrap in a long yellow cloth; she body wrap in red. She become a obeah woman, spiritual mother and priestess of Oya, Yuroba Goddess-warrior of winds, storms, and waterfalls. It was Oya who run Victor out and it was Oya who plague the doctor and laugh and drink afterwards. It was Oya who well up the tears inside Blossom and who spit the bread out of Blossom mouth.

Quite here, Oya did search for Blossom. Quite here, she find she.

Black people on Vaughan Road recognized Blossom as gifted and powerful by she carriage and the fierce look in she eyes. She fill she rooms with compelling powder and reliance smoke, drink rum and spit it in the corners, for the spirits who would enter Blossom obeah house in the night. Little by little people began to find out that Blossom was the priestess of Oya, the Goddess. Is through Oya, that Blossom reach prosperity.

"Oya arriwo Oya, Oya arriwo Oya, Oya kauako arriwo, Arripiti O Oya."

Each night Oya would enter Blossom, rumbling and violent like thunder and chant heroically and dance, slowly and majestically, she warrior dance against suffering. To see Oya dancing on one leg all night, a calabash holding a candle on she head, was to see beauty. She fierce warrior face frighten unbelievers. Then she would drink nothing but good liquor, blowing mouthfuls on the gathering, granting favours to the believers for an offering.

The offerings come fast and plentiful. Where people was desperate, Blossom, as Oya, received food as offering, boxes of candles and sweet oil. Blossom sent to Trinidad for calabash gourds and herbs for healing, guided by Oya in the mixing and administering.

When Oya enter Blossom, she talk in old African tongues and she body was part water and part tree. Oya thrash about taking Blossom body up to the ceiling and right through the walls. Oya knife slash the gullets of white men and Oya pitch the world around itself. Some nights, she voice sound as if it was coming from a deep well; and some nights, only if you had the power to hear air, could you listen to Oya.

Blossom fame as a obeah woman spread all over, but only among those who had to know. Those who see the hoary face of Suffering and feel he vibrant slap could come to dance with Oya—Oya freeness dance.

"Oya O Ologbo O de, Ma yak ba Ma Who! leh, Oya O Ologo O de, Ma yak ba Ma Who! leh, Oya Oh de arriwo, Oya Oh de cumale."

Since Oya reach, Blossom live peaceful. Is so, Blossom start in the speakeasy business. In the day time, Blossom sleep, exhausted and full of Oya warrior dance and laughing. She would wake up in the afternoon to prepare the shrine for Oya entrance.

On the night that Oya didn't come, Blossom sell liquor and wait for she, sitting against the window.

An Interview with Dionne Brand

☆

Dagmar Novak

You've lived in Canada for many years—in fact, since you were seventeen. In your first years here, what were the positive as well as the negative aspects of being an immigrant?

Basically, I really didn't think of myself as an immigrant *per se*. Yes, I came from another country, but I didn't think that the worlds were that far apart, and I knew that the problems that I would have would not stem from my being an immigrant, but would stem from my being black. If I had been white, within a generation my family would have been assimilated. I could escape being an immigrant, but along with the black people who have lived in this country for three centuries, I would not escape my race at any point. Racism was the focus of my encounter with Canada, not immigrancy.

In your short story "Blossom" there is a definite feeling of separateness between black and white. Indeed, there is a distrust and hatred of whites. Can you comment on Blossom's alienation and her refusal to assimilate?

I think that Blossom's distrust of whites is not based on some personal craziness of hers. It's based on historical practice. It is based on historical events which place her as a black woman in the world at this point in time. Her distrust of whites is not personal paranoia: it has something to do with the social conditions that she finds herself in. She finds herself in a city of whites, where her relation to them is one of subordination. She works for them; they exploit her labour through her race; they oppress her through sexual harassment. The whites in the story are not Blossom's only antagonists, though whites might read the story that way. Blossom also frees herself of an exploiting husband. What Blossom hates is suffering and the suffering of black peoples.

Is there something in "Blossom" that is universal?

I'm sure there might be, but when I start to write a story, I never begin from what might be universal. In fact, I'm wary of appeals to universality. It seems to me that only works written by writers who are not white are called upon to prove or provide universality. White literature is never called upon to commit itself in this way, but all other literature must abandon its specific projects to fit into the understanding of white literature as the expression of white sensibilities. White critics have a preoccupation with rationalizing, homogenizing meanings into white cultural codes which are, of course, loaded with historical relations of power. Universal, therefore, means white. In that context, I do not care about what is universal. I write about what is specific.

Despite the fact that you've lived in Canada for years, would you say that your racial background has affected your writing in Canada?

Yes. I've heard other writers talk about being on the margins of Canadian writing. I find myself in the middle of black writing. I'm in the centre of black writing, and those are the sensibilities that I check to figure out something that's truthful. I write out of a literature, a genre, a tradition, and that tradition is the tradition of black writing. And whether that black writing comes from the United States as African American writing or African Caribbean writing or African writing from the continent, it's in that tradition that I work. I grew up under a colonial system of education, where I read English literature, and I liked it because I love words. But within that writing, there was never my presence. I was absent from that writing. That writing was predicated on imperial history and imperial aspirations—British or American. That imperial history included black slavery. It included the decimation of native peoples. And if the literature nurtured on this is presented to you as great art and you are absent, or the forms or shapes in which you are included are derided, then you know that this literature means to erase you or to kill you. Then you write yourself.

In "Blossom" it seems to me that the past is alive in an almost mystical way.

Yes, each time I write, I find that I've got to go back. I have to go back five hundred years to come back again. Blossom had to go back to come back again to make everything beautiful, to understand anything about the world that she was living in. She had to dig into that past of hers which she retained; she becomes an Obeah woman because that was one of the things that black people in the Americas managed to retain, some sense of a past that is not a past controlled by those things that seem to control her now. I think that one of the reasons why we have been able to survive in the Americas, as a people, has been because of what we have been able to hold and preserve. You just have to look at black culture today and, despite the real hardship that we continue to suffer, you also have to look at things like the music that we make or the literature that we write. So, there is an antagonistic discourse that we continually engage in—in order to keep alive.

Of course, there are anti-discriminatory laws, but it seems as if there is no real spirit behind those laws.

It's also not even individual; it's within institutions. I came here in 1970 and went to find a job. I talked on the phone to the person about the job, and the guy was very enthusiastic on the phone. And I went there and I saw consternation on his face—and the job wasn't there. When I got back home, I called and the job was there. Every black person can tell you a similar story.

What does this do to you? What kind of effect does it have?

Personally, you have to develop an armour to deal with it. Collectively, what you do is organize against it. Because, you see, you can't deal with racism on your own—because you will go crazy. What you do is what black communities have done since we landed on these shores.

But how do you change people's minds, their hearts?

I don't think it's up to black people to change white sensibilities. I think it is up to white people to do that. I think that racism is not our problem. I think it's a white problem. I think we can fight against it. I think it's our job to fight for good laws, to fight for equality, but in terms of doing things like changing white attitudes, white people have to do that work.

For you as a writer, has multiculturalism—as an official Canadian policy—had any benefits, or any detrimental effects?

I think what it does essentially is to compartmentalize us into little cultural groups who have dances and different foods and Caribana. But it doesn't address real power.

Real power?

Real power—which is economic power and political power. I think multiculturalism makes the Canadian population think they're doing really nice things: isn't it nice that we can accept "these" people?

But "these" people remain "these" people. You know, I've been living in this country for twenty years. I am sure there's a guy who emigrated from England five years ago who feels more of this country than I. And I'm sure that there's a black person who has lived here for 150 years and feels like me.

What effect does this kind of segregation have on people in the arts?

It has never stopped us from writing or playing music or singing. I think for a lot of black artists it's a question of survival, the survival of a culture. So we cannot really depend on the Canada Council or the Ontario Arts Council or the Ministry of Multiculturalism. The black community cannot depend upon, cannot trust these institutions to maintain or nurture our cultural expression in Canada. Those institutions should be asking themselves what it is precisely that they maintain and nurture, if particular communities are not funded or are underfunded. And they should be asking themselves: what is Canadian culture? There are other literary organizations in this country, such as the Writers' Union and PEN, who seem to feel that you can quantify culture into six percent of this and two percent of that. These demographic figures are trotted out in hasty self-defense to deny charges of racism. This approach assumes that the contradictions of Canadian culture can be handled by putting them into discrete and isolated packages. Further, it assumes the ongoing dominance of white culture as justifiable and having no responsibility to change its fundamental stance.

But it must make people alien or angry or bitter?

Not really, because, you see, these institutions are a reflection of the culture in which we live. So that it's not something that only happens to us when we write to the Arts Council or the Canada Council. It's something that has happened to us everyday on the street. So we're really wise about these things, because they've been happening for years and years and years.

I noticed that in "Blossom" you portrayed two distinct worlds, the world of the whites and the world of the non-whites. Is this your sense of the divisions within Canadian society?

Of course. It isn't just my sense. There are reservations in this country; there are job ghettos for people of colour. And yes, those things have been marked out by institutions that have grown out of the building of this nation. In the end, we're all responsible for changing that.

How difficult is it to avoid the potential danger of stereotyping a racial group in order to show cultural differences?

Fundamentally, I work against stereotyping. My writing is directed against stereotypes and so I am bound to show complexity in the characters I produce. I am not trying to "show cultural differences" in my writing; I am not even trying to portray a "racial group." What you read into the text so far as that is concerned depends on your stance, your location. The question presumes a reader who is located somewhere else. The white reader may perceive cultural difference, but I am merely writing myself.

Couldn't there also be a danger in showing black men and women as always being the victims of prejudice?

Danger for whom? Racism is a fact in our lives and it is not in our interest to pretend that it does not exist. But that fact has never overwhelmed us and it is certainly not all that we live or all that I write about. I don't think that there's any more danger in it for me, in trying to look at black life, my life, than there was for James Joyce in looking at Irish life.

It seems to me that there's a great deal of anger in Blossom's life. Do you see this as being a force in her transformation?

But she also has a buoyancy. She never thinks of dying. Her anger moves her. You can be angry about silences and injustice. Those are pretty good things to be angry about. And if that anger can then move you, I think it's the real answer. In this culture, one tends to think that anger is destructive. Anger is not an emotion that's only distinguished by destructiveness. To me, it's a more complex emotion. In fact, Blossom is one of the least angry of my characters. She is a woman of mighty resilience and quick action. And this brings me to another point. I'm also wary of the word "anger" as a description for every emotion of a black character in a black work. White critics tend to describe black emotion as either angry or sad, no matter what else is going on in the text, no matter how many other emotions they are confronted by in the characters in that text. Blossom is also joyful, resigned, peaceful, excited, fearful, confused, hurt, sexual, remorseful, euphoric. . . .But the cultural codes which the critic uses to identify black characters are white cultural codes which see blacks in general as either angry in general or sad in general!

What do you see as the future for Canadian writers who are not white?

I think that we are probably the new wave of Canadian writing. Twenty years ago there was a national wave of Canadian writing which set itself up against American writing and the deluge of American culture in Canada. We are the new wave of Canadian writing. We will write about the internal contradictions.

What do you think about whites who write about native life?

I think I can say categorically that whites cannot write about native life.

Should not?

Should not. Yes, should not and cannot—not at this point in history at any rate, not in the absence of native writers having the opportunity, the possibility, and the material resources for writing about native life and having that work published and read. History has been weighted against native people in this country and weighted toward whites; this is an obvious truth for native writers. Native peoples do not need white writers to interpret their lives for them. The distortions of native life in interpretations by white writers are far too numerous and destructive to mention. If any white writer feels that he has the right to interpret native life, the shame of those distortions should make him pause, blush, and halt in his tracks. No amount of liberal good will can erase this. If anything, white writers should ponder what in their collective psyche makes them want to write about native life. Why do they need the power to do this? Why do they remain in a past of white conquest and appropriation? Why are they bent on perpetuating stereotypes, instead of breaking with that history? Now, that would make some good reading, but it would take a little more work and thinking.

Theme Questions

✿

✿ There are many forms of communication in this section—a play, a poem, an essay, a story, an interview. Do you think the ideas being conveyed in one form (the play or poem, for example) would be as powerful in another literary form? Why or why not?

✿ This section raises issues about slavery, censorship, and freedom of expression. When, if ever, do you think it is justified to limit the freedom of another human being?

✿ What are the limitations and expectations placed on women in the various settings and circumstances you read about in this section? Compare them to those in "The Yellow Wallpaper," page 9, or "A Proper Goodbye," page 101.

✿ "It is self-evident that a free society depends on a multiplicity of voices and visions, on an interplay of conflicting views." What evidence is there for and against this idea presented by Neil Bissoondath?

✿ Looking back on this unit and "Dreams: Maps of the Inner World," consider how people use dreams and their heritage as a way of finding themselves.

Language and Power

Language is the way we shape reality. It provides us with the symbols that give coherence to our world. These symbols may be more than words; they may be numbers, shapes, colours, or musical notes. In whatever form, language is the unique means of communication which makes us human.

Our thinking and our knowledge are bound up in our language. The vocabulary we use to name things, the special expressions we adopt, the symbols and metaphors we use—all of these help us convey our feelings and experiences. To learn another language, whether it be the spoken word or the symbols of music or art, is to discover the alternate and subtle shades of meanings that a new mode of expression calls into existence.

Language is *not* neutral. It is a powerful tool which socializes us and tells us what is permitted. It creates class, gender, and racial stereotypes. It can be used to manipulate our thoughts and to imprison us in someone else's version of the universe.

Language, unique and ever-changing, allows us to name things. Thus, when we use language we are not only describing the world, we are also helping to invent it. Yet there may be times when we want to unname or rename things, thus re-inventing some small part of the world. In this way, language gives us the power to free ourselves from traditional constraints.

The Treason of Images

(1928-29)

☆

René Magritte

Humpty Dumpty

☆

Lewis Carroll

However, the egg only got larger and larger, and more and more human: when she had come within a few yards of it, she saw that it had eyes and a nose and a mouth; and, when she had come close to it, she saw clearly that it was HUMPTY DUMPTY himself. "It can't be anybody else!" she said to herself. "I'm certain of it, as if his name were written all over his face!"

It might have been written a hundred times, easily, on that enormous face. Humpty Dumpty was sitting, with his legs crossed like a Turk, on the top of a high wall—such a narrow one that Alice quite wondered how he could keep his balance— and, as his eyes were steadily fixed in the opposite direction, and he didn't take the least notice of her, she thought he must be a stuffed figure after all.

"And how exactly like an egg he is!" she said aloud, standing with her hands ready to catch him, for she was every moment expecting him to fall.

"It's *very* provoking," Humpty Dumpty said after a long silence, looking away from Alice as he spoke, "to be called an egg—*very*!"

"I said you *looked* like an egg, Sir," Alice gently explained. "And some eggs are very pretty, you know," she added, hoping to turn her remark into a sort of compliment.

"Some people," said Humpty Dumpty, looking away from her as usual, "have no more sense than a baby!"

Alice didn't know what to say to this: it wasn't at all like conversation, she thought, as he never said anything to *her*; in fact, his last remark was evidently addressed to a tree—so she stood and softly repeated to herself:

> *"Humpty Dumpty sat on a wall:*
> *Humpty Dumpty had a great fall.*
> *All the King's horses and all the King's men*
> *Couldn't put Humpty Dumpty in his place again."*

"That last line is much too long for the poetry," she added, almost out loud, forgetting that Humpty Dumpty would hear her.

"Don't stand chattering to yourself like that," Humpty Dumpty said, looking at her for the first time, "but tell me your name and your business."

"My *name* is Alice, but——"

"It's a stupid name enough!" Humpty Dumpty interrupted impatiently. "What does it mean?"

"*Must* a name mean something?" Alice asked doubtfully.

"Of course it must," Humpty Dumpty said with a short laugh: "*my* name means the shape I am—and a good handsome shape it is, too. With a name like yours, you might be any shape, almost."

"Why do you sit out here all alone?" said Alice, not wishing to begin an argument.

"Why, because there's nobody with me!" cried Humpty Dumpty. "Did you think I didn't know the answer to *that*? Ask another."

"Don't you think you'd be safer down on the ground?" Alice went on, not with any idea of making another riddle, but simply in her good-natured anxiety for the queer creature. "That wall is so *very* narrow!"

"What tremendously easy riddles you ask!" Humpty Dumpty growled out. "Of course I don't think so! Why, if ever I *did* fall off—which there's no chance of—but *if* I did——" Here he pursed up his lips, and looked so solemn and grand that Alice could hardly help laughing. "*If* I *did* fall," he went on, "*the King has promised me*—ah, you may turn pale, if you like! You didn't think I was going to say that, did you? *The King has promised me*—*with his very own mouth*—to—to——"

"To send all his horses and all his men," Alice interrupted, rather unwisely.

"Now I declare that's too bad!" Humpty Dumpty cried, breaking into a sudden passion. "You've been listening at doors—and behind trees—and down chimneys—or you couldn't have known it!"

"I haven't indeed!" Alice said very gently. "It's in a book."

"Ah, well! They may write such things in a *book*," Humpty Dumpty said in a calmer tone. "That's what you call a History of England, that is. Now, take a good look at me! I'm one that has spoken to a King, *I* am: mayhap you'll never see such another: and, to show you I'm not proud, you may shake hands with me!" And he grinned almost from ear to ear, as he leant forward (and as nearly as possible fell off the wall in doing so) and offered Alice his hand. She watched him a little anxiously as she took it. "If he smiled much more the ends of his mouth might meet behind," she thought: "And then I don't know *what* would happen to his head! I'm afraid it would come off!"

"Yes, all his horses and all his men," Humpty Dumpty went on. "They'd pick me up again in a minute, *they* would! However, this conversation is going on a little too fast: let's go back to the last remark but one."

"I'm afraid I ca'n't quite remember it," Alice said, very politely.

"In that case we start afresh," said Humpty Dumpty, "and it's my turn to choose a subject—" ("He talks about it just as if it was a game!" thought Alice.) "So here's a question for you. How old did you say you were?"

Alice made a short calculation, and said "Seven years and six months."

"Wrong!" Humpty Dumpty exclaimed triumphantly. "You never said a word like it!"

"I thought you meant 'How old *are* you?'" Alice explained.

"If I'd meant that, I'd have said it," said Humpty Dumpty.

Alice didn't want to begin another argument, so she said nothing.

"Seven years and six months!" Humpty Dumpty repeated thoughtfully. "An uncomfortable sort of age. Now if you'd asked *my* advice, I'd have said 'Leave off at seven'—but it's too late now."

"I never ask advice about growing," Alice said indignantly.

"Too proud?" the other enquired.

Alice felt even more indignant at this suggestion. "I mean," she said, "that one ca'n't help growing older."

"*One* ca'n't, perhaps," said Humpty Dumpty; "but *two* can. With proper assistance, you might have left off at seven."

"What a beautiful belt you've got on!" Alice suddenly remarked. (They had had quite enough of the subject of age, she thought: and, if they really were to take turns in choosing subjects, it was *her* turn now.) "At least," she corrected herself on second thoughts, "a beautiful cravat, I should have said—no, a belt, I mean—I beg your pardon!" she added in dismay, for Humpty Dumpty looked thoroughly offended, and she began to wish she hadn't chosen that subject. "If only I knew," she thought to herself, "which was neck and which was waist!"

Evidently Humpty Dumpty was very angry, though he said nothing for a minute or two. When he *did* speak again, it was in a deep growl.

"It is a—*most*—*provoking*—thing," he said at last, "when a person doesn't know a cravat from a belt!"

"I know it's very ignorant of me," Alice said, in so humble a tone that Humpty Dumpty relented.

"It's a cravat, child, and a beautiful one, as you say. It's a present from the White King and Queen. There now!"

"It is really?" said Alice, quite pleased to find that she *had* chosen a good subject after all.

"They gave it me," Humpty Dumpty continued thoughtfully as he crossed one knee over the other and clasped his hands round it, "they gave it me—for an un-birthday present."

"I beg your pardon?" Alice said with a puzzled air.

"I'm not offended," said Humpty Dumpty.

"I mean, what *is* an un-birthday present?"

"A present given when it isn't your birthday, of course."

Alice considered a little. "I like birthday presents best," she said at last.

"You don't know what you're talking about!" cried Humpty Dumpty. "How many days are there in a year?"

"Three hundred and sixty-five," said Alice.

"And how many birthdays have you?"

"One."

"And if you take one from three hundred and sixty-five what remains?"

"Three hundred and sixty-four, of course."

Humpty Dumpty looked doubtful. "I'd rather see that done on paper," he said.

Alice couldn't help smiling as she took out her memorandum-book, and worked the sum for him:

$$\begin{array}{r} 365 \\ \underline{1} \\ 364 \end{array}$$

Humpty Dumpty took the book and looked at it carefully. "That seems to be done right——" he began.

"You're holding it upside down!" Alice interrupted.

"To be sure I was!" Humpty Dumpty said gaily, as she turned it round for him. "I thought it looked a little queer. As I was saying, that *seems* to be done right—though I haven't time to look it over thoroughly just now—and that shows that there are three hundred and sixty-four days when you might get un-birthday presents——"

"Certainly," said Alice.

"And only *one* for birthday presents, you know. There's glory for you!"

"I don't know what you mean by 'glory,'" Alice said.

Humpty Dumpty smiled contemptuously. "Of course you don't—till I tell you. I meant 'there's a nice knock-down argument for you!'"

"But 'glory' doesn't mean 'a nice knock-down argument,'" Alice objected.

"When *I* use a word," Humpty Dumpty said, in rather a scornful tone, "it means just what I choose it to mean—neither more nor less."

"The question is," said Alice, "whether you *can* make words mean so many different things."

"The question is," said Humpty Dumpty, "which is to be master—— that's all."

Alice was too much puzzled to say anything; so after a minute Humpty

Dumpty began again. "They've a temper, some of them—particularly verbs: they're the proudest—adjectives you can do anything with, but not verbs—however, *I* can manage the whole lot of them! Impenetrability! That's what *I* say!"

"Would you tell me please," said Alice, "what that means?"

"Now you talk like a reasonable child," said Humpty Dumpty, looking very much pleased. "I meant by 'impenetrability' that we've had enough of that subject, and it would be just as well if you'd mention what you mean to do next, as I suppose you don't mean to stop here all the rest of your life."

"That's a great deal to make one word mean," Alice said in a thoughtful tone.

"When I make a word do a lot of work like that," said Humpty Dumpty, "I always pay it extra."

"Oh!" said Alice. She was too much puzzled to make any other remark.

"Ah, you should see 'em come round me of a Saturday night," Humpty Dumpty went on, wagging his head gravely from side to side, "for to get their wages, you know."

(Alice didn't venture to ask what he paid them with; and so you see I ca'n't tell *you*.)

"You seem very clever at explaining words, Sir," said Alice. "Would you kindly tell me the meaning of the poem called 'Jabberwocky'?"

"Let's hear it," said Humpty Dumpty. "I can explain all the poems that ever were invented—and a good many that haven't been invented just yet."

This sounded very hopeful, so Alice repeated the first verse:

> " '*Twas brillig, and the slithy toves*
> *Did gyre and gimble in the wabe:*
> *All mimsy were the borogoves,*
> *And the mome raths outgrabe.*' "

"That's enough to begin with," Humpty Dumpty interrupted: "there are plenty of hard words there. '*Brillig*' means four o'clock in the after-noon—the time when you begin *broiling* things for dinner."

"That'll do very well," said Alice: "and '*slithy*'?"

"Well, '*slithy*' means 'lithe and slimy.' 'Lithe' is the same as 'active.' You see it's like a portmanteau—there are two meanings packed up into one word."

"I see it now," Alice remarked thoughtfully: "and what are '*toves*'?"

"Well '*toves*' are something like badgers—they're something like lizards—and they're something like corkscrews."

"They must be very curious-looking creatures."

"They are that," said Humpty Dumpty; "also they make their nests under sun-dials—also they live on cheese."

"And what's to '*gyre*' and to '*gimble*'?"

"To '*gyre*' is to go round and round like a gyroscope. To '*gimble*' is to make holes like a gimlet."

"And '*the wabe*' is the grass-plot round a sun-dial, I suppose?" said Alice, surprised at her own ingenuity.

"Of course it is. It's called '*wabe*' you know, because it goes a long way before it, and a long way behind it— —"

"And a long way beyond it on each side," Alice added.

"Exactly so. Well then, '*mimsy*' is 'flimsy and miserable' (there's another portmanteau for you). And a '*borogove*' is a thin shabby-looking bird with its feathers sticking out all around—something like a live mop."

"And then '*mome raths*'?" said Alice. "I'm afraid I'm giving you a great deal of trouble."

"Well, a '*rath*' is a sort of green pig: but '*mome*' I'm not certain about. I think it's short for 'from home'—meaning that they'd lost their way, you know."

"And what does '*outgrabe*' mean?"

"Well, '*outgribing*' is something between bellowing and whistling, with a kind of sneeze in the middle: however, you'll hear it done, maybe— down in the wood yonder—and, when you've once heard it, you'll be *quite* content. Who's been repeating all that hard stuff to you?"

"I read it in a book," said Alice. "But I *had* some poetry repeated to me much easier than that, by— Tweedledee, I think it was."

"As to poetry, you know," said Humpty Dumpty, stretching out one of his great hands, "I can repeat poetry as well as other folk, if it comes to that— —"

"Oh, it needn't come to that!" Alice hastily said, hoping to keep him from beginning.

"The piece I'm going to repeat," he went on without noticing her remark, "was written entirely for your amusement."

Alice felt that in that case she really *ought* to listen to it; so she sat down, and said "Thank you" rather sadly,

> *"In winter, when the fields are white,*
> *I sing this song for your delight— —*

only I don't sing it," he added as an explanation.

"I see you don't," said Alice.

"If you can *see* whether I'm singing or not, you've sharper eyes than most," Humpty Dumpty remarked severely. Alice was silent.

> *"In spring, when woods are getting green,*
> *I'll try and tell you what I mean:"*

"Thank you very much," said Alice.

> *"In summer, when the days are long,*
> *Perhaps you'll understand the song:*
>
> *In autumn, when the leaves are brown,*
> *Take pen and ink, and write it down."*

"I will, if I can remember it so long," said Alice.

"You needn't go on making remarks like that," Humpty Dumpty said: "They're not sensible, and they put me out."

> *"I sent a message to the fish:*
> *I told them 'This is what I wish.'*
>
> *The little fishes of the sea,*
> *They sent an answer back to me.*
>
> *The little fishes' answer was*
> *'We cannot do it, Sir, because——'"*

"I'm afraid I don't quite understand," said Alice.

"It gets easier further on," Humpty Dumpty replied.

> *"I sent to them again to say*
> *'It will be better to obey.'*
>
> *The fishes answered, with a grin,*
> *'Why, what a temper you are in!'*
>
> *I told them once, I told them twice:*
> *They would not listen to advice.*
>
> *I took a kettle large and new,*
> *Fit for the deed I had to do.*
>
> *My heart went hop, my heart went thump:*
> *I filled the kettle at the pump.*
>
> *Then some one came to me and said*
> *'The little fishes are in bed.'*

> *I said to him, I said it plain,*
> *'Then you must wake them up again.'*
>
> *I said it very loud and clear:*
> *I went and shouted in his ear."*

Humpty Dumpty raised his voice almost to a scream as he repeated this verse, and Alice thought, with a shudder, "I wouldn't have been the messenger for *anything*!"

> *"But he was very stiff and proud:*
> *He said, 'You needn't shout so loud!'*
>
> *And he was very proud and stiff:*
> *He said 'I'd go and wake them, if——'*
>
> *I took a corkscrew from the shelf:*
> *I went to wake them up myself.*
>
> *And when I found the door was locked,*
> *I pulled and pushed and kicked and knocked.*
>
> *And when I found the door was shut,*
> *I tried to turn the handle, but——"*

There was a long pause.

"Is that all?" Alice timidly asked.

"That's all," said Humpty Dumpty. "Good-bye."

This was rather sudden, Alice thought: but, after such a *very* strong hint that she ought to be going, she felt that it would hardly be civil to stay. So she got up, and held out her hand. "Good-bye, till we meet again!" she said as cheerfully as she could.

"I shouldn't know you again if we *did* meet," Humpty Dumpty replied in a discontented tone, giving her one of his fingers to shake: "you're so exactly like other people."

"The face is what one goes by, generally," Alice remarked in a thoughtful tone.

"That's just what I complain of," said Humpty Dumpty. "Your face is the same as everybody has—the two eyes, so——" (marking their places in the air with his thumb) "nose in the middle, mouth under. It's always the same. Now if you had the two eyes on the same side of the nose, for instance—or the mouth at the top—that would be *some* help."

"It wouldn't look nice," Alice objected. But Humpty Dumpty only shut his eyes, and said "Wait till you've tried."

Alice waited a minute to see if he would speak again, but, as he never opened his eyes or took any further notice of her, she said "Good-bye!" once more, and, getting no answer to this, she quietly walked away: but she couldn't help saying to herself, as she went, "of all the unsatisfac- tory — —" (she repeated this aloud, as it was a great comfort to have such a long word to say) "of all the unsatisfactory people I *ever* met — —" She never finished the sentence, for at this moment a heavy crash shook the forest from end to end.

What Language Do Bears Speak?

✪

Roch Carrier

Following our own morning ritual, to which we submitted with more conviction than to the one of saying our prayers when we jumped out of bed, we ran to the windows and lingered there, silent and contemplative, for long moments. Meanwhile, in the kitchen, our mother was becoming impatient, for we were late. She was always afraid we'd be late...Life was there all around us and above us, vibrant and luminous, filled with trees; it offered us fields of daisies and it led to hills that concealed great mysteries.

The story of that morning begins with some posters. During the night, posters had been put up on the wooden poles that supported the hydro wires.

"Posters! They've put up posters!"

Did they announce that hairy wrestlers were coming? Far West singers? Strong men who could carry horses on their shoulders? Comic artists who had 'made all America collapse with laughter'? An international tap-dance champion? A sword swallower? Posters! Perhaps we'd be allowed to go and see a play on the stage of the parish hall—if the curé declared from the pulpit that the play wasn't immoral and if we were resourceful enough to earn the money for a ticket. Posters! The artists in the photographs would gradually come down from the posters until they inhabited our dreams, haunted our games and accompanied us, invisible, on our expeditions.

"There's posters up!"

We weren't allowed to run to the posters and, trembling, read their marvellous messages; it was contrary to maternal law to set foot outside before we had washed and combed our hair. After submitting to this painful obligation we were able to learn that we would see, in flesh and blood, the unsurpassable Dr. Schultz, former hunter in Africa, former director of zoos in the countries of Europe, former lion-tamer, former elephant-hunter, and former free-style wrestling champion in Germany, Austria, and the United Kingdom, in an unbelievable, unsurpassable

174

show— "almost unimaginable." Dr. Schultz would present dogs that could balance on balls, rabbit-clowns, educated monkeys, hens that could add and subtract; in addition, Dr. Schultz would brave a savage bear in an uneven wrestling match "between the fierce forces of nature and the cunning of human intelligence, of which the outcome might be fatal for one of the protagonists."

We had seen bears before, but dead ones, with mouths bleeding, teeth gleaming. Hunters like to tell how their victims had appeared to them: ". . .standing up, practically walking like a man, but a big man, hairy like a bear; and then it came at me roaring like thunder when it's far away behind the sky, with claws like knives at the end of his paws, and then when I fired it didn't move any more than if a mosquito'd got into its fur. Wasn't till the tenth bullet that I saw him fall down. . ." Loggers, too, had spotted bears and some, so they said, had been so frightened their hair had turned white.

Dr. Schultz was going to risk his life before our eyes by pitting himself against this merciless beast. We would see with our own eyes, alive before us, not only a bear but a man fighting a bear. We'd see all of that!

A voice that reached the entire village, a voice that was magnified by loudspeakers, announced that the great day had arrived: "At last you can see, in person, the unsurpassable Dr. Schultz, the man with the most scars in the world, and his bear— a bear that gets fiercer and fiercer as the season for love comes closer!"

We saw an old yellow bus drive up, covered with stars painted in red, pulling a trailer on whose sides we could read: DR. SCHULTZ AND ASSOCIATES UNIVERSAL WONDER CIRCUS LTD. The whole thing was covered with iron bars that were tangled and crossed and knotted and padlocked. A net of clinking chains added to the security. Between messages, crackling music made curtains open at the windows and drew the children outdoors. Then the magical procession entered the lot where we played ball in the summer. The motor growled, the bus moved forward, back, hesitated. At last it found its place and the motor was silent. A man got out of the bus. He stood on the running-board; twenty or thirty children had followed the circus. He considered us with a smile.

"Hi, kids," he said.

He added something else, words in the same language, which we'd never heard before.

"Either he's talking bear," said my friend Lapin, "or he's talking English."

"If we can't understand him," I concluded, "It must be English."

The man on the running-board was still talking; in his strange language he seemed to be asking questions. Not understanding, we listened, stupefied to see Dr. Schultz in person, alive, come down from the posters.

"We talk French here," one of us shouted.

Smiling again, Dr. Schultz said something else we didn't understand.

"We should go get Monsieur Rancourt," I suggested.

Monsieur Rancourt had gone to Europe to fight in the First World War and he'd had to learn English so he could follow the soldiers in his army. I ran to get Monsieur Rancourt. Panting behind his big belly, he hurried as fast as he could. He was looking forward to speaking this language. He hadn't spoken it for so many years he wasn't sure, he told me, that he could remember it. As soon as he saw the man from the circus he told me: "I'm gonna try to tell him hello in English."

"Good day sir! How you like it here today?" ("I remember!" Monsieur Rancourt rejoiced, shouting with delight. "I didn't forget!")

Dr. Schultz moved towards Monsieur Rancourt, holding out his hand. A hand wearing a leather glove, in the middle of summer.

"It's because of the bear bites," my friend Lapin explained to me.

"Apparently the *Anglais* can't take the cold," said one of our friends whose mother's sister had a cousin who worked in an *Anglais* house in Ontario.

The man from the circus and Monsieur Rancourt were talking like two old friends meeting after a number of years. They even laughed. In English, Monsieur Rancourt laughed in a special way, "a real English laugh," we judged, whispering. In French, Monsieur Rancourt never laughed; he was surly. We listened to them, mouths agape. This English language which we'd heard on the radio, in the spaces between the French stations when we turned the tuning knob, we were hearing now for real, in life, in our village, spoken by two men standing in the sun. I made an observation: instead of speaking normally, as in French, instead of spitting the words outside their lips, the two men were swallowing them. My friend Lapin had noticed the same thing, for he said:

"Sounds like they're choking."

Suddenly something was overturned in the trailer; we could hear chains clinking, a bump swelled out the canvas covering and we saw a black ball burst out—the head of a bear.

Dr. Schultz and Monsieur Rancourt had rolled up their shirtsleeves and they were comparing tattoos.

"The bear's loose!"

The animal ran out on the canvas, came down from the roof of the bus and jumped to the ground. How could we tell that to Dr. Schultz who didn't understand our language, whose back was turned to the trailer and who was completely absorbed in his conversation?

"Monsieur Rancourt!" I shouted. "The bear's running away!"

There was no need to translate. The man from the circus had understood. Waving a revolver, he sped towards the bear, which was fleeing into a neighbouring field. He shouted, pleaded, threatened.

"What's he saying?" we asked Monsieur Rancourt.

"Words that English children don't learn till they're men."

"He must be saying the same words my father says when a cow jumps over the fence. They aren't nice."

Dr. Schultz, whom we had seen disappear into the oats, came back after a long moment and spoke to Monsieur Rancourt, who ran to the village. The men who were gathered at the general store rushed off to find other men; they took out traps, rifles, ropes. While the mothers gathered up their children who were scattered over the village, the men set out, directed by fat Monsieur Rancourt. Because of his experience in the war, he took charge of the round-up. Dr. Schultz had confided to him, we learned later:

"That bear's more important than my own wife."

They mustn't kill it, then, but bring it back alive.

The show was to begin in the early afternoon. Dr. Schultz, who had gone with the men into the forest, came back muttering; we guessed that he was unhappy. At his trailer he opened the padlock, unfastened the crossed iron bars, pulled out the pegs and undid the chains. We saw him transform his trailer into a stage, with the help of a system of pulleys, ropes and tripods. Suddenly we were working with the circus man: we carried boxes, held out ropes, unrolled canvas, stuck pickets in the ground, lined up chairs. Dr. Schultz directed our labours. Small, over-excited men that we were, we had forgotten he was speaking a language we didn't understand.

A piece of unrolled canvas suspended from a rope, which was held in place by stakes, formed a circular enclosure. It resembled a tent without a roof; we had built it. We were proud; would we, as long as we lived, ever have another day as beautiful as this one? From now on we were part of the circus.

At last it was time for the show. The music cried out as far as the horizon. In the stands there were mostly women: the men were still pursuing the lost bear.

In gleaming leather boots, in a costume sparkling with gilt braid, Dr. Schultz walked out on the stage. He said a few words and the crowd applauded fervently; the spectators no doubt considered it a mark of prowess to speak with such ease a language of which they couldn't utter a single word.

He opened a cage and a dozen rabbits came out. On the back of each he hung a number. At the other end of the platform was a board with holes cut out of it. Above each hole, a number. The man from the circus gave an order and the rabbits ran to the holes that bore their numbers. Unbelievable, wasn't it? We all raised rabbits, but our animals had never learned anything more intelligent than how to chew clover. Our hands were burning, so much had we applauded our friend Dr. Schultz. Next came the trained dogs' act: one danced a waltz; another rode around a track on a bicycle while his twin played a drum. We applauded our great friend hard enough to break our metacarpals.

The acrobatic chimpanzee's act had scarcely begun when a great uproar drowned the music from the loudspeakers. The canvas wall shook, it opened, and we saw the captured bear come in. The men from the village were returning it to its master, roaring, furious, screaming, clawing, kicking, gasping, famished. The men from the village, accustomed to recalcitrant bulls and horses, were leading it with strong authority; they had passed ropes around its neck and paws so the furious animal had to obey. Monsieur Rancourt was speaking French and English all at once.

When he saw his bear, Dr. Schultz let out a cry that Monsieur Rancourt didn't translate. The men's hands dropped the ropes: the bear was free. He didn't notice immediately. We heard his harsh breathing, and his master's too. The hour had come: we were going to see the greatest circus attraction in the Americas, we were going to see with our own eyes the famous Dr. Schultz, our friend, wrestle a giant black bear.

No longer feeling the ropes burning its neck, no longer submitting to the strength of the men who were tearing it apart, the bear stood up, spread its arms and shot forward with a roar. The bear struck Dr. Schultz like a mountain that might have rolled onto him. The bear and our friend tumbled off the stage. There was a ripple of applause; all the men together would never have succeeded in mustering half the daring of Dr. Schultz. The bear got up again, trampled on the great tamer of wild beasts and dived into the canvas enclosure, tearing it with one swipe of its claws before disappearing.

Dr. Schultz had lost his jacket and trousers. His body was streaked with red scratches. He was weeping.

"If I understand right," said Monsieur Rancourt, "He's telling us that the bear wasn't *his* bear..."

"It isn't *his* bear..."

The men shook and spluttered with laughter as they did at the general store when one of them told a funny story.

The men laughed so hard that Monsieur Rancourt could no longer hear Dr. Schultz's moans as he lay bleeding on the platform. The undertaker apologized for the misunderstanding.

"That bear was a bear that talked English, though, because I didn't understand a single word he said."

Scholar Studies Ancient Language of China's Women

✩

BEIJING (Reuter)—On elegant paper fans and in delicate, cloth-bound diaries, many women in ancient China once transcribed their innermost secrets in a written language that no man could understand.

Called everything from "the witches' script" to the first language of women's liberation, the flowing ideographs were passed from mother to daughter in a secret literary tradition that defied China's male-dominated establishment.

The script, known as "nushu" or "women's calligraphy," now survives only among a dwindling handful of elderly women in one county of the mountainous Hunan province.

A team of male scholars has embarked on a sweeping research project to analyze the writing and preserve it for its historical and linguistic value.

"Women don't seem interested in it any more," said Chen Qiguang, a professor at Beijing's Central Institute of Nationalities who has been the driving force behind efforts to save the script.

Nushu, made up of 2000 individual characters, has been used by women in Hunan for at least 1000 years, Qiguang said in an interview.

Lovingly written on the frail paper pages of crumbling diaries, the characters of nushu are simpler and more fluid than the complex ideographs of standard Chinese.

While Qiguang believes nushu may originally have been adapted from common Chinese characters, he said the two languages now have significant differences.

"Chinese characters represent individual meanings, but nushu characters represent only sounds," Qiguang said. "It is really quite complicated on its own."

Research into the origins of the language has centred on Yang Huanyi, an 83-year-old resident of Jiangyong county in Hunan. Qiguang believes she may be the last woman left in China fully literate in nushu.

Huanyi, who had not practised her nushu in almost four decades, has helped visiting scholars compile dictionaries of nushu characters and decipher older nushu writings, Qiguang said.

Qiguang's research has been primarily linguistic, but he said the nushu writings are equally valuable because they shed light on a secret women's world that received little space in China's official histories.

In their books of nushu, women discussed their views of such events as the 1840-42 Opium War with Britain and the Japanese invasion of China in the 1930s, Qiguang said.

"They would describe how the bombs fell from planes, and how people died on the ground," Qiguang said. "Some of these are valuable historical documents."

The women also used nushu to write about their own private tribulations in a world run by men.

Nushu booklets and songs were traditional gifts between women before marriage, offering advice on how to manage if a husband leaves on a long trip and how to cope with your mother-in-law, as well as lamenting the fact that marriage effectively cuts a woman's ties with her friends and family.

"The women would get together and sing songs written in nushu," Qiguang said. "They had powerful feelings of sisterhood."

The tradition of nushu began to fade in the 1930s when women were given more opportunities for formal education, including instruction in standard Chinese, Qiguang said.

Qiguang said the fruits of his research, with two other scholars, would be published early next year as a 900-page book containing original and translated versions of 400 pieces of nushu writing.

Naming of Parts

✡

Henry Reed

Today we have naming of parts. Yesterday,
We had daily cleaning. And tomorrow morning,
We shall have what to do after firing. But today,
Today we have naming of parts. Japonica
Glistens like coral in all of the neighboring gardens,
      And today we have naming of parts.

This is the lower sling swivel. And this
Is the upper sling swivel, whose use you will see,
When you are given your slings. And this is the piling swivel,
Which in your case you have not got. The branches
Hold in the gardens their silent, eloquent gestures,
      Which in our case we have not got.

This is the safety-catch, which is always released
With an easy flick of the thumb. And please do not let me
See anyone using his finger. You can do it quite easy
If you have any strength in your thumb. The blossoms
Are fragile and motionless, never letting anyone see
      Any of them using their finger.

And this you see is the bolt. The purpose of this
Is to open the breech, as you see. We can slide it
Rapidly backwards and forwards: we call this
Easing the spring. And rapidly backwards and forwards
The early bees are assaulting and fumbling the flowers:
      They call it easing the Spring.

They call it easing the Spring: it is perfectly easy
If you have any strength in your thumb: like the bolt,
And the breech, and the cocking-piece, and the point of
balance,
Which in our case we have not got; and the almond-blossom
Silent in all of the gardens and the bees going backwards and
    forwards,
        For today we have naming of parts.

Languages (1) and (2)

☆

Gwendolyn MacEwen

Languages (1)

This is a country where you have to know more than one language to survive; knowing only one language will do you no good at all. Once they found a woman babbling in some crazy unknown tongue, so they put her in a madhouse for years and years where she kept on babbling. Then someone understood her language and found out that her husband and child had been killed, and she had been trying to tell people ever since. But by now she really was crazy; her mind was a pattern in plaid. They put her in an old folks' home where she babbled less and less until she stopped it altogether and said nothing, and finally died. The language she had spoken was Ukrainian, which is not one of the official languages, so it will definitely do you no good at all. But knowing only one language of any kind in this country will do you no good; you simply have to know more than one to survive.

Languages (2)

When we were fifteen my girlfriend and I used to sit in the back seats of Dundas Street streetcars and whip out our violins and play Bach's Concerto for 2 Violins in D Minor all the way to Yonge Street. This was to startle people and make them notice us. Then we walked barefoot all over downtown before it became a fad in the Sixties, also to startle people and make them notice us. Some of these things worked, but the one thing that never worked was when we sat in the back seats of streetcars and spoke loudly in a language we made up on the spur of the moment, syllable by syllable. We didn't realize that in this country one more language, especially one more unofficial language, would do you no good at all, although knowing only one language of any kind in this country would also do you no good; you had to know more than one to survive. All those mangled feet, all those wounded alphabets, all those illicit violins.

The Stranglehold of English Lit.

☆

Felix Mnthali

(*for Molara Ogundipe-Leslie*)

Those questions, sister,
those questions
         stand
         stab
         jab
     and gore
too close to the centre!

For if we had asked
why Jane Austen's people
carouse all day
and do no work

would Europe in Africa
have stood
the test of time?
and would she still maul
the flower of our youth
in the south?
Would she?

Your elegance of deceit,
Jane Austen,
lulled the sons and daughters
of the dispossessed
into a calf-love
with irony and satire
around imaginary people.

While history went on mocking
the victims of branding irons
and sugar-plantations
that made Jane Austen's people
wealthy beyond compare!

Eng. Lit., my sister,
was more than a cruel joke—
it was the heart
of alien conquest.

My Poetry

✩

Takamura Kōtarō

My poetry is not part of western poetry;
The two touch, circumference against circumference,
But never quite coincide...
I have a passion for the world of western poetry,
But I do not deny that my poetry is formed differently.
The air of Athens and the subterranean fountain of Christianity
Have fostered the pattern of thought and diction of western poetry;
It strikes through to my heart with its infinite beauty and strength—
But its physiology, of wheatmeal and cheese and *entrecôtes*,
Runs counter to the necessities of my language.
My poetry derives from my bowels—
Born at the farthest limits of the far east,
Bred on rice and malt and soya beans and the flesh of fish,
My soul—though permeated by the lingering fragrance of Gandhara
And later enlightened by the "Yellow Earth" civilization of a vast
    continent
And immersed in the murmuring stream of Japanese classics—
Now marvels excitedly at the power of the split atom...
My poetry is no other than what I am,
And what I am is no other than a sculptor of the far east.
For me the universe is the prototype of composition,
And poetry is the composed counter-points.
Western poetry is my dear neighbor,
But the traffic of my poetry moves on a different path...

She Unnames Them

☆

Ursula K. LeGuin

Most of them accepted namelessness with the perfect indifference with which they had so long accepted and ignored their names. Whales and dolphins, seals and sea otters consented with particular grace and alacrity, sliding into anonymity as into their element. A faction of yaks, however, protested. They said that "yak" sounded right, and that almost everyone who knew they existed called them that. Unlike the ubiquitous creatures such as rats and fleas, who had been called by hundreds or thousands of different names since Babel, the yaks could truly say, they said, that they had a *name*. They discussed the matter all summer. The councils of the elderly females finally agreed that though the name might be useful to others it was so redundant from the yak point of view that they never spoke it themselves and hence might as well dispense with it. After they presented the argument in this light to their bulls, a full consensus was delayed only by the onset of severe early blizzards. Soon after the beginning of the thaw, their agreement was reached and the designation "yak" was returned to the donor.

Among the domestic animals, few horses had cared what anybody called them since the failure of Dean Swift's attempt to name them from their own vocabulary. Cattle, sheep, swine, asses, mules, and goats, along with chickens, geese, and turkeys, all agreed enthusiastically to give their names back to the people to whom—as they put it—they belonged.

A couple of problems did come up with pets. The cats, of course, steadfastly denied ever having had any name other than those self-given, unspoken, ineffably personal names which, as the poet named Eliot said, they spend long hours daily contemplating—though none of the con-templators has ever admitted that what they contemplated is their names and some onlookers have wondered if the object of that meditative gaze might not in fact be the Perfect, or Platonic, Mouse. In any case, it is a moot point now. It was with the dogs, and with some parrots, lovebirds, ravens, and mynahs, that the trouble arose. These verbally talented individuals insisted that their names were important to them, and flatly refused to part with them. But as soon as they understood that the issue was precisely one of individual choice, and that anybody who wanted to be called Rover, or Froufrou, or Polly, or even Birdie in the personal sense, was perfectly free to do so, not one of them had the least objection to parting with the lowercase (or, as regards German creatures, upper-case) generic appellations "poodle," "parrot," "dog," or "bird," and all the Linnaean qualifiers that had trailed along behind them for two hundred years like tin cans tied to a tail.

The insects parted with their names in vast clouds and swarms of ephemeral syllables buzzing and stinging and humming and flitting and crawling and tunnelling away.

As for the fish of the sea, their names dispersed from them in silence throughout the oceans like faint, dark blurs of cuttlefish ink, and drifted off on the currents without a trace.

None were left now to unname, and yet how close I felt to them when I saw one of them swim or fly or trot or crawl across my way or over my skin, or stalk me in the night, or go along beside me for a while in the day. They seemed far closer than when their names had stood between myself and them like a clear barrier: so close that my fear of them and their fear of me became one same fear. And the attraction that many of us felt, the desire to smell one another's smells, feel or rub or caress one another's scales or skin or feathers or fur, taste one another's blood or flesh, keep one another warm—that attraction was now all one with the fear, and the hunter could not be told from the hunted, nor the eater from the food.

This was more or less the effect I had been after. It was somewhat more powerful than I had anticipated, but I could not now, in all conscience, make an exception for myself. I resolutely put anxiety away, went to Adam, and said, "You and your father lent me this—gave it to me, actually. It's been really useful, but it doesn't exactly seem to fit very well lately. But thanks very much! It's really been very useful."

It is hard to give back a gift without sounding peevish or ungrateful, and I did not want to leave him with that impression of me. He was not paying much attention, as it happened, and said only, "Put it down over there, O.K.?" and went on with what he was doing.

One of my reasons for doing what I did was that talk was getting us nowhere, but all the same I felt a little let down. I had been prepared to defend my decision. And I thought that perhaps when he did notice he might be upset and want to talk. I put some things away and fiddled around a little, but he continued to do what he was doing and to take no notice of anything else. At last I said, "Well, goodbye, dear. I hope the garden key turns up."

He was fitting parts together, and said, without looking around, "O.K., fine, dear. When's dinner?"

"I'm not sure," I said. "I'm going now. With the—" I hesitated, and finally said, "With them, you know," and went on out. In fact, I had only just then realized how hard it would have been to explain myself. I could not chatter away as I used to do, taking it all for granted. My words now must be as slow, as new, as single, as tentative as the steps I took going down the path away from the house, between the dark-branched, tall dancers motionless against the winter shining.

Theme Questions

✡

✡ "Must a name mean something?" asks Alice. What power do names and naming have? How does language work to actually *shape* our reality?

✡ Do we behave differently in different languages, or in circumstances or activities that have a special language (e.g., sports, games, professions)? Explain.

✡ The language developed among Chinese women is considered "the first language of women's liberation." How does language help a group to unite, to discuss its experience, and to transmit its values and its history?

✡ Are there experiences or actions—in war, civil strife, prejudice, governmental activities—which might be terrible or contemptible, yet which are tamed by innocent language?

Risk

To risk is to place oneself deliberately on the edge—to take a chance, to court danger, to invite the possibility of disaster. We often admire those who undertake a challenge, in spite of knowing the dangers. Such people embrace the limits of being human. They tempt us to move away from the security of the centre. Because of our fascination with the idea of the risk-taker, artists and writers often use the theme of risk as a way of exploring the boundaries of human experience and the relationship we have with the forces of nature.

Society often looks with ambivalence on those who take risks; it encourages boldness, admires courage, and envies commitment—yet it fears the consequences. Sometimes risk-takers fail, but failure itself can be seen as noble and heroic, a fitting reminder of the limitations of human life. There are those who define their lives and their creativity only in terms of risk; some are called heroes, others fools. Who can say what risks are important and which should be avoided? What are we, after all, without risk?

Landscape with the Fall of Icarus

✩

Pieter Bruegel the Elder

The Story of Daedalus and Icarus

✩

Ovid

Homesick for homeland, Daedalus hated Crete
And his long exile there, but the sea held him.
"Though Minos blocks escape by land or water,"
Daedalus said, "surely the sky is open,
And that's the way we'll go. Minos' dominion
Does not include the air." He turned his thinking
Toward unknown arts, changing the laws of nature.
He laid out feathers in order, first the smallest,
A little larger next it, and so continued,
The way that pan-pipes rise in gradual sequence.
He fastened them with twine and wax, at middle,
At bottom, so, and bent them, gently curving,
So that they looked like wings of birds, most surely.
And Icarus, his son, stood by and watched him,
Not knowing he was dealing with his downfall,
Stood by and watched, and raised his shiny face
To let a feather, light as down, fall on it,
Or stuck his thumb into the yellow wax,
Fooling around, the way a boy will, always,
Whenever a father tries to get some work done.
Still, it was done at last, and the father hovered,
Poised, in the moving air, and taught his son:
"I warn you, Icarus, fly a middle course:
Don't go too low, or water will weigh the wings down;
Don't go too high, or the sun's fire will burn them.
Keep to the middle way. And one more thing,
No fancy steering by star or constellation,
Follow my lead!" That was the flying lesson,
And now to fit the wings to the boy's shoulders.
Between the work and warning the father found
His cheeks were wet with tears, and his hands trembled.
He kissed his son (*Good-bye*, if he had known it),

Rose on his wings, flew on ahead, as fearful
As any bird launching the little nestlings
Out of high nest into thin air. *Keep on,*
Keep on, he signals, *follow me!* He guides him
In flight—O fatal art!—and the wings move
And the father looks back to see the son's wings moving.
Far off, far down, some fisherman is watching
As the rod dips and trembles over the water,
Some shepherd rests his weight upon his crook,
Some ploughman on the handles of the ploughshare,
And all look up, in absolute amazement,
At those air-borne above. They must be gods!
They were over Samos, Juno's sacred island,
Delos and Paros toward the left, Lebinthus
Visible to the right, and another island,
Calymne, rich in honey. And the boy
Thought *This is wonderful!* and left his father,
Soared higher, higher, drawn to the vast heaven,
Nearer the sun, and the wax that held the wings
Melted in that fierce heat, and the bare arms
Beat up and down in air, and lacking oarage
Took hold of nothing. *Father!* he cried, and *Father!*
Until the blue sea hushed him, the dark water
Men call the Icarian now. And Daedalus,
Father no more, called "Icarus, where are you!
Where are you, Icarus? Tell me where to find you!"
And saw the wings on the waves, and cursed his talents,
Buried the body in a tomb, and the land
Was named for Icarus.

Musée des Beaux Arts

✿

W.H. Auden

About suffering they were never wrong,
The Old Masters: how well they understood
Its human position; how it takes place
While someone else is eating or opening a window or just walking
　　dully along;
How, when the aged are reverently, passionately waiting
For the miraculous birth, there always must be
Children who did not specially want it to happen, skating
On a pond at the edge of the wood:
They never forgot
That even the dreadful martyrdom must run its course
Anyhow in a corner, some untidy spot
Where the dogs go on with their doggy life and the torturer's horse
Scratches its innocent behind on a tree.

In Brueghel's *Icarus*, for instance: how everything turns away
Quite leisurely from the disaster; the plowman may
Have heard the splash, the forsaken cry,
But for him it was not an important failure; the sun shone
As it had to on the white legs disappearing into the green
Water; and the expensive delicate ship that must have seen
Something amazing, a boy falling out of the sky,
Had somewhere to get to and sailed calmly on.

Fall of Icarus: Breughel

☆

Joseph Langland

Flashing through falling sunlight
A frantic leg late plunging from its strange
Communicating moment
Flutters in shadowy waves.

Close by those shattered waters—
The spray, no doubt, struck shore—
One dreamless shepherd and his old sheep dog
Define outrageous patience
Propped on staff and haunches,
Intent on nothing, backs bowed against the sea,
While the slow flocks of sheep gnaw on the grass-thin coast.
Crouched in crimson homespun an indifferent peasant
Guides his blunt plow through gravelled ground,
Cutting flat furrows hugging this hump of land.
One partridge sits immobile on its bough
Watching a Flemish fisherman pursue
Fish in the darkening bay;
Their stillness mocks rude ripples rising and circling in.

Yet that was a stunning greeting
For any old angler, peasant, or the grand ship's captain,
Though sent by a mere boy
Bewildered in the gravitational air,
Flashing his wild white arms at the impassive sea-drowned sun.

Now only coastal winds
Ruffle the partridge feathers,
Muting the soft ripping of sheep cropping,
The heavy whisper
Of furrows falling, ship cleaving,
Water lapping.

Lulled in the loose furl and hum of infamous folly,
Darkly, how silently, the cold sea suckles him.

Poem Improvised Around a First Line*

Gwendolyn MacEwen

the smoke in my bedroom which is always burning
worsens you, motorcycle Icarus;
you are black and leathery and lean and
you cannot distinguish between sex and nicotine

anytime, it's all one thing for you—
cigarette, phallus, sacrificial fire—   *↗ penis shape*
all part of that grimy flight
on wings axlegreased from Toronto to Buffalo
for the secret beer over the border—

now I long to see you fullblown and black
over Niagara, your bike burning and in full flame
and twisting and pivoting over Niagara
and falling finally into Niagara
and tourists coming to see your black leather wings
hiss and swirl in the steaming current—

now I long to give up cigarettes
and change the sheets on my carboniferous bed;
O baby, what Hell to be Greek in this country—
without wings, but burning anyway.

---

*The first line around which it was improvised has disappeared.

writting poem about/to "old flame"

David

Earle Birney

I

David and I that summer cut trails on the Survey,
All week in the valley for wages, in air that was steeped
In the wail of mosquitoes, but over the sunalive week-ends
We climbed, to get from the ruck of the camp, the surly

Poker, the wrangling, the snoring under the fetid
Tents, and because we had joy in our lengthening coltish
Muscles, and mountains for David were made to see over,
Stairs from the valleys and steps to the sun's retreats.

II

Our first was Mount Gleam. We hiked in the long afternoon
To a curling lake and lost the lure of the faceted
Cone in the swell of its sprawling shoulders. Past
The inlet we grilled our bacon, the strips festooned

On a poplar prong, in the hurrying slant of the sunset.
Then the two of us rolled in the blanket while round us the cold
Pines thrust at the stars. The dawn was a floating
Of mists till we reached to the slopes above timber, and won

To snow like fire in the sunlight. The peak was upthrust
Like a fist in a frozen ocean of rock that swirled
Into valleys the moon could be rolled in. Remotely unfurling
Eastward the alien prairie glittered. Down through the dusty

Skree on the west we descended, and David showed me
How to use the give of shale for giant incredible
Strides. I remember, before the larches' edge,
That I jumped a long green surf of juniper flowing

Away from the wind, and landed in gentian and saxifrage
Spilled on the moss. Then the darkening firs
And the sudden whirring of water that knifed down a fern-hidden
Cliff and splashed unseen into mist in the shadows.

III

One Sunday on Rampart's arête a rainsquall caught us,
And passed, and we clung by our blueing fingers and bootnails
An endless hour in the sun, not daring to move
Till the ice had steamed from the slate. And David taught me

How time on a knife-edge can pass with the guessing of fragments
Remembered from poets, the naming of strata beside one,
And matching of stories from schooldays. . . . We crawled astride
The peak to feast on the marching ranges flagged

By the fading shreds of the shattered stormcloud. Lingering
There it was David who spied to the south, remote,
And unmapped, a sunlit spire on Sawback, an overhang
Crooked like a talon. David named it the Finger.

That day we chanced on the skull and the splayed white ribs
Of a mountain goat underneath a cliff-face, caught
On a rock. Around were the silken feathers of hawks.
And that was the first I knew that a goat could slip.

IV

And then Inglismaldie. Now I remember only
The long ascent of the lonely valley, the live
Pine spirally scarred by lightning, the slicing pipe
Of invisible pika, and great prints, by the lowest

Snow, of a grizzly. There it was too that David
Taught me to read the scroll of coral in limestone
And the beetle-seal in the shale of ghostly trilobites,
Letters delivered to man from the Cambrian waves.

V

On Sundance we tried from the col and the going was hard.
The air howled from our feet to the smudged rocks
And the papery lake below. At an outthrust we baulked
Till David clung with his left to a dint in the scarp,

Lobbed the iceaxe over the rocky lip,
Slipped from his holds and hung by the quivering pick,
Twisted his long legs up into space and kicked
To the crest. Then grinning, he reached with his freckled wrist

And drew me up after. We set a new time for that climb.
That day returning we found a robin gyrating
In grass, wing-broken. I caught it to tame but David
Took and killed it, and said, "Could you teach it to fly?"

VI

In August, the second attempt, we ascended The Fortress,
By the forks of the Spray we caught five trout and fried them
Over a balsam fire. The woods were alive
With the vaulting of mule-deer and drenched with clouds all the morning,

Till we burst at noon to the flashing and floating round
Of the peaks. Coming down we picked in our hats the bright
And sunhot raspberries, eating them under a mighty
Spruce, while a marten moving like quicksilver scouted us.

VII

But always we talked of the Finger on Sawback, unknown
And hooked, till the first afternoon in September we slogged
Through the musky woods, past a swamp that quivered with frog-song,
And camped by a bottle-green lake. But under the cold

Breath of the glacier sleep would not come, the moon-light
Etching the Finger. We rose and trod past the feathery
Larch, while the stars went out, and the quiet heather
Flushed, and the skyline pulsed with the surging bloom

Of incredible dawn in the Rockies. David spotted
Bighorns across the moraine and sent them leaping
With yodels the ramparts redoubled and rolled to the peaks,
And the peaks to the sun. The ice in the morning thaw

Was a gurgling world of crystal and cold blue chasms,
And seracs that shone like frozen saltgreen waves.
At the base of the Finger we tried once and failed. Then David
Edged to the west and discovered the chimney; the last

Hundred feet we fought the rock and shouldered and kneed
Our way for an hour and made it. Unroping we formed
A cairn on the rotting tip. Then I turned to look north
At the glistening wedge of giant Assiniboine, heedless

Of handhold. And one foot gave. I swayed and shouted.
David turned sharp and reached out his arm and steadied me,
Turning again with a grin and his lips ready
To jest. But the strain crumbled his foothold. Without

A gasp he was gone. I froze to the sound of grating
Edge-nails and fingers, the slither of stones, the lone
Second of silence, the nightmare thud. Then only
The wind and the muted beat of unknowing cascades.

VIII

Somehow I worked down the fifty impossible feet
To the ledge, calling and getting no answer but echoes
Released in the cirque, and trying not to reflect
What an answer would mean. He lay still, with his lean

Young face upturned and strangely unmarred, but his legs
Splayed beneath him, beside the final drop,
Six hundred feet sheer to the ice. My throat stopped
When I reached him, for he was alive. He opened his gray

Straight eyes and brokenly murmured "over...over."
And I, feeling beneath him a cruel fang
Of the ledge thrust in his back, but not understanding,
Mumbled stupidly, "Best not to move," and spoke

Of his pain. But he said, "I can't move. . . .If only I felt
Some pain." Then my shame stung the tears to my eyes
As I crouched, and I cursed myself, but he cried,
Louder, "No, Bobbie! Don't ever blame yourself.

I didn't test my foothold." He shut the lids
Of his eyes to the stare of the sky, while I moistened his lips
From our water flask and tearing my shirt into strips
I swabbed the shredded hands. But the blood slid

From his side and stained the stone and the thirsting lichens,
And yet I dared not lift him up from the gore
Of the rock. Then he whispered, "Bob, I want to go over!"
This time I knew what he meant and I grasped for a lie

And said, "I'll be back here by midnight with ropes
And men from the camp and we'll cradle you out." But I knew
That the day and the night must pass and the cold dews
Of another morning before such men unknowing

The ways of mountains could win to the chimney's top.
And then, how long? And he knew. . .and the hell of hours
After that, if he lived till we came, roping him out.
But I curled beside him and whispered, "The bleeding will stop.

Bob?" His eyes brightening with fever upbraided me.
I could not look at him more and said, "Then I'll stay
With you." But he did not speak, for the clouding fever.

I lay dazed and stared at the long valley,
The glistening hair of a creek on the rug stretched
By the firs, while the sun leaned round and flooded the ledge,
The moss, and David still as a broken doll.

I hunched to my knees to leave, but he called and his voice
Now was sharpened with fear. "For Christ's sake push me over!
If I could move. . . .Or die. . . ." The sweat ran from his forehead,
But only his eyes moved. A hawk was buoying

Blackly its wings over the wrinkled ice.
The purr of a waterfall rose and sank with the wind.
Above us climbed the last joint of the Finger
Beckoning bleakly the wide indifferent sky.

Even then in the sun it grew cold lying there. . . .And I knew
He had tested his holds. It was I who had not. . . .I looked
At the blood on the ledge, and the far valley. I looked
At last in his eyes. He breathed, "I'd do it for you, Bob."

IX

I will not remember how nor why I could twist
Up the wind-devilled peak, and down through the chimney's empty
Horror, and over the traverse alone. I remember
Only the pounding fear I would stumble on It

When I came to the grave-cold maw of the bergschrund. . .reeling
Over the sun-cankered snowbridge, shying the caves
In the névé. . .the fear, and the need to make sure It was there
On the ice, the running and falling and running, leaping

Of gaping greenthroated crevasses, alone and pursued
By the Finger's lengthening shadow. At last through the fanged
And blinding seracs I slid to the milky wrangling
Falls at the glacier's snout, through the rocks piled huge

On the humped moraine, and into the spectral larches,
Alone. By the glooming lake I sank and chilled
My mouth but I could not rest and stumbled still
To the valley, losing my way in the ragged marsh.

I was glad of the mire that covered the stains, on my ripped
Boots, of his blood, but panic was on me, the reek
Of the bog, the purple glimmer of toadstools obscene
In the twilight. I staggered clear to a firewaste, tripped

And fell with a shriek on my shoulder. It somehow eased
My heart to know I was hurt, but I did not faint
And I could not stop while over me hung the range
Of the Sawback. In blackness I searched for the trail by the creek

And found it. . . .My feet squelched a slug and horror
Rose again in my nostrils. I hurled myself
Down the path. In the woods behind some animal yelped.
Then I saw the glimmer of tents and babbled my story.

I said that he fell straight to the ice where they found him,
And none but the sun and incurious clouds have lingered
Around the marks of that day on the ledge of the Finger,
That day, the last of my youth, on the last of our mountains.

Mt. Lefroy

☆

Lawren Harris

Lawren Harris, 1885-1970 *Mt. Lefroy* 1930 oil on canvas 133.5 × 153.5 cm.
McMichael Canadian Art Collection Purchase 1975 1975.7

Prometheus

A Greek myth

☆

Retold by W.T. Jewkes

You will remember how Prometheus the Titan made man out of clay and helped his cousin Zeus to win the war of rebellion against Cronus. One would think that he might have won Zeus's undying thanks, but unfortunately for Prometheus, he presumed too much on Zeus's gratitude. As a result he made Zeus angry and had to suffer severe punishment.

Prometheus was very pleased with man but felt that there was a great deal left to be desired in his creation. His brother, Epimetheus, whose name means "he who thinks afterward," had had a hand in helping him make man; but true to his name, he had used up all his raw materials in giving man just a body more versatile than that of the animals. Prometheus realized that in this state man would not know how to take advantage of his upright posture. What man needed, he saw, was to have the chance to develop his mind. Athene, the goddess of wisdom, had already given Prometheus the knowledge of how to build houses, to add and subtract, to chart a course by the stars, to heal illness, and these, and many other useful arts, he soon passed on to mankind. But still man did not have enough to satisfy Prometheus. So he decided to give man the divine gift of fire.

At first Zeus did not seem to object to this idea. But trouble came when Prometheus played a joke on Zeus. It began one day when the gods were gathered together to decide which portions of the sacrificial bull should be offered to them as a gift. Since he was the most clever god, Prometheus was asked to make the decision.

"Well," he said, thinking to show them how silly they were to argue over such a matter, "give me an hour or two and I will have an answer for you."

So while the gods went off for a noontime nap, Prometheus took a bull, killed it, dismembered it, and flayed its hide. Then he made two bags from the hide. Into one he stuffed all the flesh of the bull; and on top of the flesh, at the mouth of the bag, he stuffed the bull's stomach, the least tempting part of the animal. Into the other bag, he put first the bones and then on top, at the mouth of the bag, he placed the animal's juicy fat.

When the gods returned in the early afternoon, they saw the two bags placed on a large flat stone.

"Now," said Prometheus craftily, "I've decided that the best way to resolve the argument is to let Zeus be guided by what he sees. Let the father of the gods and men choose which of these two bags he most would like. Whatever the bag contains shall hereafter be the portion of sacrifice given to the gods."

Zeus was pleased at the idea and quickly stepped up to inspect the bags. Of course, he let his greedy eyes be his guide and chose the bag whose mouth was stuffed with the fragrant fat. When the rest of the contents of the bag had been dumped on the ground, however, and he saw only a pile of dry bones, Zeus knew he had been tricked. He was furious.

"Very well, Prometheus," he raged, "so you want to make me look a fool before the other gods, do you? Well, you'll be sorry you did! You want to give mankind the gift of fire, but now you can't. I won't allow it. Let men eat their flesh raw, just as they always have!"

But Prometheus was a very persistent god. A few days later, when he thought that perhaps Zeus would not be looking, he got Athene to let him steal at night into the fire-chamber of Olympus by the back door. There, in the center of the chamber stood the flaming chariot of the sun, where Apollo had left it after its day's journey. He took a rush torch that was lying in a corner of the hall, lit it from the fiery chariot, and soon had a bright, live piece of charcoal. This he put into the hollow stalk of a giant fennel that he had brought with him, to keep it glowing, but also to hide its light. Then he quickly stole out of the chamber and came down to earth where men were sleeping. Quietly he gathered together some dry leaves and twigs, and putting his live coal in amongst them, he soon had a blazing bonfire going. At last he stepped behind a large oak tree to watch what would happen.

As it grew light, the men who dwelt near the grove got up from their beds of fern to begin the tasks of the day. Soon the news of the strange new spirit, bright as the sun, hot like the sun, so hot that it devoured logs and branches with noisy greed, spread throughout the region. Men came and gathered around the place, gazing in wonder and awe. Soon the bolder ones moved near to the fire, but it was so hot that they quickly retreated. Prometheus watched for a while, delighted with his exploit, but soon it became clear to him that he would have to instruct men in how to treat this new plaything, so that they remained in control. It would not do for fire to become their master instead of their servant. So he stepped out from behind the oak tree and called the men to him.

"This is a gift that I bring to you from Olympus, mortals. It is called 'fire,' and is stolen from the sun. But it's a dangerous gift and you must learn to treat it well. It is greedy for wood and needs to be fed constantly, but if you feed it too much, it will rage out of control and kill you. If ever it does get out of control, you can subdue it with only one thing—water. Treat it with respect and it will be the key to much happiness."

At first the men were afraid at what Prometheus told them. Stolen from the sun? Brought down from Olympus? Surely it was death to meddle with such a thing. But Prometheus meanwhile had taken up the raw haunches of a deer that lay close by. Spitting them on a sharp stick, he held them over the fire, and soon the tempting smell of roast venison brought the men hungrily to the fire's edge. In no time at all they were gulping down the delicious, hot morsels greedily. Then Prometheus showed them how to make torches by dipping branches in pitch and igniting them at the fire. He showed them also how to smelt metal from the ore in rocks. All in all, he thought, surveying men as they happily and busily went about practicing their new skills, a good day's work.

But that night Zeus happened to look down from Olympus onto the face of the earth, and there he saw something that his eyes could hardly believe. All over the landscape he spotted the glow of fires, and by the firelight he saw men cooking their food, warming their cold hands. The fires were driving back the darkness. Some men had made crude forges on which they were already beating out rough weapons, and plowshares, and nails, and iron bands to bind planks together to make ships. Others were fashioning iron rims for the wheels of chariots. Others were refining gold from the earth and making ornaments and coins. It was not hard for Zeus to guess who had been responsible for this. Only one god would have had the gall to defy his command. In his rage, he let out a roar of thunder that split the heavens in two and sent mortals scurrying into their caves and huts.

"Prometheus!" he shouted. "Where's Prometheus? Let him come here at once. If he won't come, bring him by force!"

But Prometheus was already nearby. He knew there would be trouble, but he approached the cloud-gatherer's throne boldly. Zeus frowned blackly on him.

"What have you done, you fool?" he demanded hotly. "You knew my command. Man was not to have the gift of fire. No god can defy my power and get away with it!"

"Father of the gods and men," replied Prometheus quietly, "I won't say I did obey your command. But surely, it seemed to me, you would take pity on the race of men. See how much happier they are, now that they have fire."

"Maybe they are and maybe they aren't," Zeus stormed. "Now that they have that gift, there's no telling what they'll do. Soon they will be so proud of their accomplishments that they will think they are as great as the gods. Who knows, they might even try to storm Olympus itself!"

"Whatever they do, they can never be as powerful as you," declared Prometheus reassuringly. "You can always destroy them if they do."

"I'm not going to wait that long," raged the thunderer. "I'm going to consume them all now, once and for all, in the hugest fire you ever saw!"

But Zeus had second thoughts.

"On the other hand," he said, "I think I'll have myself some sport. What you say is true—I can always destroy them if they storm heaven. In the meantime, I think I'll watch them with their new plaything. I'm not so sure it will bring them only happiness. Soon, mark my words, they'll be at war in those chariots, killing one another with those swords and spears. Maybe they'll do the job for me.

"But you," he went on, turning to Prometheus with his eyes flashing, "you will have to be punished for your disobedience!"

So the king of Olympus called two gods, Power and Violence, to serve as guards of Prometheus. Then he turned to Hephaestus, the lame blacksmith of heaven.

"Hephaestus," he ordered, "you go along with Prometheus and his guards. They are taking him to the rocky slope of the Caucasus. When you get there, I want you to forge the strongest iron fetters you can fashion and chain this criminal to the rocks with them. There he will stay forever, to bear the scorching heat of the sun by day and the bitter cold at night. And I will send an eagle to nest nearby. Each day it will swoop down and tear the prisoner's liver out, piece by piece. And each night the liver will repair itself, ready to make a meal for the bird the next day."

And so it was done. There Prometheus remained in torture for many and many a year. He would have been there still, except that Zeus finally relented and allowed one of the heroes to rescue him. The hero's name was Heracles. But that is another story.

The Mystery of Amelia Earhart

☆

Richard Gillespie

A gleaming silver Lockheed Electra crouches on an airstrip in the New Guinea jungle. In the cockpit sits a boyishly lanky woman with bright, bold eyes, a tousle of short curls and a startling facial resemblance to the young Charles Lindbergh. With a nod to her navigator, a lean, dark-haired man in his forties, she edges the twin throttles forward. As the engines crescendo to a scream, tropical birds burst from the bordering trees in screeching clots of color. Loaded with more than three tons of gasoline, the Electra trundles down the runway toward a cliff that falls sheer into the sea. With only yards to spare, it lurches off the ground, sails over the brink, then swoops almost to the wavetops before easing into a slow climb. In his logbook the navigator notes the time: 10 a.m., July 2, 1937. At 39, Amelia Earhart has begun her final flight. Within 24 hours she will vanish into silence and mystery, a mystery that has haunted the world's imagination for more than half a century, a mystery that is now solved.

Earhart is the most famous female aviator of all time. Second person after Lindbergh to fly the Atlantic solo, first to fly from Hawaii to the U.S. mainland, she had set speed and altitude records, written books, cofounded an airline, lent her name to a line of luggage and designed practical fashions for women. In a profession dominated by men, Earhart inaugurated a struggle that would one day open aerospace careers to women.

On March 17, 1937, Earhart took off from Oakland on her greatest adventure: a 28 595-mile [45 752 km] flight that would make her the first pilot to circle the globe near the equator. But on takeoff from Hawaii for the second leg of the trip, her landing gear collapsed and the plane belly-flopped in a shower of sparks. Back at the Lockheed factory in California, where the Electra was repaired, new aluminum was riveted to the mangled underside. These changes, which made Earhart's aircraft subtly different from every other Electra, would ultimately help to unravel the riddle of her disappearance.

Sixty-two days after the accident, Earhart started off again. But this time, still accompanied by navigator Fred Noonan, she flew east instead of west—across the U.S., the South Atlantic, Africa and India, then through the Dutch East Indies to Australia, and on to Lae, New Guinea, where she took off across 2500 miles [4000 km] of trackless ocean toward a speck of coral called Howland Island.

At Howland the U.S. Coast Guard cutter *Itasca* was standing by to guide the Electra in. At 6:15 a.m. Earhart reported that she was about 200 miles [320 km] out and asked the cutter to take a bearing on her signal. The *Itasca* explained that she was using too high a frequency and requested a Morse code signal on a lower frequency. No reply. The *Itasca* did not know that Amelia had removed her low-frequency antenna to save weight, and that, incredibly, neither she nor Noonan knew Morse code. Then at 7:41 a.m. Earhart's voice came through loud and clear: "We must be on you but cannot see you but gas is running low. Been unable to reach you by radio." At 7:50 a.m. Earhart called again: "We are circling but cannot hear you." She then asked for a signal on a very high frequency. The *Itasca* sent the signal. She received it, but her radio was unable to home in on high-frequency emissions. Her last message came at 8:45 a.m.: "We are on the line 157/337...We are running on line." The *Itasca* called and called. Silence.

What happened to Earhart and Noonan? In the 55 years since that grim morning, their disappearance has spawned a mini-industry of speculation. Hundreds of articles, a feature film, a number of television specials and more than 30 books have worried the mystery and dreamed up solutions. Many assume that Earhart ran out of fuel and crashed at sea. Others claim she was a U.S. spy who was captured by the Japanese and died on Saipan.

The public was fascinated. I wasn't. As an aviation risk manager, and later as executive director of The International Group for Historic Aircraft Recovery (TIGHAR), a nonprofit foundation, I had investigated hundreds of airplane accidents and was well aware of the difference between anecdote and evidence. I told Pat Thrasher, my wife and partner in TIGHAR, that "the Earhart thing is a sensationalized circus, and we should stay out of it." And then, on July 17, 1988, a couple of retired military aviators named Tom Gannon and Tom Willi walked into my office in Wilmington, Del.

Instead of anecdotes, they presented evidence. Step by step they recreated the exact navigational situation faced by Noonan as fuel ran low, radio navigation proved useless and no island appeared ahead. On a chart of the central Pacific they showed how, even without radio bearings, he could follow a standard procedure: aim his octant at the rising sun and plot a "line of position." Using celestial tables, Gannon pointed out that on the morning of July 2, 1937, the rising sun would have provided the precise line of position Earhart said she was running. By flying southeast along that line, Noonan could be sure that, even if he missed Howland, he would reach an island in the Phoenix group in about two hours. Clearly, it was the safest, sanest course to follow. I traced the line on the chart and read the name of the island: Nikumaroro.

Gannon then supplied a stunning piece of information: During the Navy's hunt for Earhart, no search party was ever landed on Nikumaroro (then known as Gardner Island), and only a brief inspection was made from the air—a full week after Earhart vanished. The planes were launched from the battleship *Colorado*, the only large U.S. warship in the central Pacific, which had to steam 2000 miles [3200 km] before the search could begin.

"You mean nobody really looked in the most likely place?" Gannon's silence spoke volumes. I knew then that we'd have to go after Amelia Earhart.

We checked Gannon's story against official reports from the 1937 search, and what we found floored us. The Navy had even stronger reasons than Gannon and Willi to believe that Earhart had landed on an island in the Phoenix group. Almost 24 hours after her last message to the *Itasca*, a Navy flying boat reestablished radio contact. Earhart's signal, barely audible but persistent, was also picked up by HMS *Achilles* and by stations all over the Pacific. Lockheed advised the Navy that, given the continuing signals, the plane must be on land and able to operate an engine to recharge its batteries. Pan Am stations at Hawaii, Midway and Wake Island also took radio bearings and told the Navy that triangulation "places plane [in] Phoenix group." After three days, Earhart's signal stopped.

Four days later, on July 9, three biplanes from the *Colorado* flew over Nikumaroro. They saw no airplane on the atoll, but Lt. John Lambrecht's report noted that "signs of recent habitation were clearly visible." However, "repeated circling and zooming failed to elicit any answering wave from possible inhabitants." Lambrecht decided "none were there" and flew off, unaware that those signs of recent habitation were hugely significant: Prior to 1937, Nikumaroro's last known inhabitants belonged to a work party of islanders that had departed in 1892. The searchers had gone to the most likely place, seen something that shouldn't have been there, and left without investigating. Clearly, the Navy's search, though extensive, had been tragically inadequate. What had not been done in 1937 had to be done now. We would have to search Nikumaroro.

It took a year to raise $250 000, assemble a team of volunteers and arrange a thousand logistical details, but on September 17, 1989, after a 1300-mile [2080 km] trip from Fiji by way of Pago Pago, we peered over the bow of a converted Japanese tuna trawler at a thin green line on the horizon: Nikumaroro. Three and a half miles [5.6 km] long and a quarter-mile [0.4 km] wide at most points, the atoll is only marginally habitable, a slender ringlet of jungle that surrounds a tranquil lagoon. Fresh water depends entirely upon rainfall, which some-times adds up to less than one inch [25.4 mm] a year. Nevertheless, in 1938, 17 months after Earhart disappeared, the British settled 10 Gilbert Islanders on the atoll and started a coconut plantation. In 1944, the U.S. Coast Guard built a radio outpost on the island's southeast tip. But in 1946 the station was dismantled, and in 1963 the Gilbertese left.

Deserted since then, the island is covered with scaevola, a writhing entanglement of iron-hard stalks that towered before us. We waded in with machetes, ignoring bees, spiders, rats and giant coconut crabs that have claws as big as a man's hand and can husk a coconut like you'd peel an orange. But the real enemy is heat. Temperatures in the shade exceed 100°F [38°C], and the noonday sun can literally fry an egg.

While 12 of us hacked through underbrush, four scuba divers scoured the shark-infested fringes of the reef. Nikumaroro is surrounded by a level table of hard coral that extends outward from the beach about 600 feet [183 m] before dropping almost vertically to the ocean floor 2000 feet [610 m] below. For two scorching weeks we hacked scaevola and combed beaches with metal detectors. But we found no trace of a flying machine. Suddenly it hit me: We were looking in the wrong places. Earhart would have landed on the reef flat, at low tide an ideal runway, and her plane must have washed off the reef into the abyss. To search those depths, we would need side-scan sonar. For now, we had to make do with the tools we had. After 21 days, we had found only a few interesting metal objects, including a cut-up aluminum box with a number stamped into it. But on a final sweep, three members of the expedition came upon a small grave in a remote jungle clearing. They snapped a photo and hurried back to the ship.

As Nikumaroro dropped astern, it was sobering to contemplate how little we had garnered for our quarter of a million dollars. Yet nothing that had happened—or hadn't happened—diminished the power of the evidence that had brought us to Nikumaroro. Convinced that the atoll held the key to the Earhart mystery, I resolved that TIGHAR would come back and find that key. I was unaware that a piece of it was already in our hands.

The aluminum box, like Aladdin's lamp, was full of surprises. The numbers stamped into it, 28F 4023, confirmed that it was an airplane part—a navigator's bookcase. The numbers also established that it had been designed for a Navy flying boat, the *Catalina*. But closer inspection produced an unexpected discovery: The holes drilled for screws that attached the box to the airplane were in the wrong places. This box was not suitable for mounting on a Catalina. Could it have been mounted on an Electra? The FBI's forensic experts studied the box and reported: "Nothing was found which would disqualify this artifact as having come from the Earhart aircraft." And at Purdue University, TIGHAR member Gary Quigg found a snapshot showing Earhart and Noonan standing beside the open door of the Electra just days before they vanished. Inside, under the navigator's chart table, was an object that looked like our bookcase. Was it the same box? No way to be sure.

Richard Evans, a former Coast Guardsman stationed on Nikumaroro during World War II, opened another promising line of inquiry. Evans said he had seen "a water collection device" on the island's northern shore in 1944. The Gilbertese told him they had not built it. Evans sketched a rectangular tank that bore a remarkable resemblance to the 149-gallon [676 L] fuel tanks shown in photographs of the Electra's cabin—photographs Evans had never seen. He also sketched a strip of heavy cloth mounted on poles and rigged to funnel rainwater into the tank below. The dimensions of the cloth match those of custom-made engine covers carried aboard Earhart's aircraft. Is this structure what Lieutenant Lambrecht meant by "signs of recent habitation"?

A grim new piece of the puzzle was provided by Floyd Kilts, another retired Coast Guardsman. In 1960 Kilts told the San Diego *Tribune* a story he had heard on Nikumaroro in 1946. The islanders reported that in 1938 newly arrived Gilbertese laborers had found "the skeleton of a woman and the skull of a man." Beside the woman's bones lay "a pair of American shoes, size nine narrow." Kilts's story was corroborated by a Tarawan resident named Bauro Tikana, who in 1939 clerked for Nikumaroro's British administrator. Tikana said natives had told him about bones found on "the other end of the island." And it was on "the other end of the island" that we had found a grave. Could this be the grave of Amelia Earhart?

We had to find out. We had to get back to Nikumaroro with the right equipment to excavate the grave and the right technology to explore the deep water around the island. That would require a bigger expedition and a much bigger budget. We decided to go ahead.

For the underwater search we hired Oceaneering International, the same company that found debris from the space shuttle *Challenger*. Oceaneering would provide side-scan sonar and a small robot submarine equipped with a video camera. To transport the expedition we leased the *Acania*, a 250-ton [225 t] research vessel. The operation would cost $483 000, most of it contributed by the general public. A week before D-Day we were $200 000 short. But at the last minute, friends of TIGHAR offered interest-free, unsecured loans that covered the shortfall.

On October 1, 1991, the *Acania* sailed from Honolulu with 10 TIGHAR members aboard—including seven who had taken part in the first expedition. Nine days later Nikumaroro surfaced on the horizon. From a distance the island seemed unchanged, but we got a shock when we went ashore. Fifty feet [15 m] of oceanfront jungle had been ripped out by giant waves and hurled inland.

Two days later a base camp had been established and search operations were underway in stunning heat. Kris Tague, John Clauss, Veryl Fenlason, LeRoy Knoll and Alan Olson swept the beach with metal detectors. At the grave site Dr. Tommy Love, Asya Usvitsky, Russell Matthews and I began a meticulous excavation. Aboard *Acania*, the Oceaneering team towed a sonar "fish" that scanned for wreckage.

On the eighth day, 53 cm down into the grave, we uncovered a box-shaped tangle of tiny roots about the size of an orange crate, apparently the remains of a coffin made of green wood that had sprouted. Hoping, dreading, we gathered around the grave. Using dental tools, I parted the tangle of roots and exposed a small brown bone. Then another, and another, I handed them carefully to Tommy, who inspected them under a field microscope.

"Finger? Toe?" I was wishing out loud.

"No. I'm afraid it's a tibia. These are the bones of a newborn baby."

We stood staring at the pathetic little bones as the irony of the moment sank in. We had traveled halfway around the world and spent half a million dollars—to dig up the remains of an unknown infant.

Finally I said, "We need to put this grave back the way we found it." So we carefully replaced the bones, reset the stone markers and brought fresh seashells to lay on the bare earth. Then Kris said, "Ric, I think it's important that we say something." I said what I felt. "We're sorry, little one, to disturb your rest. We've tucked you in as best we can. Sleep well."

By the middle of Day Eight, only two days before we would have to leave, we were all depressed. Despite costly preparations, the second expedition had proved even less successful than the first. All we had to hang onto was a curious find. Not far from the grave, Tommy had discovered the heel of an old shoe with the trademark: "Cat's Paw Rubber

Co., USA." A little later we retrieved the remains of what appeared to be a woman's size nine shoe sole, along with a small brass eyelet and another heel, unlabeled—perhaps the same pair of "American shoes, size nine narrow" that were spotted on the island back in 1938.

The next afternoon Pat made the discovery we had all been hoping for. In a welter of fallen palm fronds and coconuts lay a sheet of torn aluminum about two feet [61 cm] long and 18 inches [46 cm] wide. It was stitched with rows of rivet holes, and one rivet was still in place. From a corner of the sheet hung a tangled, 30-inch [76 cm] length of thin copper wire with some of its rubber insulation intact. This was clearly airplane wreckage. Had it lain hidden in the sand for years, perhaps since it was washed ashore from the wreck of the Electra, only to be churned up by the recent storm? There was reason to think so. The wire was so delicately linked to the aluminum that the connection could not have survived 10 seconds in an unruly sea. And what a wonderfully complex sheet of aluminum it was. Everything about it—the rivet, the wire, the faintly visible letters AD on its surface—told a story. We had to learn how to read that story.

Rousing our last energies, we tore that beach apart. Alan found what looked like the broken faceplate of an aircraft radio. And Veryl found a metal ring attached to a rusty four-inch steel pin. As the throb of the ship's engines announced our departure, we assembled the fruits of our labors: two dozen plastic bags, each containing an artifact. Mere debris— or aviation history's Holy Grail?

After four months of rigorous analysis, the contents of our plastic bags proved more eloquent than we had dared hope.

ARTIFACT 2-2-G-7 (Shoe Parts): The Cat's Paw heel and shoe sole were evaluated with the help of William F. Foshage, Jr. and Robert L. Oginz of the Cat's Paw division of the Biltrite Corporation in Waltham, Mass. They reported that these artifacts are the remains of the left shoe of a pair of women's 10-eyelet blucher-style Oxfords, about size nine. The heel is a Cat's Paw, replacement heel, somewhat worn. The style was made in the U.S. in the mid-1930s. Photos of Earhart in Lae confirm that this is a precise description of the shoes she was wearing when she disappeared. Footgear worn by British administrators of American servicemen was completely different, and the Gilbertese settlers always went barefoot. Conclusion: There is a high probability that Artifact 2-2-G-7 came from one of Earhart's shoes.

ARTIFACT 2-2-V-1 (Aluminum Sheet): The sheet was examined by Joseph Epperson, a metallurgist at the National Transportation Safety Board, and by Richard Horrigan, head of aircraft restoration at the Smithsonian's National Air and Space Museum. Photographs of the artifact were studied by Delbert Naser, an official at Alcoa, and by Herman Stevens, a retired Lockheed shop foreman. Using scanning electron microscopy, Epperson confirmed that the sheet is made of an alloy known as 24ST. Microscopic examination confirmed that the sheet was given a surface treatment called ALCLAD. Lockheed states that Earhart's aircraft was made of 24ST ALCLAD. The sheet is .032 inch [0.8 mm] thick and roughly 18 inches [46 cm] wide by 25 inches [64 cm] long. Since none of the edges is finished, the original sheet must have been larger. Skin #35R, which covered the area on the belly of an Electra where the rear antenna post was normally placed, is .032 inch [0.8 mm] thick and measures 38 inches [97 cm] wide by 72 inches [183 cm] long. Conclusion: Skin #35R and this sheet are compatible.

Alcoa's analysis of the last two letters of ALCLAD, which appear on the sheet, presented data that proved it was made before World War II. Identical labeling appears on an Electra built at the same time as Earhart's. Horrigan identified the rivet as type AN455 AD 3/3. Common in the mid-'30s, it was replaced by type AN470 during WWII. Lockheed specs call for AN455 AD 3/3 rivets on skin #35R of the Electra. The single-strand copper wire attached to the sheet has been identified as an antenna lead wire that was standard in the '30s but discontinued before WWII.

Stevens compared the sheet and Lockheed's repair orders. These repairs, he states, would have been carried out according to standards unfamiliar to modern mechanics, and the repaired belly would differ markedly from the belly of a standard Electra. It would, however, display a rivet pattern identical to the pattern on the sheet found on Nikumaroro. "It's the only way you could do it," Stevens says. Epperson also compared the repair order and the rivet pattern. His comment: "Looks like you've got it nailed."

Epperson further noted the singular manner in which the sheet ripped along a rivet line, then met resistance that caused the tear to jump sideways. Epperson says this indicates the presence of a reinforcing object on that line. Several photographs show clearly that the rear antenna mast on Earhart's Lockheed was mounted near the fuselage centerline in precisely the same position as the reinforcing object Epperson postulates.

When the analysis of the sheet was complete, every feature matched the Earhart aircraft. Might the same be said of some other aircraft? Most unlikely. The rivet, the labeling and the antenna wire all confirm that the aluminum sheet came from a prewar aircraft. But before World War II only three planes flew anywhere near Nikumaroro: Sir Charles Kingsford Smith's Fokker, now in a museum; a U.S. Navy Grumman Duck, which completed a 1939 mapping flight without incident; and Earhart's Electra.

What if an aircraft built before the war had been lost there during the war? No aircraft was ever reported lost near Nikumaroro. What if a prewar aircraft was lost during the war on another island, and pieces of it were brought to Nikumaroro? In all of World War II only four aircraft were known to be lost within 500 miles [800 km] of the island. None was built before the war.

Every possibility has been checked, every alternative eliminated. There is only one possible conclusion: We found a piece of Amelia Earhart's aircraft. There may be conflicting opinions, but there is no conflicting evidence. I submit that the case is solved.

Yet mystery remains. How long did Earhart and Noonan survive? Did they die of dehydration? Do their bones rest in the scaevola, picked clean by crabs? Somewhere on Nikumaroro—buried in its burning sands, hidden in its unforgiving jungle, lost among the sharks that shadow its shores—lies more wreckage, another shoe, and who knows what other silent witnesses to the last days of two brave people whose luck had run out. The story is there. The departure date for Expedition III is July 2, 1993.

An Opposing View

Richard Gillespie's bold claim that he has solved the Earhart mystery will not go unchallenged. If he is right, most other Earhart experts are wrong. Understandably disturbed, one expert, Elgen Long, asked a well-qualified aeronautical engineer to examine Gillespie's photographs and documents. Frank Schelling, head of the P-3 Aircraft Structures Branch at the U.S. Navy Aviation Depot in Alameda, Calif., said this:

Gillespie's case doesn't stand up. After studying the Lockheed repair orders and inspecting a photograph of the aluminum fragment found on Nikumaroro, I examined the belly and other surfaces of an Electra that was manufactured one year before Amelia Earhart's. During that year no structural changes were made. I saw no area of the aircraft where the fragment would fit. The fragment did not come from an Electra.

For one thing, the rivet patterns don't even come close to matching up. Rivets attach the fuselage skin to long structural members called stringers, which run the length of the fuselage. In the standard aircraft examined, these stringers are 3.5 inches [9 cm] apart in the area the fragment is supposed to have come from. But on the fragment, the rivet lines, corresponding to the location of stringers, are 4.25 inches [11 cm] apart. In addition, the rivets on the Lockheed 10 are spaced 1.5 inches [4 cm] apart; on the fragment the rivets are spaced one inch [2.5 cm] apart. The aluminum sheets on the belly of a Lockheed 10 are fastened to the keel by a double row of staggered rivets. But on the protruding flap, which would have extended across the keel, there is no trace of a second row.

Gillespie maintains that the rear antenna post was mounted where the flap protrudes. I disagree. An antenna post must be mounted on a flat surface, and the keel is V-shaped at that point.

One further point: Gillespie claims that when the aircraft was repaired by Lockheed, the stringer locations and the rivet spacing were changed. He believes that this accounts for the difference between the fragment and the structure of a standard Lockheed 10. Not so. If Lockheed's engineers had intended to change stringer locations and rivet spacing, they would have so specified in their work order. Lockheed would have repaired the aircraft as close as possible to its original configuration to maintain structural integrity.

Experts consulted by Gillespie disagree with this critique. Their observations appear in the text.

Young Woman's Blues

☆

Joyce Wieland

©Joyce Wieland 1993/VIS*ART Copyright Inc. Photo: Carlo Catenazzi,
Art Gallery of Ontario. From the University of Lethbridge Art Collections; purchase
1986 with funds provided by the Province of Alberta Endowment Fund.

Theme Questions

✿

✿ What is it that impels Icarus to fly too high, or Prometheus to steal fire from the gods? What makes certain risks worthwhile? In the modern world, what people or fictional characters would you consider to be Icarus or Prometheus figures?

✿ Risks sometimes raise moral dilemmas. How would you respond to the moral issues of life and death raised in two or more of the selections in "Risk"?

✿ Why are flight and fire often used as symbols related to wisdom, progress, risk, and danger? What other symbols might also be appropriate?

✿ By juxtaposing the familiar and the unfamiliar, writers and artists often intend to disturb our perceptions and change the way we understand ideas or see the world. How does juxtaposition work in the various selections in "Risk"?

Other Worlds:

Order Out of Chaos

Within the world we know lie many other worlds, waiting for us to explore them—an ancient and overgrown city hidden deep in a jungle, or the fossilized remains of strange, prehistoric creatures on a mountaintop in British Columbia. And as though the world we know were not enough, we speculate about worlds beyond, imagining them poised on the edge of our own.

Perhaps the most mysterious and profound other world is the one inside ourselves, and the voyages of discovery that we take as we explore it. Artists, scientists, and writers often take us on these voyages, creating works that tell us about human possibilities—about who we are, where we are going, and why we do what we do. In the process, we question our perceptions and assumptions.

Reflecting on other worlds allows us to make more sense of the one we know. And yet, as Einstein observed, even the physical order of our own universe is, in many ways, arbitrary and imagined—a convenient "fiction" designed to help us deal with what would otherwise seem to be chaos.

Tetrahedral Planetoid

☆

M.C. Escher

Physics and Reality

✡

Albert Einstein and Leopold Infeld

Science is not just a collection of laws, a catalogue of unrelated facts. It is a creation of the human mind, with its freely invented ideas and concepts. Physical theories try to form a picture of reality and to establish its connection with the wide world of sense impressions. Thus the only justification for our mental structures is whether and in what way our theories form such a link.

We have seen new realities created by the advance of physics. But this chain of creation can be traced back far beyond the starting point of physics. One of the most primitive concepts is that of an object. The concepts of a tree, a horse, any material body, are creations gained on the basis of experience, though the impressions from which they arise are primitive in comparison with the world of physical phenomena. A cat teasing a mouse also creates, by thought, its own primitive reality. The fact that the cat reacts in a similar way toward any mouse it meets shows that it forms concepts and theories which are its guide through its own world of sense impressions.

"Three trees" is something different from "two trees." Again "two trees" is different from "two stones." The concepts of the pure numbers 2, 3, 4..., freed from the objects from which they arose, are creations of the thinking mind which describe the reality of our world.

The psychological subjective feeling of time enables us to order our impressions, to state that one event precedes another. But to connect every instant of time with a number, by the use of a clock, to regard time as a one-dimensional continuum, is already an invention. So also are the concepts of Euclidean and non-Euclidean geometry, and our space understood as a three-dimensional continuum.

Physics really began with the invention of mass, force, and an inertial system. These concepts are all free inventions. They led to the formulation of the mechanical point of view. For the physicist of the early nineteenth century, the reality of our outer world consisted of particles with simple forces acting between them and depending only on the distance. He tried to retain as long as possible his belief that he would succeed in explaining all events in nature by these fundamental concepts of reality. The difficulties connected with the deflection of the magnetic needle, the difficulties connected with the structure of the ether, induced us to create a more subtle reality. The important invention of the electromagnetic field appears. A courageous scientific imagination was needed to realize fully that not the behavior of bodies, but the behavior of something between them, that is, the field, may be essential for ordering and understanding events.

Later developments both destroyed old concepts and created new ones. Absolute time and the inertial co-ordinate system were abandoned by the relativity theory. The background for all events was no longer the one-dimensional time and the three-dimensional space continuum, but the four-dimensional time-space continuum, another free invention, with new transformation properties. The inertial co-ordinate system was no longer needed. Every co-ordinate system is equally suited for the description of events in nature. . . .

The reality created by modern physics is, indeed, far removed from the reality of the early days. But the aim of every physical theory still remains the same.

With the help of physical theories we try to find our way through the maze of observed facts, to order and understand the world of our sense impressions. We want the observed facts to follow logically from our concept of reality. Without the belief that it is possible to grasp the reality with our theoretical constructions, without the belief in the inner harmony of our world, there could be no science. This belief is and always will remain the fundamental motive for all scientific creation. Throughout all our efforts, in every dramatic struggle between old and new views, we recognize the eternal longing for understanding, the ever-firm belief in the harmony of our world, continually strengthened by the increasing obstacles to comprehension.

Strange Bedfellows

✩

Jamie Findlay

It is a Saturday morning in midsummer, and a group of us have assembled at the foot of Mount Wapta, in B.C.'s Yoho National Park, for a guided day hike. We will go up Mount Wapta and then south along the backbone of the continent to a petrified sea. Formerly you could visit this place alone, but there were concerns about people taking things, and now the park authorities ask that you join one of the twice-weekly guided hikes. Today the group consists of a few weekend campers, their kids, a photographer and his wife, and me. It is a perfect morning, green and clear. By noon, keeping a steady pace, we will be back in the days when skeletons had only just entered the world. The palaeontologists up there will be able to show us around.

We wind our way up Mount Wapta, past tiny Yoho Lake, and move out onto the mountainside. The mountains are clear cut and enormous in the sunlight. If you could watch the land take its present shape, in a kind of reverse time-lapse photography, the most violent sculpting would occur before your eyes. Glaciers would move in and clobber the range, gouging out its current profile. After a while you would feel the continent drifting eastward under your feet, and the mountains would dwindle. Not long afterwards you would hear the waters coming in from the distance, and eventually the whole area would be under an ocean. With the ocean would come tiny monsters, most no longer than a few inches. All this would happen over a space of about 500-million years.

On the mountainside ahead those tiny monsters lie petrified, some as perfectly preserved as flies in amber. They are the fossils of the Burgess Shale.

Here I use the word "monster" in its taxonomic sense, to mean a creature forgotten by man and God. Some of the animals of the Burgess Shale have five eyes and long fleshy nozzles; some have the bodies of recumbent Gumbies with tentacles on top and spines below; some have the profiles of squids and the jaws of nutcrackers. Nowhere else in the world can you see so clearly the fantastic shifts and dodges of early evolution. Natural tombs like this—and they are rarer than dinosaur eggs—have a holy status in the eyes of earth scientists. The Harvard palaeontologist Stephen Jay Gould calls the Burgess creatures the most important animal fossils we know, not just because they tell us something about early life but because they tell us something about us. They have a large point to make. And we're still not sure if several are complete monsters, or just monster fragments.

The palaeontologists are waiting on the mountainside, standing beside their tents. They are very dusty. One of them, a student, explains that they stay up at the excavation site for about ten days, then go down to civilization for three days. "And what day are you on?" asks a woman in the group. "The tenth," he says, grinning, "so don't get too close." They have a tent for cooking, several for sleeping, and one for examining specimens. Their days are spent sifting through the scree above them, moving and splitting rock, looking for odd shapes in the fragments. It must be hard, tedious work, but there is always the possibility of finding some boneless horror intact, with its eyes staring and its tentacles upraised; and there are always the nights, with the stars as loud as lightning. I can think of worse summer jobs.

The palaeontologists are led by Desmond Collins of the Royal Ontario Museum in Toronto, who has been coming up to several sites in the area for the past fifteen years or so. He has some fossils for us to see. Some are nothing more than vague brush strokes in the rock, but some are beautifully articulated creatures, with legs and gills and membranes clearly discernible. Usually the earth preserves only hard animal parts like shells and bones, since tissues tend to decay after death; but through a geological accident the Shale preserves the soft parts as well—so beautifully, in fact, that in some specimens you can make out the remains of a meal in the animal's gut. All our great windows on the ancient past are smudged in some places, but the Burgess one is about as flawless as the earth can provide.

Through this window you can see many things. You can see shapes stalking and scavenging, burrowing and filtering, and shapes drifting like manta rays through the murky green water. You can see that mid-Cambrian life was not simple but extraordinarily variegated, both in its range of anatomies and in its strategies for living. And, says Gould, if you consider the streams that flowed from this great pool of life, you can see that there was nothing inevitable or even likely about our rise. One of the messages of his 1989 book, *Wonderful Life: The Burgess Shale and the Nature of History*, is that Homo sapiens is a "wildly improbable evolution-ary event," a spark in the night. "Wind back the tape of life to the early days of the Burgess Shale," he writes, "let it play again from an identical starting point, and the chance becomes vanishingly small that anything like human intelligence would grace the replay."

Now, Gould often finds large lessons in small things—the panda's thumb, the horse's toes, the flamingo's smile—but you may well wonder if he's reading too much into these tiny scribbles in the rock. The Burgess animals are over 500 million years old and as alien as anything on earth. What can they possibly tell us about our emergence?

Up close, not much. But stand back and look at them from our late vantage point on the curve of life, and you will see some of the immense country that lies between them and us. The Burgess animals are as distant, in aeons, as the Crab Nebula, and so well preserved that they light a long way beyond their particular parish of space and time. By them you can make out the shape of early evolution, and a bit of what came later. You can't see much in the way of particulars, but it's the perspective that counts. You get a sense of how long the road has been, how many possibilities lie behind us. And that makes it a lot easier to imagine the world empty of Homo sapiens.

The old joke in palaeontology, Gould tells us, describes mammalian evolution as a tale of teeth mating to produce slightly altered descendent teeth. Bones, shells, teeth—this is all palaeontologists have to go on, and it's not much. If you were to follow back the vertebrate line through the aeons, using only the fossil record as your guide, you would be walking through a lot of empty landscapes. Primates would take to the trees, and then come down as something like large hedgehogs, but you wouldn't see it happen. The dinosaurs would move around on the horizon briefly—their bones are large and relatively numerous—but after this you would slowly enter twilight. The living world would slide out of focus. Shapes would skitter by in the jungles, and dimple the surfaces of pools, but the details of their forms would lie under shadow. As you walked back you would feel the continents drifting together and melding, and off in the darkness life would return to the seas. The moon would grow larger, the days shorter. After you entered the Cambrian period the darkness would be almost complete.

Then you would come to the Burgess Shale, where the seas of the past would be lit up like a public aquarium.

Before you would be a marine reef as it was about 530 million years ago. You would see tiny flecks of flesh with multiple eyes, worms with tentacles and bristles, a caterpillar-like thing crawling about on sponges, something large that swam like a manta ray but was not a manta ray. You might see round armoured animals called trilobites, among the commonest fossils from the Cambrian. (Bones have not yet made their appearance, but a number of animals here have the first kinds of skeletons—shells and "spiny skins" such as those of present-day sea urchins.) You might see a spiked, plated walnut shell crawling across the sea bottom, its plates arranged like shingles on a roof, and a creature that looked like a combination of a water strider and a crab.

If any era might be considered the cradle of life, this is it. Nothing in the rocks before the time of the Burgess Shale matches the wild efflorescence that marked the mid-Cambrian. Not only is the Shale a relatively clean window, but it looks out on a particularly riotous and uninhibited time in evolution.

Needless to say, this world is not only empty of human beings but empty of anything that even hints at human beings. There are no whales, no seals, no dolphins, no sea turtles or snakes, no sharks. Those categories—mammals, jawed fishes, reptiles—have not yet come into existence. Biologists classify animals according to certain attributes, or combinations of attributes, that have persisted as exemplars for a long time. But at this period life is still young, and the biological moulds have not yet been cast. Nature is still trying out various effects. As a result many of the creatures look like hodgepodges. . . . [The] first great lesson of the Burgess Shale [is that] there are not just a few animal designs here, a few bizarre variations on a single invertebrate theme. In this small quarry in B.C., says Gould, there is "a range of disparity in anatomical design never again equalled and not matched today by all the creatures in all the world's oceans." Our world certainly has more species, but back then, according to Gould, there were more body plans—more basic templates. Cambrian life was indeed a wonderful life.

Another palaeontologist might argue with Gould about the extent of disparity in anatomical design, and how to gauge that disparity, but his general point seems sound enough. A lot of different anatomies were floating around then. We tend to think of evolution as a tree, its roots few and small, its foliage rich and varied. But the Shale suggests that evolution resembles, in some ways, an inverted tree. The first great pulse of life, as caught by the Burgess Shale, contains a large spectrum of anatomies—a spectrum that was gradually pruned over time.

(Normally these soft-bodied novelties would decay quickly after their death, but this particular Cambrian cranny is unique. The reef slopes down into stagnant waters that are almost devoid of oxygen and scavenger. The reef-dwellers will be periodically swept down into the abyss by small avalanches of sediment, and there they will come to rest in a perfect natural tomb. With no oxygen or scavengers, little decay will take place. Silt will penetrate into the spaces between every gill and bristle, and the preserved animals will eventually be pressed almost flat by the weight of the sediment. Seas will rise and fall, the surface of the earth will buckle and roil, and in half a billion years palaeontologists will be walking around here asking each other if this thing with the eyes could possibly be an arthropod.)

So why did so many of these wonderful Cambrian experiments die out? Were they maladaptive, or too weird for their own good? Gould doesn't think so. When we look at the Burgess creatures, he says, there is in most cases no way we can choose the winners and losers on the basis of their adaptations. The lace crab was elegant and streamlined; yet it turned out to be an evolutionary dead end. The caterpillar-like thing crawling about on the sponge, *Aysheaia*, doesn't seem to have anything particular to set it apart from the other worm-like creatures there; yet it was the probable ancestor of today's insects—one of the great success stories of evolution.

From this Gould concludes that a large element of luck entered into the survival of the Burgess Shale animals. Many of the creatures that triumphed were not necessarily marked for success; they simply won the lottery. . . .

If all this is true, then it follows that the stream of evolution that flowed from the time of the Burgess Shale is one remote possibility out of many. If modern life had arisen from a few simple forms that differed little, any replay would have gone essentially the way of the original. The stream would have followed the same basic course. But if life got its initial push from a large diverse group of models, and arose from a few of those models largely by the luck of the draw, then a replay could easily have gone a different way. This is why the Burgess Shale is of more than local interest. It represents one of the first great springs of evolution, and (remotely) of us.

Gould certainly looks at it that way. In the epilogue to his book he describes *Pikaia*, a small ribbon-like creature that resembles a worm and was classified as such by Walcott. It is not a worm, however, for worms are invertebrates. *Pikaia* has a notochord, a rod running along its back. It is the first known member of our own phylum, *Chordata*, and may be considered (at least for Gould's rhetorical purposes) our ancestor. "Wind the tape of life back to Burgess times, and let it play again," says Gould on the last page of his book. "If *Pikaia* does not survive in the replay, we are wiped out of future history—all of us, from shark to robin to orangutan. And I don't think that any handicapper, given Burgess evidence as known today, would have granted very favourable odds for the persistence of *Pikaia*.

Maybe not. It certainly doesn't look like much, lying there eyeless in the Cambrian mud. But surely the emergence of a thinking being doesn't hang on the survival of this one tiny creature. It may be that *whatever* soft-bodied streams had flowed from Cambrian times, they would have settled into the familiar grooves. Bones could have appeared later, out of any number of stocks. Maybe spines would have blossomed once more into brains. In other words, evolution might have swung around to us— or something like us—even if it had started out on a slightly different tack. No-one can argue that human beings are a fluke solely on the basis of what happened in the Cambrian.

Gould recognizes this, of course. That is why, in the last part of his book, he surveys the rest of evolution in an attempt to show that we came about at the end of a toppling-domino chain of fortuitous events, and that the whole story could have turned out differently. Consciousness would not be here, he argues, if it hadn't been for a long run of happenstance. This is where things get murky. For, if you retrace your steps from the Burgess Shale, you will find that the what-ifs are even harder to follow than the lineages.

Moving forward from the mid-Cambrian at a million years a step, you soon come to the Permian period, which began about 290-million years ago. It was an active era, geologically speaking. The Appalachian mountains were rising in North America, the Urals in Russia. Your accelerated passage through time lets you see inland oceans evaporate as if vacuumed up, leaving large deposits of salt and potash. The plains and swamps are alive with scorpions, land snails, cockroaches, and reptiles that (in the words of one scientist) look like "long alligator-covered coffee tables." Things are moving nicely towards whole new orders of monsters.

But something catastrophic happened to the living world at the end of the Permian. You don't catch much of this as you pass by—just a vague shuddering of the earth—but the age directly afterwards is unusually still. The writhings and scuttlings have diminished. The ocean shallows are virtually empty. Palaeontologists have estimated that during the late Permian, about eighty per cent of reptile species and seventy-five per cent of amphibian species died out. Trilobites disappeared, and with them, perhaps, some of the other Burgess eccentrics. There have been at least five mass extinctions in the history of the earth, but none matches the devastation of the Permian one.

Whatever caused the Permian catastrophe—and a meteorite impact is a possibility—it sure looks like one brute accident. Some creatures that had been flourishing in the quiet days of the Permian must have been perfunctorily wiped out. The adaptations that had served them well would have been useless in the drastically altered world. The cockroaches survived because cockroaches *always* survive, but a lot of other creatures may well have gotten by simply because they happened to be in the right place at the right time—on land rather than water, say. If any episode contains an element of survival by lottery, it is this kind of debacle.

There is thus a certain chanciness to evolution. Lineages take shape according to the nudges and presses of the environment. Sometimes those jostlings are relatively gentle, and the responses are predictable. But during the great extinctions, the jostlings are of such magnitude that only God can be sure of what will bounce back. Over time this lends a fortuitous character to the drift of life. Things could have turned out differently.

But the question is: how differently?

You can't see a great deal in the way of lineages, walking through these fossil landscapes, but you can see big trends. One trend is increasing complexity. If you forget about things like bacteria, you could make a case that over the aeons there has been a general movement toward more molecules, more organization, and (at least among certain animal streams) an improved ability to process information. All this suggests that maybe intelligence—some kind of intelligence—was probable from the start. After all, it is the last word in the ability to process information. Might not evolution have just wended its way naturally towards a thinking being?

Ahead looms a juncture that is particularly important in this respect. It is the death of the dinosaurs. Again, something catastrophic probably happened here, for many other organisms became extinct along with the dinosaurs. Gould is particularly interested in this episode, for he believes it was crucial to our own emergence. If the dinosaurs had not died out, he argues, mammals would not have been able to find a niche. And that would have snuffed out any prospect for mind. "Since dinosaurs were not moving toward markedly larger brains," he writes, "and since such a prospect may lie outside the capabilities of reptilian design...we must assume that consciousness would not have evolved on our planet if a cosmic catastrophe had not claimed the dinosaurs as victims."

Here in the late Cretaceous period is an opportunity (so you think) to test this assumption. Small svelte dinosaurs are scuttling by on their hind legs, dinosaurs that seem to have eyes in the front of their heads and the beginnings of opposable thumbs. They look promising. Could they have evolved into some kind of self-conscious intelligence if they had not become extinct? Who knows? The fossil record has nothing to tell us about alternative histories. It barely has anything to tell us about *actual* histories. All you can say is that these creatures disappeared relatively quickly—and you are still not sure of the reason even as you stride into the age of mammals.

Nobody knows what would have happened if the dinosaurs had not become extinct. Nobody knows if some sort of mind could have arisen in a different stream from the mammalian one. What we do know is that 10 000 things went into the making of a *human* intelligence, and this suggests that its particular character is somewhat rare. The recipe for a remembering, language-using, technology-haunted, self-conscious creature seems to involve a fairly precise chunk of history. The chances of that history repeating itself, in this or another world, are pretty small.

As you walk forward into the recent geological past you can see some of the elements that went into the making of humans. You see a four-foot missing link scampering upright near a forest. You see *Homo habilis* fashioning tools on the African savanna. After a while you start to hear language—real language, not just gibbering and gruntings. You watch the emergence of an increasingly complex social life. From the change in human physiognomy you get a sense of the anatomical alterations that went hand in hand with these developments, including the increase in brain size and the lateralization of functions. You see imagery flowering in the form of cave paintings and religious rituals. Finally you make your way down the spine of the Rockies to the Burgess quarry, where the palaeontologists—in their modern hominid form—are sipping tea in their lawn chairs. It has taken you barely a few minutes to go from the earliest primate to these most recent ones.

Now you know a bit of the story behind this story. *Homo* sapiens is an evolutionary parcel. Its skeleton, brain, and social life evolved together. Without this history, this run of circumstances, its intelligence would not have appeared in the form that it did. Whether it would have appeared at all is anyone's guess.

Gould is right in at least one respect: you can see a lot from the Burgess quarry. Few other geological eyries give you such a strong sense of the variety, the range of possibilities, out of which we took our rise. Normally we forget all about this. We look back and see a line from the most primitive vertebrates to us, and if we squint in a certain way, that line seems to assume a certain ineluctability. History rolls back to make way for our tribe. But there were alternative routes back there, at almost every juncture. There were various soft-bodied forms, and various nervous systems, and various packages of brain and bone, that might have triumphed in more favourable settings. What emerged was the cumulative work of circumstance. One thing led to another, and that to another, and so on down the ages; and the end product in all its permutations was unlikely from the start. In this sense, we are improbable creatures—

improbable as falcons or newts or any other complex animal that took shape over the aeons. In saying this I am only summarizing the observations of many eminent biologists.

It is hard to say whether we as thinking beings are a *complete* fluke, however. Granted, if you wound back the tape of life and let it run again, you wouldn't get Homo sapiens. You might not get falcons either. But you might very well get something with wings, and you might well get something vaguely like us, something intelligent.

It's not the sort of question you can answer on the basis of rocks. All you can say is that we are a cosmic rarity for the good reason that a certain stretch of history went into our making. Since that history is bound to be different on another planet, intelligent extraterrestrials—if they exist— are going to look mighty different from humans. We might not even recognize them as intelligent. They might have some reservations about us. But in both cases, we will be able to trace the peculiarities of our forms and intellects back a long way, through the vicissitudes and fortunes of our respective planets.

On the basis of all this, you can call yourself unique if you want. There is certainly nothing else around you with your particular form, your brain, the precise cut of your skeleton. But there is also nothing else around with the leg-iron jaws of those luminous deep-sea fishes, and nothing else around that literally pulls itself apart like the sea star, and nothing else around that looks quite so much like seaweed as the sea dragon. These monsters, like the Burgess ones, draw our eyes to the periphery of the world, the way shooting stars do. Even a glimpse of one is enough to leave us with an enlarged sense of space.

Klara and Lilo

☆

Miriam Waddington

What wind, you have to ask, had blown them to the Rancho Rio Cantara, these two freckled, brightly coloured old birds with their big busts and stomachs, dyed hair, and German accents? For that matter, what wind had blown me to the Rancho that winter? There must be hundreds of spas in Mexico, so why did I decide to spend my midwinter break at this one and no other? Especially as it's so hard to get to from Toronto. You have to fly to Dallas, change for Guadalajara, and then take a taxi that bumps you over twenty-five miles of cobblestone road into a national park famous for its high altitude and healing hot springs.

The Rancho took only fifty guests. Most of them were Yoga devotees, psychics, and spiritual healers with a few retired couples thrown in who came to bathe in the mineral springs. It was a little like a kibbutz in that we all had our own adobe huts, each with its own fireplace, yet we ate communally at long wooden tables in the dining room. Conversation at meal times, although not elevating, was at least not about the body, its health or diet, but mostly about new ways to get in touch with your unconscious. To this end the Rio Cantara offered Felsenkreis, Alexander method, Yoga and Acupuncture, and there were guests who would cast your horoscope, read your palm, or tell your fortune from the vibrations of your aura. There was also a weathered little woman from Seattle who played the guitar and sang old cowboy numbers like "I'm Sending you a Big Bouquet of Roses" and "Her Name was Lil and She was a Beauty and Lived in a House of Ill Repute-y"—songs I hadn't heard since my college days.

One Friday morning after Yoga class I was settling down to read in one of the lounge chairs around the pool. I had just opened Anita Brookner's *Providence* when one of the freckled ladies who had arrived the day before sat down beside me. She wanted to talk. At first I wasn't too happy about it; I remembered the arrival of the two sisters—for such they turned out to be—and how they had looked like a couple of beat-up parrots with half their feathers missing and the other bedraggled half sticking out every which way under garish red and yellow sun-hats. The one now at my side was still wearing the sun-hat and a dressmaker bathing-suit from the nineteen-thirties. But her face, under her dyed red hair, was composed and all her feathers were back in place.

I resigned myself to not reading, shut my book, and listened. Klara had a low voice with gravel caught in its timbre, which emphasized her heavy Viennese accent. To this day I don't know why she chose me to sit beside, except that I look Jewish, but after that day Klara always sought me out at the poolside. Her sister Lilo was a swimmer, and spent most mornings doing lengths. Sometimes she stopped and chatted with us for a few minutes, but mostly she was in the pool.

Even now, four years later, when I close my eyes I see the pool and the steamy vapours rising from the river that flows through the ranch. And I hear the blur of murmuring sound from which Klara's voice always emerges with slow vibrancy and careful succinctness. She is talking, always talking. About what? First it's the past. Given the place and time they lived in, it's a life like other Jewish lives—in no way remarkable. In the thirties they were Jews living in Vienna, yes, but who thought about it? "We weren't always old and dumpy like now," Klara smiles out of her very clear, very large green eyes. They're shallow as a wading pool with an opaque skin of calmness that doesn't let you really look into them.

Klara talks. Lilo is a book-keeper—"You should have seen her. So pretty, fair, with rosy cheeks and best of all she's afraid of no one." She, Klara, the older sister, is a children's doctor. "It wasn't easy even before the war, no, not even then. But when has it ever been easy?" But she persists and in 1938 she is working in a children's clinic in one of Vienna's poor sections. She laughs. "I was an idealist. Not practical like Lilo, who when she reads in the paper that Jews aren't allowed to sit on park benches with Austrians, wastes no time, lines up outside the British Consulate and gets a visa to emigrate to England. As a maid. Some maid! A Jewish girl who can't even boil water, her head is so full of numbers. Only numbers interest her. It's still the same."

But in those days everyone was working in factories in England, even the maids. Only immigrants were left to work in the rich houses— mostly German girls. Where was it she worked? Somewhere in the north, in a castle where everybody freezes and they don't give a maid enough to eat. "And Lilo is writing me come, begging me, 'Come, don't wait.' But I don't want to leave. Just think, there are so many little children! I love my work and they are still keeping me in the clinic. My director is not so bad, not all the Austrians hate Jews. Things will get better, it has to be.

"But Lilo pesters me. She runs everywhere, to all the offices, she sends me papers. They come and three days later there is war, and I am a maid with Lilo in the same castle. We keep each other warm at night, we sleep in sweaters, I knit socks. Thursday is our day off and all us maids go to the village, we meet in a café, we have tea. The English—you know how tea is their life."

And the rest of the story? Again ordinary. I've heard it all, read it all before, I don't know why I'm listening except that Klara makes it interesting. Maybe it's her voice, or the sun, or this out-of-the-way place. I hear how neither Klara nor Lilo marry, there's just no time. Lilo is busy going to night school, learning English. Soon she has a job, but Klara isn't so lucky. She has no talent for the language. "Your verb to be—am, were, was, be, be—all those bees." She can never learn it. And how can you be a doctor for children without English? Besides, she has no money. The best she can do is work as a technical assistant in a children's clinic in Leeds. "About Leeds what can I say? The people, they're good, they're kind, they're nice, but after Vienna, who can live in Leeds?"

When the war is over the sisters get a letter from an uncle in Montreal. They write back and forth and the upshot is, he brings them over. "You needed a sponsor and all kinds of papers, not like today." But at least they're together. She and Lilo get an apartment on Van Horne near Victoria, in those days a nice Jewish district if you know Montreal. Lilo has no trouble—right away she starts to work for an accountant. But Klara is miserable. For her to learn English is like climbing the Alps. And friends in Vienna, those who are left, begin to write and urge her to come back. They need doctors in Vienna, even her old clinic that was bombed has been rebuilt.

But she hesitates. She feels ashamed that she wants to go back after what they did to the Jews, and she doesn't want to leave Lilo. But what kind of life can she have in Montreal? She misses her work. Children don't have prejudices, they don't know from anti-Semitism. When she decides to go back—in 1951, to be exact—Lilo agrees just so long as they can meet twice a year for three weeks in winter and again in summer.

Klara stops talking. I open my eyes and she smiles at me. I smile back. One thing I notice. Although Klara talks freely and enjoys it, she always becomes vague when I ask her the details about how she got back to Vienna. And I don't probe—I've met enough refugees to know that you don't ask. You listen.

She does say something that stays in my mind. "You know, to survive is not always the most important thing, I didn't want to live my life only or mostly as a survivor, to have the idea to save my life always uppermost. What kind of a life could I have in Leeds, in Montreal? I was an outsider, I didn't fit in, I was not at home. What is a person without a life's work, if there is no purpose except to stay alive? I wanted to breathe the air I grew up in, no matter how everything changed. I knew that the earth, the air, the forests of my childhood would always be the same, would always know my footsteps when I returned.

"And I wanted to feel useful, to heal children, to talk to their mothers in the only language I knew. I said to myself, 'Klara, there are more important things than survival. To survive and live half-dead is no kind of life.'" She sighs and ends with one of those remarks older people like to make to younger ones. "Yes, in life you pay for everything."

Then these serious matters are lost, in a welter of appealing trivialities. Such as the matter of Klara's man-friend. He's a bachelor. Like herself, he never married. They have dinner together every day except for the six weeks she spends with Lilo. How long have they been together? Without blinking an eyelash she tells me: "Thirty-three years." It works very well—they each have their own apartment, their own bank account, their own tastes. Of course he misses her while she's with Lilo, but she needs that time, not only because of Lilo, but to refresh herself. For example, up to this year she and Lilo have always gone to the Canaries in winter. Klara gives me a precise description of the wonderful little hotel they patronize there. I take out my notebook and write down the name of the hotel and the proprietor and all the details. She is even more enthusiastic about their summer getaway in the mountains, and her eyes light up as she tells me about Merano in the Italian Dolomites. I've never heard of it, but I listen to a description of the Hotel Peterhof, its location, the names of the proprietors, and the way they had it decorated with everything handmade, handcarved, and handwoven. I can see the fresh white linen curtains with their embroidered borders, the breakfast room with its blue earthenware cups, the lime tree outside the back windows, and the road that runs in front of the hotel separating it from a spring-fed mountain lake. I had never known anyone who had been to the Dolomites, but there and then I made up my mind to spend my next European holiday near Merano at Klara's Hotel Peterhof.

So the week passed. We did Yoga every morning and joined the group hike to explore the surrounding country. Afterwards people bathed naked in the walled pool set aside for that purpose, or sat under umbrellas by the main pool. In the afternoons some guests went for a walk. The next village was two kilometres away over rough cobblestones—fine if you had good shoes with thick soles, but there was an easier walk if you followed the river that ran through the Rancho for about half a mile to a waterfall.

One afternoon Klara and I decide to walk there. The path is sandy and narrow and we have to walk single file. The sand is so fine and white that it's hard to plough through it with our shoes on. So we take them off and walk barefoot, scuffing our feet through the warm sand.

The walk takes longer than we think and the landscape doesn't appeal to my Canadian eyes. It's all stunted and gnarled trees, craggy rocks, and wide-hipped hills that sprawl sloppily against a woundingly hot sky. The sun beats down on us, so we're glad when we reach the waterfall. We leave our shoes on the bank, take off our T-shirts, and pick our way carefully over a series of flat rocks to where the water slips over the ledge and cascades down in a shower. We sit and let the water splash over us, enjoying its warmth and telling each other how healthy it is, with our skins absorbing all those good minerals. We talk about the winter we're missing, with its dark nights and rain. It is utterly quiet except for an occasional bird and the sound of water, which soothes us until we're almost nodding. But we don't let ourselves fall asleep; instead we get up and climb up the bank to the opposite side so we can take a different way home. Klara needs a hand to get up the bank—she's seventy, after all—and we start back. Our feet are still wet and the sand on this side of the river is damp too. This is the shady side. Klara walks ahead of me. My feet are big and make deep marks in the sand. I see with satisfaction that at least my feet aren't flat; the arch doesn't sink into the sand but forms a crescent in each footprint.

I glance ahead to see how Klara's feet are doing. I read somewhere that old people's feet are nearly always flat and I want to know if that's true. I see Klara walking a few yards ahead, but realize with a start that she isn't leaving any footprints in the sand. None at all! At first I'm puzzled. Then I'm sort of scared. How can it be? I can't really let myself believe it. Should I say something? Should I ask her? No, it's better to just keep walking, pretend I haven't noticed.

I try to rationalize. I tell myself maybe it's because she's so small. Small yes, but not exactly light; and certainly not light enough. Maybe there are no footprints because the sand is dry up ahead where she's walking. When I get there I see it isn't dry; it's the same sand that sucks at my feet and makes me sink heavily into it.

I begin to wonder if there isn't something odd about Klara. I don't believe in all that psychic stuff about auras and reincarnation that's floating around at the spa. At the same time Klara's clothes are terribly old-fashioned. And what about her hair? Dyes are a lot better these days than what Klara's using. And Klara did something few other Jews have done. She went back to Vienna and turned her back on America. She said some odd things too. "To survive is not all-important"—that isn't a Jewish thought. She also said it's better to be dead than half dead. A lot of Jews would find that idea disloyal, as if she were dismissing everything that survivors lived through and suffered. And to go back to Vienna? It's all very well to lose yourself in work, to find a purpose in life through your work, but who do you talk to at night, after work? Who do you go to the movies with, or how exchange recipes? Of course I know the answer to that—Klara has a man friend. I wonder if he knows she doesn't leave footprints? And if he knows, does he care? I'm not even sure that I care. I just can't help wondering.

When it comes time for the sisters to leave, Klara gives me her address. "You must come to visit me next time you're in Europe," she urges. "Come to Vienna and stay with me. I have an extra room for when Lilo comes." And she carefully writes out her address and phone number. I give her my Toronto address too—I would enjoy seeing her again. I like her exactness, her precision, the pragmatism, the lack of sadness.

I tell her not to expect me in Vienna, but I promise to go to Merano, to the Hotel Peterhof. We say all these things as Klara and Lilo are getting into the taxi. They are wearing their red and yellow sun-hats, and as the taxi lurches out of the Rancho they open the window and wave.

A year later I went to Merano and looked for the Hotel Peterhof at the address Klara had given me. There was no Hotel Peterhof. There had been one long ago before the war, but it had been used by German soldiers during the occupation and on its site now stood a row of high-rise condominiums.

As for Klara and Lilo themselves: I wrote to Dr Klara in Vienna but my letter was returned. When I made further inquiries I learned that she had never left Austria, had never joined Lilo, but died in a concentration camp in 1942. As for Lilo, her apartment house in Montreal was real enough, but she was no longer there. Neighbours told me that she had drowned years ago in a lake in the Laurentians where she had a cottage.

I still think about Klara walking ahead of me in the sand, leaving no footprints. I can't seem to get her out of my mind, and when I close my eyes she's always there: "Look, we were not always so old and dumpy," and "Lilo had such rosy cheeks and was afraid of no one," and "To survive is not always the only thing or the best thing." I keep telling myself that the wind that blew those two into the Rancho Rio Cantara that day in February must be the same wind that has now spirited them away, complete with sun-hats and flowered dresses, to a place where Klara heals little children in a clinic that never closes, while Lilo, the champion swimmer, swims endless lengths in a sunlit pool where the summer never ends.

Hands

☆

Oliver Sacks

Madeleine J. was admitted to St. Benedict's Hospital near New York City in 1980, her sixtieth year, a congenitally blind woman with cerebral palsy, who has been looked after by her family at home throughout her life. Given this history, and her pathetic condition—with spasticity and athetosis, i.e., involuntary movements of both hands, to which was added a failure of the eyes to develop—I expected to find her both retarded and regressed.

She was neither. Quite the contrary: she spoke freely, indeed eloquently (her speech, mercifully, was scarcely affected by spasticity), revealing herself to be a high-spirited woman of exceptional intelligence and literacy.

"You've read a tremendous amount," I said. "You must be really at home with Braille."

"No, I'm not," she said. "All my reading has been done for me—by talking-books or other people. I can't read Braille, not a single word. I can't do *anything* with my hands—they are completely useless."

She held them up, derisively. "Useless godforsaken lumps of dough—they don't even feel part of me."

I found this very startling. The hands are not usually affected by cerebral palsy—at least, not essentially affected: they may be somewhat spastic, or weak, or deformed, but are generally of considerable use (unlike the legs, which may be completely paralysed—in that variant called Little's disease, or cerebral diplegia).

Miss J.'s hands were *mildly* spastic and athetotic, but her sensory capacities—as I now rapidly determined—were completely intact: she immediately and correctly identified light touch, pain, temperature, passive movement of the fingers. There was no impairment of elementary sensation, as such, but, in dramatic contrast, there was the profoundest impairment of perception. She could not recognise or identify anything whatever—I placed all sorts of objects in her hands, including one of my own hands. She could not identify—and she did not explore; there were no active "interrogatory" movements of her hands—they were, indeed, as inactive, as inert, as useless, as "lumps of dough."

This is very strange, I said to myself. How can one make sense of all this? There is no gross sensory "deficit." Her hands would seem to have the potential of being perfectly good hands—and yet they are not. Can it be that they are functionless—"useless"—because she had never used them? Had being "protected," "looked after," "babied" since birth prevented her from the normal exploratory use of the hands which all infants learn in the first months of life? Had she been carried about, had everything done for her, in a manner that had prevented her from developing a normal pair of hands? And if this were the case—it seemed far-fetched, but was the only hypothesis I could think of—could she now, in her sixtieth year, acquire what she should have acquired in the first weeks and months of life?

Was there any precedent? Had anything like this ever been described—or tried? I did not know, but I immediately thought of a possible parallel—what was described by Leont'ev and Zaporozhets in their book *Rehabilitation of Hand Function*. . . . The condition they were describing was quite different in origin: they described a similar "alienation" of the hands in some two hundred soldiers following massive injury and surgery—the injured hands felt "foreign," "lifeless," "useless," "stuck on," despite elementary neurological and sensory intactness. Leont'ev and Zaporozhets spoke of how the "gnostic systems" that allow "gnosis," or perceptive use of the hands, to take place, could be "dissociated" in such cases as a consequence of injury, surgery and the weeks- or months-long hiatus in the use of the hands that followed. In Madeleine's case, although the phenomenon was identical—"uselessness," "lifelessness," "alienation"—it was lifelong. She did not need just to recover her hands, but to discover them—to acquire them, to achieve them—for the first time: not just to regain a dissociated gnostic system, but to construct a gnostic system she had never had in the first place. Was this possible?

The injured soldiers described by Leont'ev and Zaporozhets had normal hands before injury. All they had to do was to "remember" what had been "forgotten," or "dissociated," or "inactivated," through severe injury. Madeleine, in contrast, had no repertoire of memory for she had never used her hands—and she felt she *had* no hands—or arms either. She had never felt herself, used the toilet herself, or reached out to help herself, always leaving it for others to help her. She had behaved, for sixty years, as if she were a being without hands.

This then was the challenge that faced us: a patient with perfect elementary sensations in the hands, but, apparently, no power to integrate these sensations to the level of perceptions that were related to the world and to herself; no power to say, "I perceive, I recognise, I will, I act," so far as her "useless" hands went. But somehow or other (as Leont'ev and Zaporozhets found with their patients), we had to get her to act and to use her hands actively, and, we hoped, in so doing, to achieve integration: "The integration is in the action," as Roy Campbell said.

Madeleine was agreeable to all this, indeed fascinated, but puzzled and not hopeful. "How *can* I do anything with my hands," she asked, "when they are just lumps of putty?"

"In the beginning is the deed," Goethe writes. This may be so when we face moral or existential dilemmas, but not where movement and perception have their origin. Yet here too there is always something sudden: a first step (or a first word, as when Helen Keller said "water"), a first movement, a first perception, a first impulse—total, "out of the blue," where there was nothing, or nothing with sense before. "In the beginning is the impulse." Not a deed, not a reflex, but an "impulse," which is both more obvious and more mysterious than either...We could not say to Madeleine "Do it!" but we might hope for an impulse; we might hope for, we might solicit, we might even provoke one...

I thought of the infant as it reached for the breast. "Leave Madeleine her food, as if by accident, slightly out of reach on occasion," I suggested to her nurses. "Don't starve her, don't tease her, but show less than your usual alacrity in feeding her." And one day it happened—what had never happened before: impatient, hungry, instead of waiting passively and patiently, she reached out an arm, groped, found a bagel, and took it to her mouth. This was the first use of her hands, her first manual act, in sixty years, and it marked her birth as a "motor individual" (Sherrington's term for the person who emerges through acts). It also marked her first manual perception, and thus her birth as a complete "perceptual individual." Her first perception, her first recognition, was of a bagel, or "bagelhood"—as Helen Keller's first recognition, first utterance, was of water ("waterhood").

After this first act, this first perception, progress was extremely rapid. As she had reached out to explore or touch a bagel, so now, in her new hunger, she reached out to explore or touch the whole world. Eating led the way—the feeling, the exploring, of different foods, containers, implements, etc. "Recognition" had somehow to be achieved by a curiously roundabout sort of inference or guesswork, for having been both blind and "handless" since birth, she was lacking in the simplest internal images (whereas Helen Keller at least had tactile images). Had she not been of exceptional intelligence and literacy, with an imagination filled and sustained, so to speak, by the images of others, images conveyed by language, by the *word*, she might have remained almost as helpless as a baby.

A bagel was recognized as round bread, with a hole in it; a fork as an elongated flat object with several sharp lines. But then this preliminary analysis gave way to an immediate intuition, and objects were instantly recognised as themselves, as immediately familiar in character and "physiognomy," were immediately recognised as unique, as "old friends." And this sort of recognition, not analytic, but synthetic and immediate, went with a vivid delight, and a sense that she was discovering a world full of enchantment, mystery, and beauty.

The commonest objects delighted her—delighted her and stimulated a desire to reproduce them. She asked for clay and started to make models, her first model, her first sculpture, was of a shoehorn, and even this, somehow imbued with a peculiar power and humour, with flowing, powerful, chunky curves reminiscent of an early Henry Moore.

And then—and this was within a month of her first recognitions— her attention, her appreciation, moved from objects to people. There were limits, after all, to the interest and expressive possibilities of things, even when transfigured by a sort of innocent, ingenuous, and often comical genius. Now she needed to explore the human face and figure, at rest and in motion. To be "felt" by Madeleine was a remarkable experience. Her hands, only such a little while ago inert, doughy, now seemed charged with a preternatural animation and sensibility. One was not merely being recognised, being scrutinised, in a way more intense and searching than any visual scrutiny, but being "tasted" and appreciated meditatively, imaginatively, and aesthetically, by a born (a newborn) artist. They were, one felt, not just the hands of a blind woman exploring, but of a blind artist, a meditative and creative mind, just opened to the full sensuous and spiritual reality of the world. These explorations too pressed for representation and reproduction as an external reality.

She started to model heads and figures, and within a year was locally famous as the Blind Sculptress of St. Benedict's. Her sculptures tended to be half to three-quarters life size, with simple but recognisable features, and with a remarkably expressive energy. For me, for her, for all of us, this was a deeply moving, an amazing, almost a miraculous, experience. Who would have dreamed that basic powers of perception, normally acquired in the first months of life, but failing to be acquired at this time, could be acquired in one's sixtieth year? What wonderful possibilities of late learning, and learning for the handicapped, this opened up. And who could have dreamed that in this blind, palsied woman, hidden away, inactivated, over-protected all her life, there lay the germ of an astonishing artistic sensibility (unsuspected by her, as by others) that would germinate and blossom into a rare and beautiful reality, after remaining dormant, blighted, for sixty years?

The Ones Who Walk Away from Omelas

☆

Ursula K. LeGuin

With a clamour of bells that set the swallows soaring, the Festival of Summer came to the city of Omelas, bright-towered by the sea. The rigging of the boats in the harbour sparkled with flags. In the streets between houses with red roofs and painted walls, between old moss-grown gardens and under avenues of trees, passed great parks and public buildings, processions moved. Some were decorous: old people in long stiff robes of mauve and grey, grave master workmen, quiet, merry women carrying their babies and chatting as they walked. In other streets the music beat faster, a shimmering of gong and tambourine, and the people went dancing, the procession was a dance. Children dodged in and out, their high calls rising like the swallows' crossing flights over the music and the singing. All the processions wound towards the north side of the city, where on the great water-meadow called the Green Fields boys and girls, naked in the bright air, with mud-stained feet and ankles and long, lithe arms, exercised their restive horses before the race. The horses wore no gear at all but a halter without bit. Their manes were braided with streamers of silver, gold, and green. They flared their nostrils and pranced and boasted to one another; they were vastly excited, the horse being the only animal who has adopted our ceremonies as his own. Far off to the north and west the mountains stood up half encircling Omelas on her bay. The air of morning was so clear that the snow still crowning the Eighteen Peaks burned with white-gold fire across the miles of sunlit air, under the dark blue of the sky. There was just enough wind to make the banners that marked the racecourse snap and flutter now and then. In the silence of the broad green meadows one could hear the music winding through the city streets, farther and nearer and ever approaching, a cheerful faint sweetness of the air that from time to time trembled and gathered together and broke out into the great joyous clanging of the bells.

Joyous! How is one to tell about joy? How describe the citizens of Omelas?

They were not simple folk, you see, though they were happy. But we do not say the words of cheer much any more. All smiles have become archaic. Given a description such as this one tends to make certain assumptions. Given a description such as this one tends to look next for the King, mounted on a splendid stallion and surrounded by his noble knights, or perhaps in a golden litter borne by great-muscled slaves. But there was no king. They did not use swords, or keep slaves. They were not barbarians. I do not know the rules and laws of their society, but I suspect that they were singularly few. As they did without monarchy and slavery, so they also got on without the stock exchange, the advertisement, the secret police, and the bomb. Yet I repeat that these were not simple folk, not dulcet shepherds, noble savages, bland utopians. They were not less complex than us. The trouble is that we have a bad habit, encouraged by pedants and sophisticates, of considering happiness as something rather stupid. Only pain is intellectual, only evil interesting. This is the treason of the artist: a refusal to admit the banality of evil and the terrible boredom of pain. If you can't lick 'em, join 'em. If it hurts, repeat it. But to praise despair is to condemn delight, to embrace violence is to lose hold of everything else. We have almost lost hold; we can no longer describe a happy man, nor make any celebration of joy. How can I tell you about the people of Omelas? They were not naïve and happy children—though their children were, in fact, happy. They were mature, intelligent, passionate adults whose lives were not wretched. O miracle! but I wish I could describe it better. I wish I could convince you. Omelas sounds in my words like a city in a fairy tale, long ago and far away, once upon a time. Perhaps it would be best if you imagined it as your own fancy bids, assuming it will rise to the occasion, for certainly I cannot suit you all. For instance, how about technology? I think that there would be no cars or helicopters in and above the streets; this follows from the fact that the people of Omelas are happy people. Happiness is based on a just discrimination of what is necessary, what is neither necessary nor destructive, and what is destructive. In the middle category, however— that of the unnecessary but undestructive, that of comfort, luxury, exuberance, etc.—they could perfectly well have central heating, sub-way trains, washing machines, and all kinds of marvellous devices not yet invented here, floating light-sources, fuelless power, a cure for the common cold. Or they could have none of that: it doesn't matter. As you like it. I incline to think that people from towns up and down the coast have been coming in to Omelas during the last days before the Festival on very fast little trains and double-decked trams and that the train station of Omelas is actually the handsomest building in town, though plainer than the magnificent Farmers' Market. But even granted trains, I fear that Omelas so far strikes some of you as goody-goody. Smiles, bells, parades, horses, bleh. If so, please add an orgy. If an orgy would help, don't hesitate. Let us now, however, have temples from which issue beautiful nude priests and priestesses already half in ecstasy and ready to copulate with any man or woman, lover or stranger, who desires union with the deep godhead of the blood, although that was my first idea. But really it would be better not to have any temples in Omelas—at least, not manned temples. Religion yes, clergy no. Surely the beautiful nudes can just wander about, offering themselves like divine soufflés to the hunger of the needy and the rapture of the flesh. Let them join the processions. Let tambourines be struck above the copulations, and the glory of desire be proclaimed upon the gongs, and (a not unimportant point) let the offspring of these delightful rituals be beloved and looked after by all. One thing I know there is none of in Omelas is guilt. But what else should there be? I thought at first there were no drugs, but that is puritanical. For those who like it, the faint insistent sweetness of *drooz* may perfume the ways of the city, *drooz* which first brings a great lightness and brilliance to the mind and limbs, and then after some hours a dreamy languor, and wonderful visions at last of the very arcana and inmost secrets of the Universe, as well as exciting the pleasure of sex beyond all belief; and it is not habit-forming. For more modest tastes I think there ought to be beer. What else, what else belongs in the joyous city? The sense of victory, surely, the celebration of courage. But as we did without clergy, let us do without soldiers. The joy built upon successful slaughter is not the right kind of joy; it will not do, it is fearful and it is trivial. A boundless and generous contentment, a magnanimous triumph felt not against some outer enemy but in communion with the finest and fairest in the souls of all men everywhere and the splendour of the world's summer: this is what swells the hearts of the people of Omelas, and the victory they celebrate is that of life. I really don't think many of them need to take *drooz*.

Most of the processions have reached the Green Fields by now. A marvellous smell of cooking goes forth from the red and blue tents of the provisioners. The faces of small children are amiably sticky; in the benign grey beard of a man a couple of crumbs of rich pastry are entangled. The youths and girls have mounted their horses and are beginning to group around the starting line of the course. An old woman, small, fat, and laughing is passing out flowers from a basket, and tall young men wear her flowers in their shining hair. A child of nine or ten sits at the edge of the crowd, alone, playing on a wooden flute. People pause to listen, and they smile, but they do not speak to him, for he never ceases playing and never sees them, his dark eyes wholly rapt in the sweet, thin magic of the tune.

He finishes and slowly lowers his hands holding the wooden flute.

As if the little private silence were the signal, all at once a trumpet sounds from the pavilion near the starting line: imperious, melancholy, piercing. The horses rear on their slender legs and some of them neigh in answer. Sober-faced, the young riders stroke the horses' necks and soothe them, whispering, "Quiet, quiet, there my beauty, my hope..." They begin to form in rank along the starting line. The crowds along the racecourse are like a field of grass and flowers in the wind. The Festival of Summer has begun.

Do you believe? Do you accept the festival, the city, the joy? No? Then let me describe one more thing.

In a basement under one of the beautiful public buildings of Omelas, or perhaps in the cellar of one of its spacious private homes, there is a room. It has one locked door, and no window. A little light seeps in dustily between cracks in the boards, second-hand from a cobwebbed window somewhere across the cellar. In one corner of the little room a couple of mops, with stiff, clotted, foul-smelling heads, stand near a rusty bucket. The floor is dirt, a little damp to the touch, as cellar dirt usually is. The room is about three paces long and two wide: a mere broom closet or disused tool room. In the room a child is sitting. It could be a boy or a girl. It looks about six, but actually is nearly ten. It is feeble-minded. Perhaps it was born defective, or perhaps it has become imbecile through fear, malnutrition, and neglect. It picks its nose and occasionally fumbles vaguely with its toes or genitals, as it sits hunched in the corner farthest from the bucket and the two mops. It is afraid of the mops. It finds them horrible. It shuts its eyes, but it knows the mops are still standing there; and the door is locked; and nobody will come. The door is always locked; and nobody ever comes, except that sometimes—the child has no understanding of time or interval—sometimes the door rattles terribly and opens, and a person, or several people, are there. One of them may come in and kick the child to make it stand up. The others never come close, but peer in at it with frightened, disgusted eyes. The food bowl and the water jug are hastily filled, the door is locked, the eyes disappear. The people at the door never say anything, but the child, who has not always lived in the tool room, and can remember sunlight and its mother's voice, sometimes speaks. "I will be good," it says. "Please let me out. I will be good!" They never answer. The child used to scream for help at night, and cry a good deal, but now it only makes a kind of whining, "eh-haa, eh-haa," and it speaks less and less often. It is so thin there are no calves to its legs; its belly protrudes; it lives on a half-bowl of corn meal and grease a day. It is naked. Its buttocks and thighs are a mass of festered sores, as it sits in its own excrement continually.

They all know it is there, all the people of Omelas. Some of them have come to see it, others are content merely to know it is there. They all know that it has to be there. Some of them understand why, and some do not, but they all understand that their happiness, the beauty of their city, the tenderness of their friendships, the health of their children, the wisdom of their scholars, the skill of their makers, even the abundance of their harvest and the kindly weathers of their skies, depend wholly on this child's abominable misery.

This is usually explained to children when they are between eight and twelve, whenever they seem capable of understanding; and most of those who come to see the child are young people, though often enough an adult comes, or comes back, to see the child. No matter how well the matter has been explained to them, these young spectators are always shocked and sickened at the sight. They feel disgust, which they had thought themselves superior to. They feel anger, outrage, impotence, despite all the explanations. They would like to do something for the child. But there is nothing they can do. If the child were brought up into the sunlight out of that vile place, if it were cleaned and fed and comforted, that would be a good thing, indeed; but if it were done, in that day and hour all the prosperity and beauty and delight of Omelas would wither and be destroyed. Those are the terms. To exchange all the goodness and grace of every life in Omelas for that single, small improvement: to throw away the happiness of thousands for the chance of the happiness of one: that would be to let guilt within the wall indeed.

The terms are strict and absolute; there may not even be a kind word spoken to the child.

Often the young people go home in tears, or in a tearless rage, when they have seen the child and faced this terrible paradox. They may brood over it for weeks or years. But as time goes on they begin to realize that even if the child could be released, it would not get much good of its freedom: a little vague pleasure of warmth and food, no doubt, but little more. It is too degraded and imbecile to know any real joy. It has been afraid too long ever to be free of fear. Its habits are too uncouth for it to respond to humane treatment. Indeed, after so long it would probably be wretched without walls about it to protect it, and darkness for its eyes, and its own excrement to sit in. Their tears at the bitter injustice dry when they begin to perceive the terrible justice of reality, and to accept it. Yet it is their tears and anger, the trying of their generosity and the acceptance of their helplessness, which are perhaps the true source of the splendour of their lives. Theirs is no vapid, irresponsible happiness. They know that they, like the child, are not free. They know compassion. It is the existence of the child, and their knowledge of its existence, that makes possible the nobility of their architecture, the poignancy of their music, the profundity of their science. It is because of the child that they are so gentle with children. They know that if the wretched one were not there snivelling in the dark, the other one, the flute-player, could make no joyful music as the young riders line up in their beauty for the race in the sunlight of the first morning of summer.

Now do you believe in them? Are they not more credible? But there is one more thing to tell, and this is quite incredible.

At times one of the adolescent girls or boys who go to see the child does not go home to weep or rage, does not, in fact, go home at all. Sometimes also a man or woman much older falls silent for a day or two, and then leaves home. These people go out into the street, and walk down the street alone. They keep walking, and walk straight out of the city of Omelas, through the beautiful gates. They keep walking across the farmlands of Omelas. Each one goes alone, youth or girl, man or woman. Night falls; the traveller must pass down village streets, between the houses with yellow-lit windows, and on out into the darkness of the fields. Each alone, they go west or north, towards the mountains. They go on. They leave Omelas, they walk ahead into the darkness, and they do not come back. The place they go towards is a place even less imaginable to most of us than the city of happiness. I cannot describe it at all. It is possible that it does not exist. But they seem to know where they are going, the ones who walk away from Omelas.

Theme Questions

✿

✿ Why do we envision other worlds? How do these other worlds help us to see our own world from a fresh perspective?

✿ Other worlds can be real or imagined, or sometimes both. Einstein and Infeld said, for instance, that science "is a creation of the human mind, with its freely invented ideas and concepts." How does this idea relate to the worlds encountered in this section?

✿ Utopia is sometimes defined as a perfect society. Is it possible for a society to have all of its needs met and, at the same time, offer happiness to all its individual members? What are the implications of finding out that our own happiness is a condition of other people's misery, as in "The Ones Who Walk Away from Omelas"?

✿ Are there other worlds in our collective past as well as in our future and our imaginations? Have we lost some worlds in our long history?

Acknowledgements

☆

Every effort has been made to trace the original sources of materials contained in this book. The publisher would be pleased to hear from copyright holders to rectify any errors or omissions.

Page 4: From THE COMPLETE LETTERS OF VINCENT VAN GOGH. By permission of Little, Brown (Inc.) in conjunction with New York Graphic Society
Page 41: From *Traditional Chinese Tales* translated by Chi-Chen Wang.
Page 44: Excerpt from *Maps and Dreams* © 1981, 1988 by Hugh Brody, published by Douglas and McIntyre. Reprinted by permission.
Page 54: From *Stones* by Timothy Findley. Copyright © Pebble Productions, 1988. Reprinted by permission of Penguin Books Canada Ltd.
Page 74: Reprinted by permission of the publishers from REVOLUTION IN TIME: CLOCKS AND THE MAKING OF THE MODERN WORLD by David S. Landes, Cambridge, Mass.: The Belknap Press of Harvard University Press, Copyright © 1983 by the President and Fellows of Harvard College.
Page 76: From Lewis Carroll, *Alice in Wonderland*, Donald J. Gray ed., W.W. Norton, Inc. 1971.
Page 86: Jorge Luis Borges, *Labyrinths*. Translated by Harriet de Onis. Copyright © 1962, 1964 by New Directions Publishing Corp. Reprinted by permission of New Directions Publishing Corp.
Page 95: Reproduced by permission of G.F. Clutesi, Clutesi Agencies.
Page 97: From LOST IN TRANSLATION by Eva Hoffman. Copyright © 1989 by Eva Hoffman. Used by permission of the publisher, Dutton, an imprint of New American Library, a division of Penguin Books USA Inc.
Page 99: Reprinted with permission from *Chinatown Ghosts* by Jim Wong-Chu (Arsenal Pulp Press, 1986).
Page 101: Copyright Katherine Judith Alexander.
Page 112: Copyright Gerald Moore and Ulli Beier.
Page 113: From David Suzuki, *Metamorphosis*. Reprinted with permission of Stoddart Publishing Co. Ltd., Don Mills, ON.
Page 120: Reprinted by permission of the author.
Page 128: Reprinted with the permission of Mosaic Press, 1252 Speers Rd., Units 1 & 2, Oakville, ON L6L 5N9, from *Italian Canadian Voices*, edited by Caroline Morgan DiGiovanni, copyright 1984.
Page 139: "Heritage" by Neil Bissoondath. Reprinted with the permission of the author. Copyright 1990.

Page 148: Dionne Brand, "Blossom: Priestess of Oya, Goddess of winds, storms, and waterfalls" from *San Souci*.

Page 156: "An Interview with Dionne Brand" from *Other Solitudes: Canadian Multicultural Fictions*, Linda Hutcheon and Marion Richmond eds., © Linda Hutcheon and Canadian Publishing Foundation 1990. Reprinted by permission of Oxford University Press Canada.

Page 165: From Lewis Carroll, *Alice in Wonderland*, Donald J. Gray ed. W.W. Norton Inc., 1971.

Page 174: From Roch Carrier, *The Hockey Sweater and Other Stories*. Reprinted with permission of Stoddart Publishing Co. Ltd., Don Mills, ON.

Page 180: Reprinted with permission of Reuters.

Page 182: © The Executor of Henry Reed's Estate 1991. Reprinted from Henry Reed's *Collected Poems* edited by Jon Stallworthy (1991) by permission of Oxford University Press.

Page 184: From *Afterworlds* by Gwendolyn MacEwen. Used by permission of the Canadian Publishers, McClelland & Stewart, Toronto.

Page 186: Reprinted by permission of the author.

Page 188: "My Poetry" by Takamura Kōtarō. Translated by Ninomiya Takamichi and D.J. Enright. © D.J. Enright through Watson, Little Ltd., London.

Page 195: From Ovid, *Metamorphoses*, translated by Rolfe Humphries, Indiana University Press.

Page 197: From W.H. AUDEN: COLLECTED POEMS by W.H. Auden, ed. by Edward Mendelson. Copyright 1940 and renewed 1968 by W.H. Auden. Reprinted by permission of Random House, Inc.

Page 198: From William A. Heffernan *et al*, *Literature Art and Artifact*, Harcourt Brace Jovanovich, 1987.

Page 200: Reprinted with the permission of the author's family.

Page 201: From *The Collected Poems of Earle Birney*. Used by permission of the Canadian Publishers, McClelland & Stewart, Toronto.

Page 209: From W.T. Jewkes, *Man the Myth-Maker*, Harcourt Brace Jovanovich, 1981.

Page 213: Richard Gillespie, *Life* Magazine © 1992 The Time Inc. Magazine Company. Reprinted with permission.

Page 227: Copyright © 1938 by Albert Einstein and Leopold Infeld. © Renewed 1966 by Albert Einstein and Leopold Infeld. Reprinted by permission of Simon & Schuster Inc.

Page 229: Reprinted by permission of the author.

Page 238: Miriam Waddington: "Klara and Lilo" from *The Last Landscape*, copyright © Miriam Waddington 1992. Reprinted by permission of Oxford University Press Canada.

Page 224: From Oliver Sacks, *The Man Who Mistook His Wife for a Hat*. Reprinted by permission of International Creative Management, Inc. Copyright © 1970 by Dr. Oliver Sacks.

Page 249: "The Ones Who Walk Away from Omelas" from *The Wind's Twelve Quarters* by U.K. LeGuin. © Ursula K. LeGuin 1973, 1975.

Author/Artist Index

☆